NARVIK

DIE WEHRMACHT IM KAMPF

NARVIK

The Struggle of Battle Group Dietl in the Spring of 1940

ALEX BUCHNER

Translated by
JANICE W. ANCKER

Series editor:
MATTHIAS STROHN

CASEMATE
Philadelphia & Oxford

AN AUSA BOOK
Association of the United States Army
2425 Wilson Boulevard, Arlington, Virginia, 22201, USA

Published in the United States of America and Great Britain in 2020 by
CASEMATE PUBLISHERS
1950 Lawrence Road, Havertown, PA 19083, USA
and
The Old Music Hall, 106–108 Cowley Road, Oxford OX4 1JE, UK

Originally published as Die Wehrmacht im Kampf 18: Alex Buchner, *Die Kämpfe der Gruppe Dietl im Frühjahr 1940* (Scharnhorst Buchkameradschaft GmbH, Neckargemünd, 1958)

Hardback Edition: ISBN 978-1-61200-917-9
Digital Edition: ISBN 978-1-61200-918-6

A CIP record for this book is available from the British Library

Printed and bound in the United States of America by Sheridan

Typeset by Versatile PreMedia Service (P) Ltd

For a complete list of Casemate titles, please contact:

CASEMATE PUBLISHERS (US)
Telephone (610) 853-9131
Fax (610) 853-9146
Email: casemate@casematepublishers.com
www.casematepublishers.com

CASEMATE PUBLISHERS (UK)
Telephone (01865) 241249
Email: casemate-uk@casematepublishers.co.uk
www.casematepublishers.co.uk

Front cover: The 8,514 ton German supply ship *Alster*, which was captured by the Royal Navy destroyer HMS *Icarus* on 11 April 1940 off Narvik. The ship was brought back to the UK where it was renamed *Empire Endurance*. (IWM HU 104686)

Contents

Translator's Note

Today the rusted hulk of the wrecked destroyer *Georg Thiele* can still be seen on the rocks of a fjord near Narvik, and there are diving tours of the sunken ships in Narvik harbour. For me, this translation has also been something of a deep-sea dive of its own, providing a glimpse into a world of assumptions and values of times past. Although I frequently had to come up for air, I did my best to leave the tone and historical integrity of this work intact.

I wish to thank my husband, Col Ret C. J. Ancker III for his valuable insight and help with military and weapons terminology.

Janice W. Ancker

Foreword

The German invasion of Norway in 1940 was the first large amphibious operation of World War II. In many ways, the odds were against the German troops: the threat from the British Royal Navy, questions of resupply for a prolonged fight, and other issues meant that a surprise attack was the only option for the Wehrmacht. So swift was the planning for the invasion that, allegedly, the German general tasked with the invasion based his plan on a Baedeker travel guide. It was a gamble, but, like many other gambles in the first half of World War II, it paid off for the Germans. In this operation, the fight for Narvik was probably the most dramatic episode. It was a 'close-run thing' and the Germans came close to defeat: a force of 4,600 German soldiers (2,000 mountain troops and 2,600 sailors from sunk German warships) faced an Allied expeditionary force of approximately 25,000 men, supported by Norwegian troops. Heavily outnumbered and suffering significant naval losses, the German troops stood no realistic chance of success. Narvik, which had been seized by the Germans on 9 April 1940, fell into Allied hands again on 28 May. Hitler was even contemplating issuing an order allowing the German troops to be interned in Sweden. In the end, the Germans prevailed, not least because of greater strategic issues and the German invasion of France, which made the withdrawal of Allied troops necessary. The Germans reoccupied Narvik on 8 June 1940, and Norway remained occupied by the Germans until the end of World War II.

The tenacity of the German soldiers was impressive. And yet, the operation came at a cost, in particular for the German navy, which lost 10 destroyers in the struggle for Narvik. In this book, the author describes these events in detail and the book therefore offers a good overview of the fight for Narvik from the German perspective. It is, however, a book of its time. It was published in Germany in 1958, when the interest of German writers and the public alike concentrated on tactical and operational matters. The wider implications of Nazi ideology, atrocities, and such like, were not comfortable topics for an immediate post-war Germany. This is reflected in this book. Generalleutnant Dietl, who commanded the German troops in Narvik, is praised for his obvious military abilities. His clear support for the Nazi ideology remains unmentioned. The author of this book is not alone in this; for instance, the German Army named a barracks after Dietl, and the name was only changed in 1995. Dietl's support for the National Socialists does not negate the impressive military achievement at Narvik, but the actions there have to be seen in the wider context of the Nazi war of aggression.

Prof. Matthias Strohn, M.St., DPhil, FRHistS
Head of Historical Analysis,
Centre for Historical Analysis and Conflict Research
Visiting Professor of Military Studies,
University of Buckingham

Introduction

Much has been written about Narvik, the battle of the German destroyers and mountain troops, and their confrontation with the much superior enemy. Most writing on this subject so far, however, has been based on personal experiences and written in narrative form. Other publications of important military-historical significance focus on political and military developments in the northern European area of operations and descriptions of the overall campaign in Norway, with emphasis on the operations of the German navy (Kriegsmarine).

To avoid duplicating these efforts, the present work will shift focus away from those kinds of depictions, referring to them only briefly where such material is essential to the understanding of the context.

Drawing on the wealth of available material, this volume attempts to provide a complete and coherent overview of the battles in the area of Narvik. This work will go into essential details of the experience, and as much as is possible within its parameters, illustrate the high level of achievement of both troops and commanders and the enormous burden borne by all.

The fighting, which lasted for eight weeks, was carried out by a unit of fighters who had to rely on themselves alone, and was distinguished by the combat expertise of the individual combatants and the creativeness and tactical excellence of General Dietl's leadership.

It was a battle of mountain soldiers, sailors, and paratroopers, standing shoulder to shoulder, fighting under extreme physical and psychological conditions – all for the sake of Narvik, an objective that had taken on symbolic meaning.

Alex Buchner,
First Lieutenant, Ret.

Glossary of Rank Equivalents

German	English
Army	
General der Infanterie	General of Infantry, equivalent to Lieutenant-General
Generalleutnant	Lieutenant-General
Generalmajor	Major-General
Oberst	Colonel
Oberstleutnant	Lieutenant-Colonel
Major	Major
Hauptmann	Captain
Oberleutnant	First Lieutenant
Leutnant	Lieutenant
Stabsfeldwebel	Staff Sergeant
Oberfeldwebel	First Sergeant
Feldwebel	Sergeant
Navy	
Kommodore	Commodore
Kapitän zur See	Captain
Fregattenkapitän	Commander
Korvettenkapitän	Lieutenant Commander
Leutnant zur See	Ensign

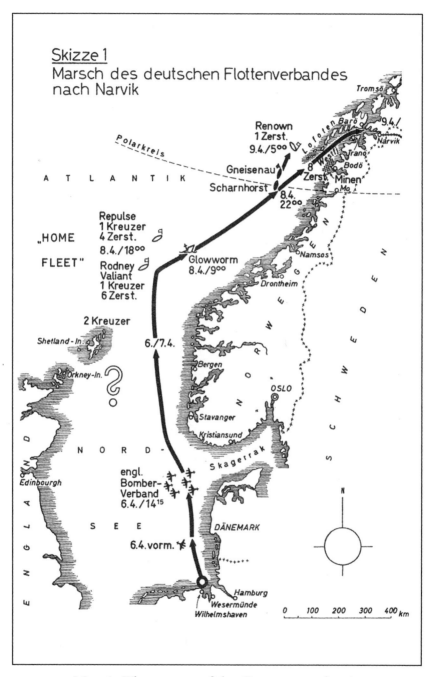

Map 1: The voyage of the German naval units

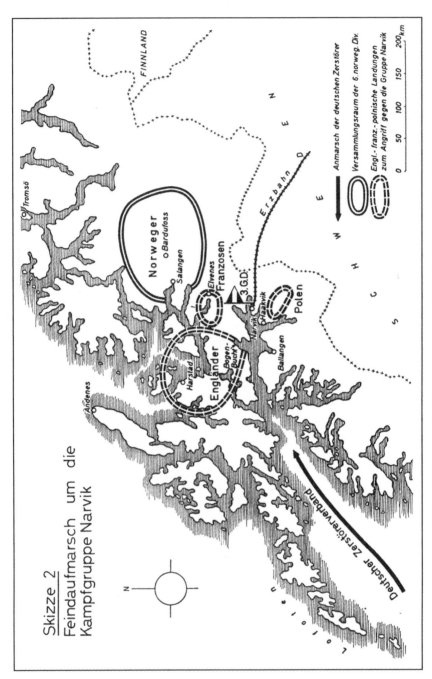

Map 2: Enemy deployment around Battle Group Narvik

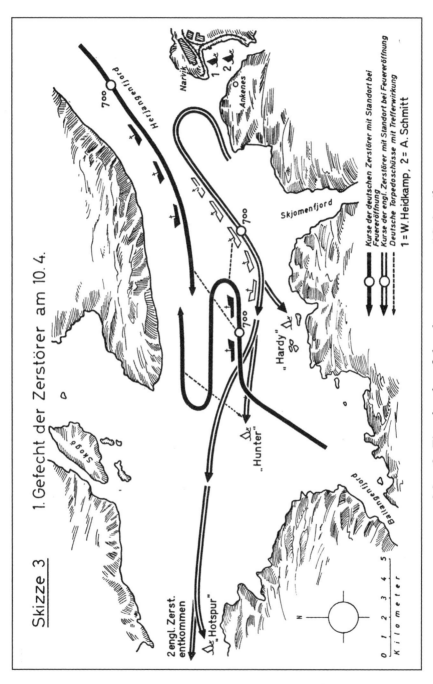

Map 3: First battle of the destroyers on 10 April

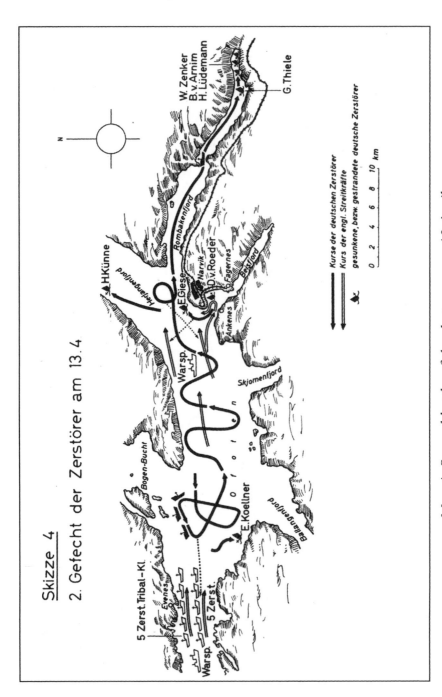

Map 4: Second battle of the destroyers on 13 April

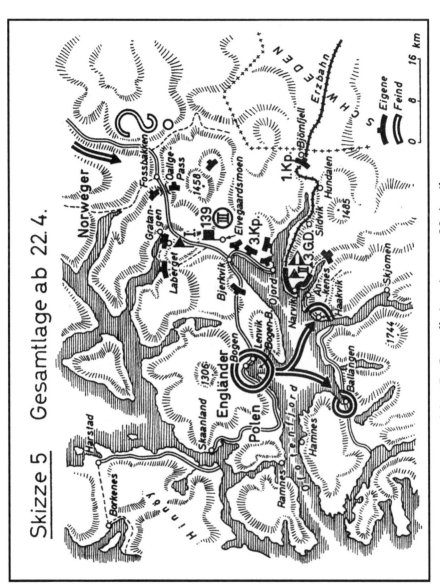

Map 5: Overall situation on 22 April

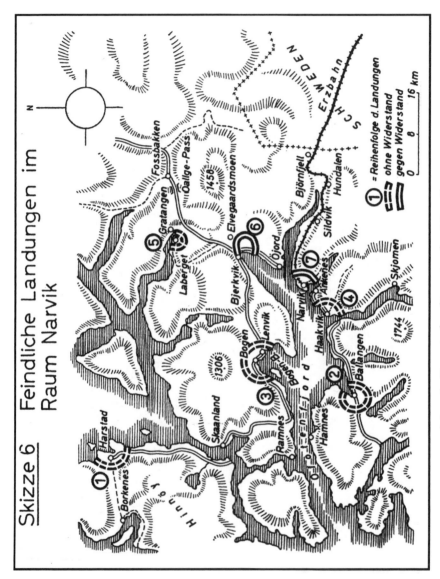

Map 6: Enemy landings in the Narvik area

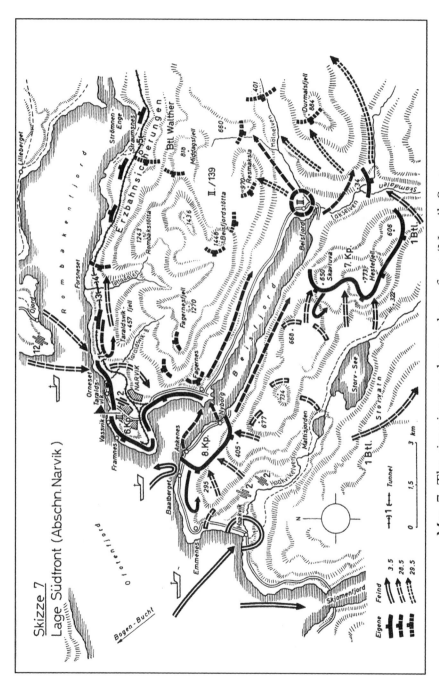

Map 7: The situation on the southern front/Narvik Sector

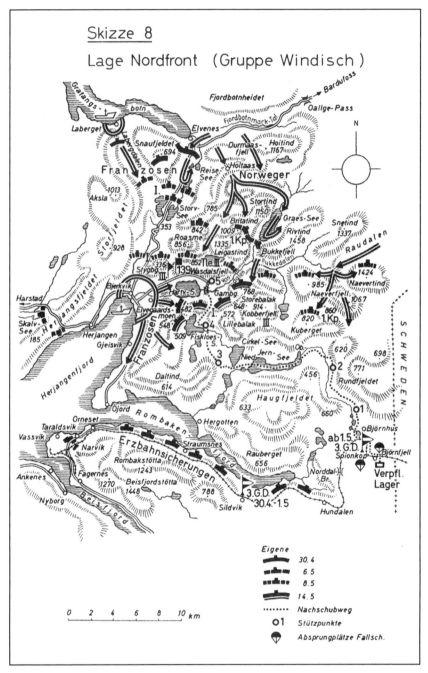

Map 8: Situation at the northern front/Group Windisch

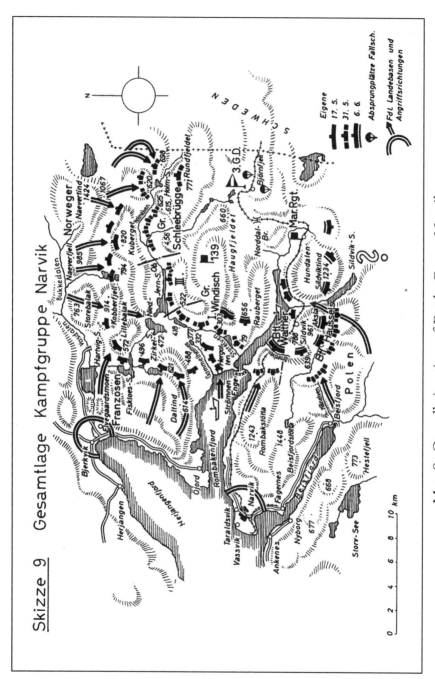

Map 9: Overall situation of Battle Group Narvik

CHAPTER I

The Voyage to Narvik

The deployment of the German warships (Map 1)

In the afternoon of 6 April 1940, the reinforced 139th Mountain Infantry Regiment and staff from the 3rd Mountain Division, under the command of Generalleutnant Dietl, arrived in Bremerhaven. Having come from an assembly area in Berlin, they would continue on into Wesermuende harbour, where a group of destroyers awaited their arrival (for units and their designations see Appendix 1).

Boarding began immediately. The long Columbus Pier thundered with the sound of spiked mountain boots, as company after company of mountain infantry soldiers clambered aboard the ships, weighed down by heavy rucksacks, dangling with gear, with machine guns shouldered. These were men who had come from the Alps, the Dolomites, and the Karawanks – destination unknown.

The loading of the destroyers ran quickly and efficiently. The boarding plan had been organised weeks earlier, on 28 March 1940, in Wilhelmshaven by the commander of the destroyers and the Ia (division operations officer) of the 3rd Mountain Division.[1] The entire regiment and its reinforcements would be quartered on the 10 destroyers, in cramped conditions, and with enough rations only for the voyage. According to the operations plan for this mission, *Weserübung Nord* (Weser Exercise North), only the men and their personal equipment and weapons were to be taken on board (see Appendix 6). Everything else – armour, flak, and the bulk of the munitions, food, and other items – would follow in the so-called Export Echelon, or *Ausfuhrstaffel*. Precise timing was crucial, and the transport of the troops had to be expedited.

During transport, the troops were kept together as units on their respective destroyers, close together and battle-ready, with their heavy weaponry including heavy machine guns, medium mortars, and light infantry guns. Each destroyer took on between 200 and 250 men, who had to be packed into every possible corner. The division command and staff, however, found themselves separated from one another, with Generalleutnant Dietl on the lead destroyer *Wilhelm Heidkamp* and a portion of the staff on the destroyer *Bernd von Arnim*.

The men had never before taken part in a naval transport as a unit, and almost every man was seeing the sea for the first time. Despite much speculation and rumour, the men knew nothing of their destination or mission.

Under the darkness of darkness on 6 April, at 2300 hrs, the destroyers left the piers and followed the Weser River downstream. Then, lights dimmed, they sailed out into the open North Sea. Thus began the journey into the Norwegian Sea to their destination, 1,200 nautical miles to the north. Only now were the men informed of their destination and mission (see Appendix 6). They were headed for Narvik, the Norwegian iron ore town, north of the Arctic Circle. This operation would be one of the boldest and most daring in the history of modern naval warfare, filled with drama and extraordinary turns of luck. No one was certain what awaited them there – whether the Norwegians would remain neutral as they had been so far, or whether they would rise up in defence of their harbour. There was no guarantee that the destroyers would even reach the appointed destination, as the entire journey would take place under the watchful eye of the powerful British Home Fleet.

At approximately 0300 hrs, the destroyers linked up with the battleships *Gneisenau* and *Scharnhorst*, which were assigned to protect and secure the approach to Narvik against heavy enemy surface vessels. Travelling with Group Narvik was Group Trondheim, comprised of the heavy cruiser *Admiral Hipper* and four destroyers. The overall fleet commander was Admiral Lütjens.

The primary mission was to transport the troops safely to the designated area at the specified time, and battle was therefore to be avoided if at all possible during the approach. Because speed and the element of surprise were crucial, even the usual man-overboard procedures were to be dispensed with (see Bibliography, 40). Per orders, the commander of the destroyers and his ships were to be at Narvik harbour on 9 April at 0500 hrs, at which time the troops would put ashore.

The German ships set out on 7 April at 0510 hrs, at a speed of about 22 knots. At dawn the convoy was covered by air, at first only with Me 109 fighters, later with long-distance He 111 aircraft.

The fleet passed through an area in which Britain had unquestioned control of the waters and would be able to bring in far superior forces. Still, the German fleet commander placed complete trust in the speed of his ships, on the meticulously guarded secrecy of the mission, and on the element of surprise. Due to increasing cloudiness and rain storms, visibility was less than ideal, but the enemy's reconnaissance would also face the same challenge. By mid-morning, however, a British aircraft sighted the German fleet; at midday, two British reconnaissance aircraft appeared and reported that the German fleet was moving north at high speed (see Bibliography, 1). At 1415 hrs, from high altitude, 12 British bombers attacked the fleet, although with little effect.

The British were fully aware of the objectives of the German fleet in the Baltic Sea. They had already deployed light combat vessels in the area and added further, heavier units, planning to engage the Germans in battle; at 1730 hrs, *Radio Tower Report 1707* stated that British admiralty cruisers and destroyers were deployed and headed toward the advancing German fleet (see Bibliography, 44). But in the pitch black, rainy night of 7 April, with constantly deteriorating visibility, the German fleet managed to pass undetected through the dangerous channel between the Shetland Islands and the Norwegian coast. With this they had made their first significant breakthrough.

During the night, the brisk south–west wind had brought heavy swells up to Force 8, so that they could no longer maintain their speed of advance of 26 knots. The destroyers pitched violently in the rough seas, and to avoid collisions they had to be spread out far apart from one another.

On the morning of 8 April, with its ships still widely scattered by the storm, the fleet stood somewhere off Trondheim. Despite an already significant loss of time, the fleet commander ordered a slower pace to allow the lagging destroyers to close in. In the rough waters, the ships listed as much as 50 degrees and became difficult to steer. All ships incurred heavy external damage, as well as engine and steering problems. Motorcycles, munitions crates, machinery, and heavy weapons, although firmly lashed down, were ripped overboard by the powerful breakers.[2] Wounded men with fractures and sprains were found on almost all the ships, and 10 men had been washed overboard. The mountain troops also found themselves seasick, which was made all the worse by the cramped conditions on board.

That morning, without warning, the British destroyer *Glowworm* appeared, and at 0900 hrs, engaged in a running battle with the destroyer *Bernd von Arnim*. After the *Admiral Hipper* rushed to join the battle, *Glowworm* was set on fire and sunk.[3] Shortly after this first enemy engagement, *Admiral Hipper* and the four destroyers belonging to Group Trondheim were released from the fleet to continue on to their assigned position.

Battle Group Narvik plunged further on into the stormy seas of the North Atlantic. At 1358 hrs, a German Dornier Do 26 reconnaissance aircraft reported a large British force of two battleships, one heavy cruiser, and six destroyers in the waters off the Orkneys. Moving north-north-east, it was clear that this enemy unit was headed toward the German fleet. To provide security for as long as possible, fleet commander Admiral Lütjens decided to escort the 10 Narvik destroyers as far as the entry to Vestfjord. According to short-range radar, several large enemy ships lay at about 190 nautical miles (19km)[sic] distance, but the German fleet was able to evade them.

On the evening of 8 April, the German fleet arrived at Vestfjord, towards 2100 hrs. The destroyers were released from the fleet and sent on to Narvik, with best wishes for their success. Having accomplished their escort mission, the heavy ships [*Gneisenau* and *Scharnhorst*] now set a north-westerly course toward the enemy fleet reported to be out on the high seas, with the mission of protecting the landing in Narvik. On the morning of 9 April, both German battleships took part in a fierce battle with the British battleship *Renown*, which had been scouring the northern Norwegian waters for the reported German ships.

As darkness fell on the night 8/9 April, the German destroyers drew nearer their destination. This third night at sea was the toughest. The weather worsened, and the storm moved in. Coming from the south-west, the weather had so far only whipped them forward and threatened them from the rear, but now the ships met with heavy north-west winds of Force 10–11. The water was roiling, endless, and sea-green. The destroyers, slim and streamlined in design, pitched, yawed, and rolled in the turbulence. Pounded and thrown about by breaking waves, the destroyers tipped onto their sides and plunged deep into troughs. Decks and cabins were awash, and equipment was damaged and ripped from the decks. Yet on this black, starless night, drenched in sea spray, blown by rain and snow, the destroyers maintained a dogged pace, and even increased their speed to 30 knots.

Here at Vestfjord, the German destroyers found they had been favoured with some amazing good luck this time, and in double measure. First of all, the storm had hit them early in their journey. Had it arrived any later, and just a bit more to the south, they would have had to fight through the turbulent waves for an even longer time, which would have used up all their fuel reserves. They might never have reached Narvik at all (see Bibliography, 44). The bad weather had also kept them hidden and out of sight of the enemy. And, because of the raging storm, the British 2nd Destroyer Flotilla had gone to seek the protection of land near the Vestfjord, in the nearby Lofoten Islands.

At about 2200 hrs, the commander of the German destroyers assumed that he was near the southern tip of the Lofoten archipelago. He could not determine the precise position of the ships based only on the radio bearings given by the Norwegian Skraaven Station in the Lofotens.

Entry into Ofotenfjord near Narvik

Shortly before midnight at the latitude of Trano, the German destroyers' voyage on the high seas finally came to its end. The storm abated and the weather gradually became calmer. In the shelter of the Lofoten archipelago, close to land and deeper into the fjords, conditions improved.

The battle for Narvik would meet with both good fortune and bad, coincidence and fate. But at this particular moment the news was not good. At about 0300 hrs, the German Naval Group Command West intercepted an order from the Norwegian admiralty calling for the immediate cessation of all coastal radio traffic and coastal lights. The fortunate part was that this order appeared not to have gotten through everywhere, as some lights were still visible in the inner West Fjord.

The warning lights in the narrow fjord passage with its cliffs and shallows had never been adequate in any circumstance, but now, in the pitch blackness of night, there came the added challenge of heavy snow. There was almost no visibility. The only option was to follow the lights of other ships, or trail after the greenish-white foam of their wakes. By travelling in a keel-line, the destroyers were able to work their way through the narrow passage, which put tremendous pressure on the lead ship. The shoreline loomed close, the towering walls of stone stood black against the sky, but were only visible for seconds. Great finesse and careful manoeuvring were needed to avoid crashing against the cliffs, or colliding with other ships. Thus, this stretch of the journey took place under enormous tension.

The entire undertaking could have been brought to a halt early in the game by a massive air attack or an engagement with the British fleet. But this passage of ships through the narrow fjord, in darkness, crammed to the hilt as they were with mountain riflemen, many of whom were unable to swim, could also have put an end to the whole operation. The entire plan absolutely rested on these troops and their timely arrival.

After managing the narrow passage into the Vestfjord, they still had to enter the narrow passage into Ofotenfjord to reach the harbour of Narvik. On 9 April, shortly after 0400 hrs, the fleet of destroyers passed Baro at 27 knots. Under orders to ready the ships for battle, they set an easterly course toward Ofotenfjord. Here, two Norwegian patrol ships appeared, one of which radioed in cleartext: 'Eight battleships in Ofotenfjord!' But the German destroyers were allowed to continue unhindered into Ofotenfjord.

In the early morning twilight, above the perpetual heavy snow, the enormous white mountain peaks now became visible. They reached as high as 1,000 metres, rising dramatically out of the waters of the fjord, dangerously close to the ships. Still ahead lay the narrow straits of Hamnes and Ramnes, whose entrance was said to be guarded by Norwegian coastal batteries. Yet, as the destroyers moved through the narrow channel, they were not fired on. Battle-ready, and at high speed, they moved further on into Ofotenfjord until they stood in front of the town of Narvik.

The 3rd Destroyer Flotilla brought up the rear, with its three ships. Per orders, they remained at a distance, prepared to respond quickly to any challenge from the suspected coastal fortifications. While one destroyer stayed in the centre of the fjord, its guns ready to respond to fire from any mountain batteries, the two others turned, one left and one right. The reinforced 1st Company/139th Mountain Infantry Regiment unloaded its troops at Hamnes, and the reinforced 6th Company/139th unloaded at Ramnes. At their rear was the artillery unit of the Naval Artillery Command, whose mission after the takeover was to seize the coastal fortifications and capture their weapons for the German coastal defence. But still, not one enemy shot fell.

The mountain infantry shock troops climbed the steep slopes from three different sides through 2-metre deep snow. Hours later it was discovered that no mountain fortifications existed at all. There were no weapons, nor was anyone there – nothing was there but some scattered, completely empty block buildings peeking out from the deep snow. At 0800 hrs, after a futile search, the troop landing was halted, and except for some reconnaissance patrols with light machine guns who remained behind, the companies were loaded back onto the ships.

What had seemed like good fortune during their entry into Narvik harbour, however, soon turned out to be the first significant setback for Battle Group Narvik. These armed coastal fortifications were actually on record in the German Admiralty handbook, reportedly armed with heavy cannons. Now they proved to be non-existent. There had once been actual battery emplacements near Ramnes, about 100 metres up the slopes, which had been blasted out, but construction efforts had not gotten beyond the preparation phase.[4] Due to his knowledge of the area, a merchant ship captain named Lindemann had been ordered on board by the naval command. Even before departing Wesermuende, he reported that he had never known of any fortifications or guns along these straits (see Bibliography, 1).

The Germans had counted heavily on the presence of these fortifications, and their absence had grave consequences. Had they actually existed, the Germans would have been able to block the British Fleet's entrance into Ofotenfjord. The subsequent land battle, with its continuous fire from the enemy battleships and the resulting conflagration, could have been prevented.

But there was still some good fortune for the German destroyers and their cargo of mountain troops. Close to the harbour of Narvik, they were able to overcome a further challenge, which at the last moment might also have put a stop to the entire mission.

While the destroyer *Diether von Roeder* moved into a reconnaissance and security position at Baro awaiting the arrival of the crippled, slow-moving vessel *Erich Giese*, it met two Norwegian patrol ships, but disarmed them and sent them to Narvik. At last, at 0515 hrs, the lead ship of the German 1st Destroyer Flotilla stood in the harbour of Narvik in the blowing snow (see Bibliography, 40).[5]

The troops below deck had been readying for the landing and climbed up top, released at last from their miserably rough voyage. The German 4th Destroyer Flotilla, with its three destroyers, had already arrived at its assigned landing place at Herjangenfjord and had been released to proceed to Bjerkvik. Then suddenly, through the whirling snow, the Norwegian coastal defence ship *Eidsvold* appeared in the harbour. It immediately fired a loud shot at close range and signalled the destroyers to halt. It was now clear that the Norwegians were set on resistance! Despite some brief negotiations, the Norwegian ship commander remained resolute and refused all demands by the Germans to hand over Narvik. This meant a fight!

The heavy ordnance of the *Eidsvold* (two 21cm, six 15.2cm, and eight 7.6cm guns) were aimed menacingly at the German destroyers. With just one volley from these weapons, the destroyers would have been badly torn up. After a tense moment, the German lead ship *Wilhelm Heidkamp* shot a spread of four torpedoes, two of which hit their target. The *Eidsvold* burst open amidships and sank seconds later. Only eight [with more than 170 drowned] crewmen were rescued.

In the meantime two ships, *Bernd von Arnim* and *Georg Thiele*, moved closer into the harbour next to the throng of foreign merchant ships anchored there. During their docking manoeuvres, the German ships were again fired on by the Norwegians, this time by coastal defence ship *Norge*, with its Swedish-made guns. The first salvo of the 21cm and 15cm projectiles fell short of the destroyers, and the next ones went far over its head and all the way into the town of Narvik (see Bibliography, 1). *Bernd von Arnim* commenced fire with all weapons from its port side, while simultaneously, the first of the mountain infantry troops jumped off the ship from the starboard side and onto the quay. As the coastal defence ship *Norge* steamed at slow speed back and forth between the German merchant ships, the Germans fired their torpedoes. A sixth salvo finally hit the *Norge* in the stern; the seventh detonated it mid-ships. The *Norge* capsized and sank just minutes later. Ninety-seven men were pulled from the harbour waters [but at least 100 were killed].

With this, the soldiers came ashore unhindered. The movement of more than 1,200 nautical miles had been successful, and the execution time for the landing had been met almost to the hour. Despite the adversities, the German destroyer group had accomplished its mission according to the plan. The race against the British, who, as it was later learned, had also planned a landing in Narvik, was won by just hours. Despite enemy aircraft, mines, enemy U-boats, the superior British Home Fleet, and stormy seas, the German destroyers had got the mountain troops entrusted to them safely to their destination. This dangerous venture had demanded navigational art, seamanship skills, and daring. But bad weather had also worked to the advantage of the overall operation. Moreover, the crews on the destroyers had excelled at their duties, as exemplified by the helmsman on the *Diether von Roeder*, who stood at his post with only four hours relief during almost 54 turbulent hours at sea (see Bibliography, 6).

Narvik is in German hands

The landing of troops and the occupation of Narvik, like all later developments in the campaign, had its moments of intense drama and its full share of luck, both good and bad.

The swift landing of troops with their weapons and equipment took place under the cover of the destroyers, whose guns were aimed toward the city. Free from enemy interference, the soldiers either stepped directly onto the quay or were shuttled to land in small motor boats and sloops.

The mountain infantry troops of 2nd Company/139th, the first of the shock troops to go ashore, had got over their seasickness, felt revived and in excellent spirits, and were immediately ready to deploy. Once on land, unit after unit quickly fell into formation, doing their best to be exactly in their preassigned places as quickly as possible. The 7th Company/139th proceeded from the south-western side, 8th Company/139th from the north-west, both marching in the direction of Narvik. The remaining companies and battalion staffs pushed directly into the city centre (see Appendices 6, 7).

Despite the early morning hour, all 10,000 or so residents of the city of Narvik were out in the streets. Many civilians stood about and looked with astonishment upon the unaccustomed military presence and on the German soldiers themselves, who at first were thought by many to be British. This crowd of civilians, many of whom simply stood gawking, could be the very reason that the handover of Narvik was quick and bloodless. As Oberst Sundlo, the Norwegian city commander wrote:

> I developed a mental image of the situation. The Norwegian soldiers walked around and looked with astonishment upon the foreign troops. All around in the streets, everywhere, were civilians and children. No one appeared to have the slightest idea that we were at war. And right through this mass of people, the German column slipped in, hand grenades in their fists, their weapons loaded, and with an eerie, goal oriented objectivity in their entire entrance. At the first shot, such a crowd of innocent civilians would be surely make for easy prey. (see Bibliography, 3)

Among the first to land was Generalleutnant Dietl himself with his staff. He was received at once on the pier by the German consul, Wussow. Because the two Norwegian coastal defence ships had opened fire, it was also to be expected that the Norwegian ground troops would resist. The general chose not to arrange for a peace negotiator, and instead climbed into the consul's vehicle and quickly headed into the city. He knew he would have to act decisively and take immediate control of this tense, uncertain situation. Escorted only by a trooper in a Norwegian taxi with a light machine gun, Dietl arrived at the large railway bridge that connected the eastern section of Narvik with the other part of the city that lay on the Framnes Peninsula. Gathered there was a group of

Norwegian soldiers, weapons at their feet, appearing unsure of themselves. Stepping forward from this grim, indecisive-looking group, was an older officer who introduced himself as Oberst Sundlo, city commandant and commander of the Norwegian 15th Infantry Regiment.

Considering the general military situation in Norway, when German troops were landing or had landed in much of the country – and especially given the situation in Narvik, where large segments of a German division had landed from 10 destroyers followed by two battleships, whose guns were aimed and ready to fire on the city – Oberst Sundlo was ordered to hand over Narvik without resistance, thereby avoiding what promised to be a senseless spilling of blood. Sundlo, after a moment's thought, asked for an hour's respite so that he could contact his superiors at the duty station in Haarstad (Norwegian 6th Division). The general denied him this and ordered his capitulation immediately. After several minutes of deep silence, Oberst Sundlo murmured: 'I surrender the city.'

During these negotiations – which were fully successful thanks solely to Generalleutnant Dietl's decisiveness action – Norwegian Major Spjeldner slipped away unnoticed, left Narvik, and headed to the ore railway, taking with him two Norwegian companies with some 250 men. He obviously disagreed with the decision of his superior officer and was determined to put up a fight. This had the potential to become a serious matter for the Germans, as it placed him to the rear of the German battle group that controlled the route across the Swedish border.

Meanwhile, Narvik was quickly occupied and all key elements of the city were taken over, with very little armed resistance outside of one or two shots. Most of the Norwegian soldiers had returned to their quarters, where they were disarmed. One of the prisoners of war was discovered to be a nephew of Churchill, who on 24 April was flown from Narvik to Germany (see Bibliography, 40).

By midday, the majority of the 139th Mountain Infantry Regiment (the Staff and 1st and 3rd Battalions) had landed successfully at Bjerkvik (15km north of Narvik) and the nearby Elvegaardsmoen troop exercise area was taken without opposition. Some light flak cannons were emplaced as a first line of defence against an enemy aircraft attack in the harbour. Kommodore Bonte's message to the Führer's Headquarters read:

'Capture of Narvik carried out according to plan!' (For the structure of Battle Group Narvik on 9 April, see Appendix 1).

The occupation of Narvik from the enemy's perspective

Prior to the German landing in Narvik, Norway found itself in the following situation:

In northern Norway, the Norwegian 6th Division with headquarters in Haarstad was commanded by Generalmajor C. G. Fleischer, the youngest of the Norwegian generals, and an extremely energetic and capable officer. Since the previous winter, in response to the Russo–Finnish winter war of 1939–40, the division had partially mobilised and provided a so-called neutrality guard (*Neutralitätswacht*) along the Norwegian–Finnish border. In the first days of April 1940, however, it could not be considered a general mobilisation (for the structure of the division, see Appendix 5).

The commandant of the city of Narvik, Oberst Sundlo, had held that position since 1933. His [purported] long-term project had been to install heavy weapons to prevent the entry of enemy battleships into Ofotenfjord and the harbour of Narvik. The proposed installations were begun, but not finished. By the winter of 1939–40, two block houses were built as nests for medium artillery, but only in the Narvik area, and as fortifications they were unsatisfactory.

In Narvik itself was the regimental staff of the Norwegian 15th Infantry Regiment and the Narvik Detachment, consisting of one infantry company, one pioneer company, and one anti-aircraft battery. On the Elvegaardsmoen troop exercise area was the 1st Battalion/13th Infantry Regiment.[6] According to numbers provided by the German military attaché in Stockholm, Norwegian strength in the area of Narvik consisted of approximately 1,500–1,600 men, 45 light machine guns, a few heavy machine guns and trench mortars, and four anti-aircraft guns (see Bibliography, 59).

In the first week of April 1940, the two built block houses were manned and defence-ready. The trenches that had previously been blasted out and excavated were not yet manned.

Besides the ground troops, two Norwegian armoured coastal defence ships, *Eidsvold* and *Norge*, stood in Narvik harbour under the command of Kaptein Askin. Out in the fjords were several patrol ships. By 0700 hrs on 4 April, the coastal defence ships were cleared for battle. This was a full 22 hours before the German destroyers appeared. At 2000 hrs on 4 April, the *Eidsvold* was sent out to its position in front of the harbour.[7]

On the same day, at 2200 hrs, Oberst Sundlo received the call from his division in Haarstad, saying that, according to the Norwegian ambassador in London, German and British naval vessels were then in the Baltic and on their way north, with an expected arrival in Ofotenfjord at around midnight. The Germans were to be fired upon, but not the British (see Bibliography, 3). (From this it becomes quite clear that the Germans were only a few hours ahead of the British.) In this conversation, Oberst Sundlo made it known that then, as before, he considered it senseless to launch a defence of Narvik against an enemy fleet, and did not intend to bring in the battalion from Elvegaardsmoen. On orders from the division, however, 1st Battalion/13th Infantry Regiment under Major Spjeldner was called in to Narvik, arriving shortly after midnight. At 1010 hrs on 4 April, the division commander reported that the German forces were battling in Oslofjord and German battleships were on the way to Ofotenfjord. At the same time, the following order was issued: 'Narvik must be held!' Kaptein Askin, who had been notified by Oberst Sundlo, responded: 'I have received the order and confirm that we are on the way.' The ground troops in Narvik received instructions that the trenches in the north and south of the city were to be manned by a rifle and one medium gun company. The majority of the troops were ordered to stand ready near the school, where a command post was located.

With the first news of the Germans' landing, the Norwegian 1st Battalion/13th Infantry Regiment was ordered to develop a counter-attack in the direction of the harbour. It took considerable time for the inexperienced troops to become ready, and in the meantime the first German mountain riflemen had pushed their way into the town. They were ordered by Oberst Sundlo to leave Narvik within 30 minutes, or they would be fired upon. This was reportedly the amount of time still needed for the Norwegian battalion to prepare their counter-attack. In the meantime, Oberst Sundlo called the division headquarters in Haarstad and received the answer: 'You have full responsibility!' The colonel had just returned to Spjeldner's battalion when he encountered Generalleutnant Dietl, as described earlier, which ultimately led to the capitulation.

In retrospect, one can only conclude that the bloodless surrender of this small, cramped harbour at Narvik had not been necessary. The Norwegian defence measures all appeared to be tactically unwise, indifferent, and hardly constituted any serious, determined defence effort. The responsibility for this no doubt rests on Oberst Sundlo. Either because of deep-seated pro-German sentiments, or because of differences he had with his division commander in Haarstad, which he had spoken of repeatedly, or out of pure military incompetence, he failed to perform his duty.

Even with the enormous disadvantage presented by the non-existent coastal fortifications and artillery, there had been other promising means of defence against the threat of the German ships' guns. To start with, instead of staying in town, the defenders could have posted themselves in the high, rugged mountains encircling Narvik. If there had been mountain positions prepared and manned early on, the ore route could have been protected, and the fjords could have been guarded and blocked off from both sides. Had the Germans tried to storm such mountain defences, it would have cost them unsustainable losses. Another approach would have been to isolate the German troops landing in Narvik and Elvegaardsmoen, who for a certain window of time had no means of transport onto land. When the British fleet arrived as expected in the next few days, the individual German battle groups could have been pressed into tight spaces and quickly crushed.

Thus, what enabled the German ground troops to become safely established in the area was an overall failure by the Norwegian leaders in Narvik.

The first destroyer battle, 10 April (see Map 3)

There were, however, still more dramatic events and twists of fate awaiting the Narvik operation.

On the evening after the landing, Kommodore Bonte invited Generalleutnant Dietl to spend the night of 9 April aboard his ship, particularly because of the radio tower installation on board, the only one that could connect with the higher command. Dietl, however, declined the offer and remained on land.[8] Had he stayed on the destroyer that night, he would most likely have met his death the following morning along with Kommodore Bonte. His loss would have been a great misfortune for the whole battle group, as his personality, initiative, and art of leadership ultimately played a great role in helping the troops surmount the difficult times that followed.

After the troops came ashore, the 10 German destroyers were readied for the long journey back to their home ports, making storm damage repairs and refuelling runs to the tanker *Jan Wellem*. For protection from surprise enemy attacks from sea and the air, the ships were scattered in the adjoining fjords around Narvik, with a patrol ship on constant duty. In the north-east, in Herjangenfjord, lay the 4th Flotilla with three ships; to the south-west, in Ballangenfjord, was the 1st Flotilla with two ships; and in the harbour itself, which was filled with the 29 merchant ships of various nationalities, was anchored the lead ship with the four destroyers of 3rd Flotilla.

Because of a misunderstanding in the issuing of orders, the destroyer *Diether von Roeder*, which was on patrol duty at that time, did not wait around for its relief patrol to show up. In the early morning twilight of 10 April, at 0500 hrs, it [left its post in the fjord and] sailed into Narvik harbour.

A few minutes later, the British ships opened fire inside the crowded harbour. Five destroyers from the British 2nd Destroyer Flotilla under Captain Warburton-Lee had slipped unnoticed into west Ofotenfjord in the semi-darkness of early morning and the poor visibility caused by thick snow.[9]

The surprise attack by the British was a complete success. Firing their broadside guns and torpedoes, the German lead ship was turned into burning wreckage and sank in the early morning of the following day. Shortly afterward, the destroyer *Anton Schmitt* was struck mid-ship by two torpedoes, broke apart, and sank quickly. The *Dieter von Roeder*, now having entered the harbour, took one powerful hit followed by several more, and became immobilised. Five merchant steamers were sunk, nine were partially burned and run aground, and others took fatal blows and sank during the next two days. The whole of Narvik harbour had become one enormous graveyard of ships.

At around 0620 hrs, as the British destroyers turned around in the harbour, they ran into the pincer formation made by the German 4th Destroyer Flotilla as it came steaming out of Herjangenfjord, and the two destroyers of the German 1st Flotilla that broke out of Ballangenfjord. In a vigorous naval battle that began at 0645 hrs, in Ofotenfjord, the British flotilla leader *Hardy* was so shot up that it had to be beached on the southern shore of the fjord near Ballangen. Along with most of his officers, Captain Warburton-Lee was mortally wounded. The destroyer *Hotspur* received seven powerful hits, and limped, burning, from the battle arena and was later beached as well. After several direct hits, the destroyer *Hunter* became impossible to manoeuvre and was rammed by the destroyer *Hostile* following behind. *Hunter* sank immediately. Eight officers and 99 men went to the deep with the *Hunter*, and 50 survivors were rescued by German ships. The *Havock*, the ship that had brought up the rear of the British keel-line, was also badly damaged.[10]

In the last phase of the battle, after the *Georg Thiele* and *Bernd von Arnim* of the 1st Flotilla had already been badly damaged, the German ship *Erich Giese* was also struck hard.

In a rush of bow waves and foaming wake, the last two ships of the British 2nd Destroyer Flotilla swept out of Ofotenfjord, travelling west at high speed, and disappeared under clouds of black smoke.

Because they had not yet fuelled up completely, the German destroyers had to break off pursuit after half an hour. With their last available fuel, they returned to the harbour of Narvik, and anchored at 0810 hrs.

This British attack was definitely well-timed and boldly executed. The deployment of five British destroyers must, however, be understood as a one-off action that could do nothing to change the German occupation of Narvik. This kind of attack could only have gone on to succeed if the British had fully committed sufficient means and measures (immediate troop landings, for instance), which was not the case on 10 April, nor in the days that followed (see Bibliography, 44).

The initiative and responsibility for the attack by the British 2nd Destroyer Flotilla belonged to Captain Warburton-Lee, whom the British Admiralty had previously cautioned against attacking in Ofotenfjord before stronger naval forces were in place.

The first naval battle on 10 April, which had almost completely destroyed the British destroyer unit, also caused the Germans bitter losses. Two destroyers were sunk, two ships were put out of commission, and three had suffered serious battle damage. Only three destroyers remained fully functional. The human losses totalled 159 officers and sailors, among them the commander of the destroyers, Kommodore Bonte, and the majority of his staff.

In the place of the fallen Kommodore Bonte, the chief [Fregattenkapitän Erich Bey] of the 4th Destroyer Flotilla took command. Knowing that despite any victory, the condition of the German destroyers had definitely deteriorated, he had grave concerns. Because of the heavy damage that many of them had suffered, their return voyage home would now be considerably delayed. They would have to be significantly restored, and more fuel would have to be acquired.

Moreover, half of their munitions had been expended and would not be resupplied by the Export Echelon vessels, which had failed to appear.

A further obstacle was the strong enemy at the entrance to the fjord. This was discovered on 10 April by two German destroyers trying to exit the area to start on their homeward journey. In the dead of night, attempting to reach Vestfjord and then the North Atlantic, they found their egress blocked at Ofotenfjord strait by British cruisers and destroyers. At midnight, the German ships returned and tied up in the harbour.

Two days passed almost without incident until the evening of 12 April. Between 1800 and 1900 hrs, British carrier planes ran a bombing attack, causing 30 wounded and several deaths. The intervening time was used in feverish efforts to restore the destroyers enough to make them seaworthy and battle-ready. In case of more surprise attacks, a regular outpost patrol was on duty in the west part of Ofotenfjord.

At this point, the inevitable question arises as to the why the destroyers were scuttled. Given that the destroyers could not expect to breach the British blockade of the fjord entrance and return home, why were they not put to use? Their light weapons, matériel, and equipment could have been removed and brought in to reinforce the ground defence around Narvik. Their crews could have been sent at an earlier point to integrate into the ground troops. Further, the destroyers, each with five 120cm cannons, could have become floating batteries, or could have been sunk at the fjord entrances around Narvik (Beisfjord and Rombakenfjord) to form a barrier.

The destruction of the German destroyers, 13 April (Map 4)

Then came 13 April. At 1010 hrs, the acting commander of the German 4th Destroyer Flotilla received a message from Naval Command West, reporting that strong enemy forces were to be expected in the Narvik area that afternoon (see Bibliography, 1). In response, the Naval Command ordered all operational destroyers to leave the harbour and divide themselves between the adjoining fjords. They were to create a pincer effect, similar to that of 10 April, against any invading enemy ships. The *Erich Koellner*, which was no longer fully operational, was to be used as a blocking battery, and was to take position behind a rocky outcrop at the narrow entrance at Hamnes, in the western part of Ofotenfjord.[11] The destroyer *Hermann Künne* was to escort this slower-moving vessel and then continue on out to Baro as picket patrol.

Suddenly at 1215 hrs, while the remaining destroyers were busy with ongoing repair work and the refuelling, a radio message came in from the *Hermann Künne*: 'Alert! Light naval forces invading Ofotenfjord!'

No further, more precise information was received, but from out in west Ofotenfjord came the roar of gunfire.

What had happened?

At 1210 hrs, the same two destroyers that had attempted to leave for home were now trying to reach their assigned positions in the fjord. Suddenly, at a distance of about 22 nm, nine British destroyers came into view. The German destroyers immediately sounded the alarm. With enemy forces suddenly bearing down on them, the *Erich Koellner* turned and sailed toward the south coast of Ofotenfjord, finally anchoring at Djupvik. Shortly after 1300 hrs, *Erich Koellner* turned on the enemy's lead destroyers and fired hard with all weapons. They could not keep it up for long, however, and after only six salvos, they were surrounded by enemy ships. After several torpedo hits, the *Erich Köllner* caught fire and sank. Thirty-one men died, and 34 were wounded. The remaining crew and commander swam ashore, but lacking life rafts, they were unable to reach Narvik. Several days later they were captured.

At this moment, the *Hermann Künne* was moving toward the British fleet, attempting to lay a smokescreen to allow the other German destroyers to leave the harbour unseen.

After receiving the alarming radio message, the destroyers *Hans Lüdemann*, *Wolfgang Zenker*, and *Bernd von Arnim* hoisted their anchors, threw off their lines, and left their moorings at full steam. Two destroyers, not yet cleared for sailing, remained behind. A renewed battle had little prospect of success, especially considering the scarcity of ammunition. This became even more obvious when the enemy, with his overwhelming superiority, actually pulled into view. In two rows of dark blue-grey ships, the British closed in. Five large destroyers of the Tribal class – *Bedouin*, *Punjabi*, *Eskimo*, *Cossack*, and *Kimberley* – came to a stop at the northern shore of the Ofotenfjord. Four ships of the Forester class – *Icarus*, *Hero*, *Forester*, and *Foxhound* – headed southwards. Behind them appeared one more powerful steel colossus – the battleship *Warspite*, with the flag of Vice Admiral Whitworth on the masthead. Aboard the 33,000-ton ship were eight 38cm guns, along with eight 15cm and eight 10.2cm guns.

Thus, only about 35 German guns of 12.7cm calibre were confronted by 80 British guns of 12cm calibre and 16 heavy cannons as large as 38cm.

The storms had cleared, and the fjord basked in brilliant winter weather. The enemy ships came into sharp, distinct focus.

At 1240 hrs, the Germans attacked. Charging, the three lead destroyers pivoted in front of Bogen Bay and sailed diagonally across the fjord, shooting from broadside. In a zigzag course from one side of the fjord to the other, continuously firing and charging, making a series of effective hits, the broadsides battle began.

The British sailed in a line abreast, slowly edging closer in and forcing the Germans back. The whoosh and howl, boom and crack of the shots and their impacts grew louder, then echoed back a hundred fold from the snow-covered mountains. Shots flashed yellow-red, swirling black clouds tinged with yellow balled up and dissolved into long banners; from the water burst white foamy spray in ever-changing patterns. The second sea battle in Ofotenfjord had now become an inferno.

The German destroyers fought on from 1240 to 1345 hrs, at the same time being pushed further and further back into the eastern part of Ofotenfjord. Despite the oftentimes close ranges, the enemy shot poorly, and the German destroyers found themselves surrounded by a constant series of fountain-like explosions on the water. Ten planes from the aircraft carrier *Furious* also attacked without success, and had two planes shot down. But now the German fire became noticeably weaker: it would not be long before their entire supply of ammunition was exhausted.

At 1350 hrs, the commander of the German 4th Destroyer Flotilla ordered a retreat into Rombakenfjord. The destroyers were now without ammunition and completely defenceless. The crews were ordered to abandon ship, and the destroyers themselves were ordered to be scuttled or destroyed.

As the British slowly closed in, the destroyers fired off their last rounds and sailed into the Rombakenfjord. But the *Hermann Künne*, which was following at considerable distance, had not received the message to retreat. After a nearly two-hour battle in the Herjangenfjord, the destroyer missed linking up with the others, and after firing nearly all of its ammunition, finally veered off. On the north side of the rocky shore, the commander ran the ship aground and blew it up. Then the crew marched to Elvegaardsmoen, where, in the coming weeks, they would take part in the fighting on the northern front.

The destroyers, having largely escaped damage in the actual fight, now bobbed and swirled in a cloak of artificial fog in Rombakenfjord. It was here that they saw their final battle. The destroyers *Hans Lüdemann*, *Wolfgang Zenker*, and *Bernd von Arnim*, which had been the first destroyers through the fjord passage, were taken to the easternmost end of Rombakenfjord and their crews evacuated. The portholes were then opened, and, with the help of explosive shells and depth charges, the ships were sunk. The *Wolfgang Zenker* ran aground, stern first. The *Bernd von Arnim* sank after bursting apart amidships. The *Hermann Künne* did not sink immediately, but after being searched it was then destroyed by a British torpedo. It sank, keel up.

The destruction of these three destroyers took place while under guard of the destroyer *Georg Thiele*, which lay diagonally at the narrowest point of the fjord – the Stromnen Strait – blocking the entry of four pursuing British destroyers. The *Georg Thiele* fired with all weapons, was badly torn up in the process, yet with its last torpedo it inflicted severe damage on the destroyer *Eskimo*, ripping through its entire bow. The wounded *Georg Thiele* captain ran the ship with full steam toward the hard granite rocks at Sildvik in an effort to deliver the seriously wounded safely on the rocky shore. From the wreckage, which sat firmly lodged at an angle to the wall of the fjord, a lone gun shot off its last round of ammunition. Its aft portion blown up, the *Georg Thiele* then broke apart and slipped slowly into the deep waters.

In the meantime, the destroyer *Erich Giese* was also attacked. Having remained in the harbour with mechanical problems, it had undergone intense repair work. By 1350 hrs, it was somewhat seaworthy and able to sail. As soon as it left the harbour it ran into enemy fire, and as it rounded the Hook of Framnes at a sluggish 12 knots, it came under an intense attack. Around the *Erich Giese* lay five British destroyers in a half-circle, aimed in at close range –about 1,800 meters. Despite a determined defence, the *Erich Giese* was literally overwhelmed by the gunfire. Its entire munitions supply exhausted, it was enveloped in thick clouds of smoke, with fires burning on several decks. At approximately 1430 hrs, riddled with 22 direct hits, the *Erich Giese* began to burn and founder, listing further and further to one side until it sank. The remaining crew made it safely to the rocky shore of Framnes either by swimming or on one of the three life rafts filled with wounded. The *Erich Giese*, the last but one of the 10 Narvik destroyers, went down in the deep water opposite Framnes. This uneven battle against the larger enemy had cost the lives of 85 crew members from the German destroyers.

The second and final battle of the German destroyers took place in the harbour of Narvik. Here, the critically damaged *Diether von Roeder* was tied up at the mail pier and was no longer seaworthy, but still able to fire its forward guns. The battleship *Warspite* lay opposite Narvik in the Ofotenfjord in bombardment position, with its long-range guns pointed toward the city, the harbour area, and the jutting mountains in the background, apparently prepared to fight the suspected artillery positions. Three British destroyers sailed toward the harbour. After just one German salvo from the *Diether von Roeder*, one of the British destroyers caught fire and veered off. And then one more turned away, also apparently hit. Only the third destroyer, the *Cossack*, continued forward and began shooting its torpedoes. But after a few well-placed hits from the *Diether von Roeder*, *Cossack* too turned off, finally manoeuvring its way into the harbour at Ankenes, where it ran aground, burning and smouldering.

At 1440 hrs, its munitions exhausted, the *Diether von Roeder*, the last of the destroyers was sunk. Packed with depth charges, it went forecastle-first, with the stern listing portside, and finally reached the bottom of the 25-metre deep harbour.

By afternoon of 13 April, this second naval battle had come to an end. All 10 ships from the German destroyer unit lay in ruins in the fjords around the ore town of Narvik, beached, blown up, or sunk. Almost 300 German seamen, officers and sailors, had died. The majority of the crews found themselves climbing steep, slippery mountainsides through deep snow, in water-soaked clothing that quickly froze to their limbs, finding their way to the mountain rifle units where they were to reinforce the defence of the Narvik area.

In this second naval battle, the British had lost 83 men. A number of their destroyers had been hard hit, and the *Eskimo* and *Cossack* had been badly damaged.[12] On the morning of 14 April, around 0500 hrs, all British naval forces down to the last destroyer remaining in the fjords regrouped and steamed back out through the Ofotenfjord passage.

The British did not come ashore at Narvik. In this, they lost a perfect opportunity to deal a blow to Battle Group Narvik, which at that point was in its early stages of defence preparations and still vulnerable.[13]

CHAPTER 2

Consolidation of the Situation for Battle Group Narvik

Narvik – an alpine environment in winter

Before them [the Germans] stood Narvik and its environs, soon to become the battle arena, covered with towering mountain ranges, deeply carved fjords, and snowy alpine meadows.

The fjords were grey and drab, closed in all around by the white mountain walls. Like an open hand with fingers outstretched, Ofotenfjord reached deep into the countryside, branched out into the narrow Skjomenfjord toward the south; eastward lay the smaller Beisfjord, and still further eastward, Rombakenfjord, with its narrow Stromnen Strait. Finally, to the north-east lay Herjangenfjord.

Between Rombakenfjord and Beisfjord lies the town of Narvik, situated on a peninsula that extends out into the basin of the large natural harbour. In the background looms a high rocky massif. A geological depression slopes down from the train station to the harbour, dividing the town into two sections, with one section lying on the north, and the other on the south-east of this depression. This large depression also separates Narvik's peninsula, the Framnes Peninsula, from the mountainous area behind it. The peninsula, with its 100-metre elevation, rises steeply from the waters of Ofotenfjord. Also on the Framnes Peninsula is the Frydenlund district, an area with mostly wooden houses, while the business and administrative quarter of Narvik lies at the foot of the towering mountain, Fagernesfjell (Fagernes peak). The area on the outskirts of the town of Narvik is sparsely settled, with only a few small towns and fishing villages along the coastline of the fjord.

On the few existing roads, travel was interrupted by ferry services across the fjords. One road, for instance, ran along the shoreline of Beisfjord all the way to the southernmost tip of the fjord and continued along the southern shoreline of Beisfjord to Ankenes. On the other side of Ankenes was a ferry that crossed the narrow fjord channel and met the road along the edge of Ofotenfjord. This road went to Ballangen via Haakvik and Skjomenfjord. The main route out of Narvik was by ferry from Vasvik to Ojord, connecting to the Nordland road from Haarstad at the north end of Herjangenfjord. This led past Gratangsbotn village, across the Oallge pass and further on to Bardufoss and Tromso. More important than these roads, however, was the ore railway. Electric-driven and on a single track, it led up from the harbour along Rombakenfjord, climbing 500 metres to Bjornfjell and the small settlement of the same name, and then across the Norwegian–Swedish border to the iron ore mines located in Kiruna, Sweden. The 34km rail line consisted of curve after curve of track and many man-made structures, including 24 tunnels and the Norddal Bridge, which spanned over Norddal (Nord valley) at a height of about 50 metres.[1]

The area around Narvik is a pure alpine landscape in an arctic environment. On the other side of Beisfjord, to the south, an elongated chain of mountains – Ankenesfjell (295m), Hohe (677m), and Skavtuva (650m) – runs north-east and drops down into the Skamdalen. To the east of Narvik, the mountains climb up steeply to a powerful rocky massif, whose individual peaks are Fagernesfjell (1,270m), Rombakstotta (1,243m), Beisfiordstotta (1,448m), and Middagsfjell (818m). The mountain massif then drops down into an alpine meadow at the Molnelven (Moln River), then continues on at an elevation of between 500 and 800 metres to the border, 30km away.

North of Rombakenfjord stretches a high plateau ranging in elevation between 300 and 800 metres, which is dotted with numerous lakes and streams of relatively small size. This alpine terrain falls off northward into the Bukkedal and Vasdal (valleys), where Hartvik Lake lies. On the opposite side looms once again the tall, jagged mountain chain whose peaks are Bukkefjel (1,146m), Rivtind (1,468m), Leigastind (1,335,m), Roasme (856m) and Hoitind (1,176m).

Also in the west, on the other side of Ofotenfjord, lies a range of wild, rugged mountains, whose peaks include the 694-metre Snaufjeldet to the north-west, and the alpine mountain ridges of the Storfjeldet, whose tallest point is 1,015 metres. Separating them is the Labergdal (valley) that begins at Gratangsbotn.[2]

Geographically, Narvik lies north of the Arctic Circle between the 68th and 69th parallel. In terms of climate, this means a very long winter with rough weather (storms, heavy snowfall, an average temperature of minus 15 degrees centigrade), and a very short summer. From the end of May until the second half of July, the luminous midnight sun hangs in the sky continually, while in winter it hovers below the horizon.

The scant vegetation consists only of thin groves of birch and thickets growing in the many valleys and depressions. The vegetation line, or timberline, on the slopes and flanks of the mountains lies at about 600 metres.

During the period of German occupation, the whole country lay under a blanket of snow, 1–2 metres deep; after the spring melt, the valleys became swamps and quagmires.

The area of about 30 by 40 kilometres where the coming battles were to take place, made for a most difficult terrain for combat. Added to this were the very adverse climatic conditions:

> An inhospitable, sparsely settled region, which offered little or no lodging …
> … a wasteland of mountain and rock landscape with bare, steep, stone cliffs, glacier covered mountain ridges, craggy canyon fjords and valleys covered in loose stones, mountain streams and melting lakes that delayed and burdened each forward movement, and digging in was impossible on the granite …
> … the bright northern nights, no longer providing cover and concealment to our movements, gave us no rest, only enabled the attacking enemy to conduct operations in the night hours, while our own troops living in constant, heightened watchfulness …
> … at the beginning the deep snow, storms and cold temperatures, which later all turned to rain, moisture, and sogginess, and with this came additional difficulties, exertions, and privations.

Under these adverse conditions, only the very toughest soldier could so much as think about engaging the enemy, a soldier who had experienced the sweat and comradeship that comes from fighting alongside an outstanding corps of non-commissioned officers (NCOs), and under the leadership of dynamic commanders. These troops had the good fortune to serve under Generalleutnant Dietl, the commander of the battle group (*Kampfgruppe*). As a leader, a soldier, and individual, he stood as role model, soul, and motivating force; with his will, his energy, and his leadership skill, he surmounted all barriers, difficulties, and crises.

As mountain soldiers, the troops looked upon the massive arctic mountains and immediately felt at home. Although these men had the Poland campaign behind them, and were battle-proven, rigorously trained and schooled, they could not have foreseen the hard battles and even greater toil and privations that lay ahead.

Now, 1,700km from the nearest border of the Reich, Battle Group Narvik found itself completely alone and fully dependent on its own resources. The impact of this situation is illustrated in the following paragraphs.

The problematic supply situation

So far, the battle group had faced two unexpected challenges – one was the missing Norwegian coastal batteries, and the second was the surprising resistance from Norwegian troops from Narvik on the ore railway. And now two new challenges presented themselves, which had to do with commanding and controlling an isolated battle force from a distance. Provisions, in particular, became a sore problem.

In the overall plan for their deployment to northern harbours of Norway, the soldiers could bring with them on the destroyers only their most necessary equipment. Due to the small space available, the destroyers carried only the food needed until they reached their destination. To ensure speed and efficiency, all heavy equipment, artillery, anti-aircraft weapons, munitions and provisions, and so on, would arrive separately on German merchant steamers. This was called the *Ausfuhrstaffel*, or Export Echelon, whose destination was ostensibly Murmansk. But within hours of the landing in Narvik, it was discovered that only one of the ships of the Export Echelon had made it through.

Like the destroyers, the Export Echelon had departed for Narvik from harbours in Germany on 3 April. The 7,600-ton steamer *Bärenfels* left Hamburg at 0200 hrs carrying food supplies. On 8 April, it found itself stuck in the Norwegian Haugesund for lack of a harbour pilot. On 10 April, it was rerouted to Bergen, and four days later it was sunk in a British air attack. Also on 10 April, shortly before it was to arrive in Narvik, the 8,500-ton ship *Alster*, carrying munitions, was captured in the sea north of Bodo by British naval forces. The 8,500-ton steamer *Rauenfels* – carrying a 15cm battery, an 8.8cm anti-aircraft gun, a heavy infantry gun, and an anti-tank gun – was also destroyed in Ofotenfjord just short of Narvik.[3] On 9 April, the 8,000-ton tanker *Kattegatt*, which left Wilhelmshaven on 3 April, was stopped in the waters outside of Narvik by the Norwegian auxiliary ship *Nordkap*, and was scuttled by its crew.

Only the huge 12,000-ton tanker *Jan Wellem* had been able to reach Narvik, carrying fuel for the destroyers and a large quantity of provisions. The *Jan Wellem* had sailed from North Base in the Zapdnaja-Litsa Bay in the Arctic Ocean (see Bibliography, 40).[4] It had left on the evening of 6 April and arrived unchallenged in Narvik, anchoring according to plan on the late afternoon of 8 April. This fortunate ship also survived the next heavy shelling in the harbour (on 1 and 13 April) by the British, with no damage. But later, feigning damage, it was purposely sunk near the ore pier in 8 metres of water, thus avoiding bombardment from the enemy ships cruising near the harbour. The *Jan Wellem* and its valuable cargo, like the steamer *Lippe* that lay in Narvik harbour, were later unloaded in an involved procedure lasting several days and nights, which for the time being provided the only supplies for the entire battle group.

With the occupation of the Norwegian troop exercise area at Elvegaardsmoen, the staff of the 139th Mountain Infantry Regiment received the welcome news that a great number of Norwegian infantry weapons of all kinds, munitions, rations, and even clothing had become available. Although it appeared certain that the troops could be supplied from this stock for the next two to three weeks, the division's leaders were to be greatly disappointed. News arrived that due to the deep snow and expected resistance by Norwegian troops, the Norwegian airport of Bardufoss, which was 80km away, could not be reached, let alone occupied.[5] This was the only airport designated for resupply by air, and now the Norwegian army supplies could not be brought in. Because no other airport existed around Narvik, the resupply by air could only be done by airdrop or by seaplanes in the fjords, which were partially under fire from the British battleships.

After the ships of the Export Echelon failed to appear, attempts were made at the highest levels to quickly send help to Battle Group Narvik, but by that point such help would be very limited. Due to the fully deployed British counter-measures, resupply by means of transport steamers (surface vessels) was no longer possible, and on 10 April, the German Naval Warfare Command (*SKL, Seekriegsleitung*) ordered the U-boats U26, U29, and U43, which were lying in homeland ports, to be fitted out for cargo transport to Narvik. The U-boats actually departed between 2 and 16 April, each with 40–50 tons [of supplies] (mainly ammunition), but due to the apparently unsafe situation at Narvik, they were rerouted to Trondheim (see Bibliography, 1). The only possibility for a consistent resupply would have been by air-drop, but this was hindered and delayed due to the inclement weather.

To provide Battle Group Narvik with artillery, however, the Führer's headquarters ordered a mountain battery be shipped as quickly as possible (unfortunately there were no Norwegian guns found at the troop exercise area at Elvegaardsmoen). On 11 April, the commander of 2nd Company/112th Mountain Artillery Regiment (Hauptmann Lochmann) was ordered to fly to Narvik with 60 artillerymen, four 7.5cm mountain guns, munitions, communications equipment, and provisions. Next day, at 0800 hrs, 12 Ju 52s under Oberst Bauer took off from the Tempelhof airport in Berlin. Due to inclement weather, there was a necessary 24-hour stopover in Neumünster, which meant they could not take off for Oslo until 13 April. There was a two-hour refuelling stop at Oslo before going on to Narvik.

With their fighter cover forced to remain behind, at about 1830 hrs, in thickly clouded skies and heavy snow, the squadron turned across

Vestfjord toward Narvik. The transport planes, fully loaded and trying to cope with low cloud cover, could just barely fly above a thousand metres. The British ships immediately fired on them and shot down three planes filled with equipment and provisions. (At the start of the flight to Narvik, one Ju 52 had to return to Oslo due to engine damage.) With their last drops of fuel and no ground crew to guide them, the [surviving] transport planes finally touched down on the only landing surface possible – the snow-covered Hartvik Lake. They sank deep into the snow.[6]

The battery was unloaded, and on the night of 13 April, at around 2400 hrs, it reached the camp at Elvegaardsmoen.

Improvisation in capital letters

With the loss of the supply ships, this battle group may well have been the most impoverished troop ever to engage an enemy under modern-day circumstances and still live through it. This dire state of affairs went on for some time to come, compounded by an enemy who was much superior in numbers. But this was not the only challenge: the group had almost nothing in its possession. It had no artillery, heavy weapons, anti-aircraft weapons, munitions, communications equipment, field mess, vehicles, draft animals, winter kit, or mountain gear.

The radio station operated by Signal Section 463 was too weak to communicate with its counterpart station, and therefore the urgently needed communication with the homeland, as well as with Group XXI in Oslo, was impossible.

At the same time, the troops were also inadequately dressed for deployment in the mountains, which still lay in deep winter. Instead of warm winter clothing with padded anoraks, fur caps, fur vests, winter camouflage uniforms, fur-lined boots, and so forth, they wore only their normal mountain clothing, plus the long, old-style coats. Each man carried his entire kit in his rucksack. All winter equipment such as sleds, skies, snow shoes, bivouac gear, camouflage items, and so forth, were completely wanting.[7]

The mountain troops were soon joined by about 2,600 naval personnel, who had lost most of their possessions on the sunken destroyers and were totally unprepared for ground combat. They too had to be fed, equipped, and armed.

Thus, the days immediately after the landing had to be used in making the troops combat-ready and building effective defensive positions. While these vital tasks were being completed, the enemy cooperated by remaining inactive.

Because no amount of help could be brought in, the battle group had to fall back onto its own resources. Once again it was the tireless spirit of Generalleutnant Dietl and his staff who pulled together, seemingly out of thin air, all that was needed for the coming victory. Everyone, down to the last man, was inspired by Dietl's will to accomplish the seemingly impossible.

Even during the earliest stages of preparations, the naval personnel proved themselves extremely valuable, and were indispensable in technical areas. They were mostly tasked with the ferrying service in the fjords, the maintenance and running of the iron ore railway, harbour security, and the unloading of the *Jan Wellem*. To ease the shortage of artillery and anti-aircraft guns, one 3.7cm and three 2cm anti-aircraft guns, together with ammunition, were borrowed from the destroyer *Diether von Roeder* before it was blown up on 13 April. With an additional four 2cm anti-aircraft guns, the air defence was built up in the harbour, and later along the ore railway.[8]

As replacement for the missing heavy artillery, the guns on the five armed British ore steamers in the harbour were dismantled (each of the two 10.5cm guns had 30 rounds). It was primarily the German merchant ship captain, Kordludgert, and his men who toiled for three days and nights and brought six guns ashore. Two of them were conveniently mounted on open flatcars. Under Oberleutnant zur See Buch, they were installed at Tunnel 1 and at the harbour, but they were practically unusable because of the enormous smoke they produced when fired. Even the 3.7cm anti-aircraft gun was made mobile by mounting it on planks on an ore railcar. By10 April, these guns, including the 2cm anti-aircraft gun, were partially deployed in an attempt to feign a strong artillery emplacement in Narvik. This may well have deterred the enemy from coming ashore, and bought time for further strengthening of the overall defences.[9]

To further reinforce artillery at Narvik, Dietl also ordered the immediate seizure of the mountain battery that had arrived at the camp at Elvegaardsmoen. The battery was trucked to Ojord, but in the morning hours of 14 April, enemy battleships interrupted the ferry service across Rombakenfjord to Vassvik, and there was no other course but to row the dismantled weapons in small boats across the fjord, secretly and in darkness. Once they had got safely to the area of Tunnel 3, the weapons still had to be hoisted up the steep mountainside to the ore railway. After this nearly insurmountable challenge was met, and after the 1st Artillery Platoon under Leutnant Enzinger had finally arrived in Narvik, 2nd Platoon was sent back to Elvegaardsmoen and placed under the command of the 139th Mountain Infantry Regiment. The crews from the destroyers helped with the communications link-up, which was of inestimable value. On the afternoon of 10 April, on the initiative of the commander of the *Diether von Roeder*, the radio tower station (a 200-watt transmitter) was removed from the destroyer, and both radio equipment and technical personnel from the division headquarters were put at their disposal. The station was installed on the slope of Fagernesfjell, and was the only radio link with decent coverage.[10]

The naval personnel provided valuable support in the occupied zone in the area of mobility. By 16 April, technical naval personnel made the iron ore train serviceable again as far as Sildvik. When the Troeldal electrical plant was shelled and damaged, causing the electrical service to fail, they converted the ore train into a steam locomotive. In the town of Narvik, 48 privately owned lorries, six personally owned automobiles, and the entire inventory of gasoline were seized and used for necessary hauling tasks, primarily the salvaging of the provisions from the steamer *Jan Wellem*. At the same time, the ferry service across Rombakenfjord between Vassvik and Ojord was taken over, creating a direct access to the 139th Mountain Infantry Regiment assembled at Camp Elvegaardsmoen. The captured stock of Norwegian weapons, clothing, and ammunition was now able to be brought in to equip the naval company, that is, until 20 April, when the ferry was sunk by enemy ships. A further ferry service across Beisfjord, from Fagernes to Ankenes, was seized, and two small naval support stations were set up (each with two motor boats) at the end of Rombakenfjord and Beisfjord, so that the boats could unload the seaplanes and tow the planes for taking off again. The destruction of the German destroyers also meant the loss of almost all dinghies, and the Norwegians had disabled most of their cutters, so that ferry service in the fjords had to be maintained by simple row boats. The sailors provided an immeasurable service by running supply relays with these small craft, carrying provisions for all of the combat units.

The naval units formed as pure combat units were mainly deployed to secure and protect the ore railway or as naval battalions for coastal defence. A large number of the sailors also went directly into the mountain infantry companies, thereby enabling other groups and platoons to be assigned to newly formed combat units. Even though the sailors could not be expected to have the toughness, training, and experience for mountain fighting, they nevertheless fought faithfully and reliably at the most forward lines, standing shoulder-to-shoulder with their mountain infantry comrades.

With such scarcity of important basic needs, one could argue that it was only possible to survive the challenges of the Narvik battles with the support of such strong naval personnel on the ground. The German Navy adapted extremely quickly to new and unfamiliar conditions on land, not to mention the difficult tasks in the wintery mountain environment. They took on the mission assigned to them as part of the context of the overall battle, and executed it fully.

The troops soon took on a motley, generally unmilitary appearance. The destroyer crews carried a combination of navy packs, civilian articles, and bits of uniforms from the mountain infantry and Norwegian Army. In town, all skis were bought for use by reconnaissance troops and individual platoons for fast mobility in the wintery terrain. Tablecloths, bed linen, draperies, and later, white parachutes were made into camouflage clothing and covers for soldiers, weapons, and emplacements.

The German situation vis-à-vis that of the enemy in mid-April (Maps 2 and 5)

Along with ongoing efforts to organise and provision the troops, the defence measures for Narvik were developed and enlarged. Because digging into the rocky, frozen ground was impossible, the emplacements on the Framnes Peninsula and some of the heavy weapons positions on the slopes of Fagernesfjell were simply dug into the deep snow. Emplacements along the ore railway were built around the tunnels and railway cut-outs, where natural cover and shelter could be found.

By 18 April, the division headquarters had established three individual battle groups (Narvik Sector, Ore Railway (*Erzbahn*) Sector, and Group Windisch). On 1 May, the Narvik defence along the ore railway had the following structure:

Narvik Sector

(Major Haussels, Commander 2nd Battalion/139th)

Naval Battalion Erdmenger:	(Kapitän von Diest,[11] Kapitän Feiler) from tongue of land at Fagernes along the harbour as far as the ore quay.
2nd Battalion/139th:	(under command of Kapitän Wagner,[12] 7th Company, 6th Company, and a platoon from the pioneer battalion) on the Framnes Peninsula, 8th Company from Taraldsvik to Orneset.
Train Station (*Bahnhof*) Company:	(approximately 100 technical naval personnel and light infantry weapons; members of 2nd Battalion/139th without weapons) with technical missions.
Division Reserve:	Parts of 2nd Battalion/139th, in company strength, consolidated.

At the ore railway, as of 18 April, the defence area between Straumsnes and Bjørnfjell was taken over by the recently formed Naval Regiment Berger.

Ore Railway Sector

(Fregattenkapitän Berger)

Naval Battalion Holtorf:	Three companies in Straumsnes sector under command of Korvette Kapitän Holtorf.
Naval Battalion Thiele:	Three companies in the Sildvik sector under command of Fregattenkapitän Berger.
Naval Battalion Zenker:	Two companies at Hundalen sector under command of Fregattenkapitän Pönitz.
Naval Battalion von Arnim:	Two companies at Bjornfjell sector under command of Fregattenkapitän Rechel.

The enemy headquarters in northern Norway responded to the German landing in Narvik with a nationwide mobilisation.[13] From the area of Salangen, troops were on the march, even coming by lorry on the single large road, planning to counter-attack Narvik from the north. At the officers' school of the Norwegian 6th Division and the school squadron at Haarstad, the order was received to hold back the German attack as much as possible until these forces were in place. The units under Major Spjeldner near the ore railway, who had been determined to attack from the earliest moment of the occupation, were contacted via aircraft.

On 15 April, the British landed powerful forces in Haarstad, where they set up their headquarters (see Bibliography, 40). On 19 April, British landings also began in the area around Narvik. Toward 1800 hrs, one destroyer, an aircraft carrier (presumably used as a troop transport), and two steamers sailed into the centre of Bogen Bay, and began a rapid unloading process that continued until 21 April, as troops and substantial matériel were brought ashore.[14]

At the same time, British destroyers cruising in Ofotenfjord began to blockade the Narvik area and the fjord coastline.

Expansion of the occupied area

From the beginning, under the adverse conditions (difficult terrain, loss of the Export Echelon ships, and enemy counter-measures), Battle Group Narvik felt pressured into a defensive mode. The mission, as stated in the operations order of 2 April, Appendix E (see Appendix 8), was no longer an option. Division headquarters therefore decided to strengthen defensive measures around the city and harbour of Narvik, as well as along the ore railway, against the feared enemy landings. Further, the occupied area would be expanded by taking possession of as large a forward area as possible, especially to the north, in order to make room for an effective mobile defence against any Norwegian attacks that came in from that direction by land.

Another priority was to eliminate the enemy troops that had slipped out of Narvik and now stood along the ore railway, at their rear, with the intention of taking complete control of this crucial railway all the way to the Swedish border.

The enemy had been sighted by reconnaissance troops in positions at Spionkop, and on 14 April, the division commander sent in the reinforced 1st Company/139th, under Major von Schleebrügge, to attack. At 1300 hrs on 15 April, the company arrived in Hundalen by train transport, where it linked up with naval troops, adding 20 sailors and one Norwegian heavy machine gun.[15] At 0300 hrs, in the pale arctic sunlit night of 16 April, the newly reinforced company arrived on the mountain slope by ski train (with Leutnant Trautner, 21 men, and parts of Company Trupp). Two attack groups, which consisted of most of the company, started their advance. At the last minute, the Norwegians blew up the large Norddal Bridge, but only damaged it slightly. Then, in a fierce battle, the retreating enemy was thrown by storm from the strongly defended Bjornfjell border station and was totally defeated.

German casualties totalled only one dead and seven wounded. The Norwegians, however, suffered many deaths; nine officers and about 60 men were taken prisoner, some of whom were wounded. Some 150–300 men escaped to safety across the border into Sweden. Valuable items captured in this first land battle included 12 machine guns, 150 pairs of skis, and many other pieces of equipment. Furthermore, a Norwegian plane which landed to make contact with the [now defeated] enemy unit, was stopped from taking off again by German machine-gun fire. Its crew (a major and a lieutenant) were captured. A further outcome of the battle was that a German reconnaissance troop from the 2nd Battalion/139th was released from captivity.[16]

With this well-executed foray, the German units had fought their way through to the Swedish border and secured their rear. The platoon of the 83rd Mountain Pioneer Battalion (under Leutnant Brandt) repaired the battle damage on the huge Norddal Bridge, and by 3 May, this route to the border was usable once more. The ability to use this third and last section of the railway line would facilitate some small-scale troop transport, as well as enable supplies to be stocked up and cached in the mountains, initially at Hundalen and later at Bjornfjell. The most significant factor, however, was that it enabled a direct overland connection through neutral Sweden. To a limited extent, Sweden allowed civilian transportation (evacuation of some of the civilian population, shipwrecked crews of commercial ships, etc.) and also permitted relief transports with provisions and clothing for the German troops in Narvik. (On 23 April, a train arrived in Bjornfjell containing provisions, three train cars filled with clothing and one with medical equipment. On the same train were 30 signal personnel in civilian clothing.) The transport of troops, weapons, and other kinds of war-related equipment was not allowed.[17] Despite this, it was possible to use this transport to supply the battle groups with a number of specialists, disguised as civilians.

On 18 April, after the naval personnel had taken over security for the area around Bjornfjell, 1st Company/139th was placed under the command of the 39th Mountain Infantry Regiment at Hartvik Lake, and was transferred back to the division reserves at Bjornfjell on 24 April.

The majority of the 39th Mountain Infantry Regiment that landed at Bjerkvik – now called Group Windisch – had begun their advance north in order to seize the Oallge Pass which lay north-east of Gratangsbotn. Even as early as the afternoon of 10 April, the forward-most units of the 1st Battalion (minus the 1st and 3rd Companies, but including the attached 13th Company) pushed forward on the solitary, snow-covered Nordland road, their progress greatly hampered by the deep snow and shortage of vehicles. By mid-morning of 11 April, 2nd Company moved into Elvenes, at the end of the Gratangsbotn fjord, an area that was free of enemy forces. Toward the Oallge Pass, a clash occurred between the German ski reconnaissance troops that were patrolling far forward and a small Norwegian group that was retreating (the Officers' School of the Norwegian 6th Division). By 16 April, the area around Elvenes was occupied, with 13th Company located at Laberget, one platoon at Elvenes, and two platoons from 2nd Company in front of the pass.

In the following days, it became apparent that the enemy in the north had decided to shift to the offensive. Reconnaissance reported that 15 lorries carrying troops were coming from the direction of Salangen. On 17 April, a British destroyer attempted a landing at Laberget on small, open boats, but was blocked by security there. On 18 April, Generalleutnant Dietl issued the order to attack and occupy Oallge Pass, in anticipation of an enemy advance from the north. The pass was then occupied, again by the 2nd Company, with only few casualties (two dead and three wounded), which completely pushed the weaker enemy back. From the beginning, the commander of 1st Company/139th, Major Stautner, feared a detour around his far advanced units from across the mountains by the Norwegians, who were mobile in winter conditions, and therefore organised his battalion into especially deep echelons. These were about 20km deep, and included the following defence positions: security platoon at Laberget, 2nd Company on Oallge Pass, heavy weapons and parts of the 5th Company/139th in a support position at Elvenes, and 13th Company/139th in backup position forward of Storv Lake, with the battalion command post behind it.

Prior to 23 April, there was essentially no enemy contact. The battalion lay behind defensive structures constructed of snow trenches, and by clearing the road, maintained communication and supply from the rear. Reconnaissance troops who were sent out, ran into only weak, hesitant enemy soldiers, who quickly fell back and moved off.

The regimental staff of the 139th (under Oberst Windisch) had stayed on in Bjerkvik, while the majority of the 3rd Battalion/139th was at Camp Elvegaardsmoen with half of a mountain battery. The eastern shore of Herjangenfjord from Ojord to Gjeisvik was secured by the 3rd Company/139th. On 19 April, Naval Battalion Kothe (3rd Company), now battle-ready, was allocated the coastal security for the adjoining stretch of coast between Gjeisvik and Bjerkvik.

Until 16 April, the Nordland road, which ran from Haarstad through the mountain terrain west of Herjangenfjord, was secured only by a platoon from the 3rd Battalion/139th near the small village of Herjangen. This platoon moved on farther south-west to Skalve Lake and carried out reconnaissance as far as Bogen Bay.[18] While the enemy was securing its landings, the weaker German troops prevailed, even against entire enemy companies, by employing deception. By feigning a powerful force on the west side of Herjangenfjord, they caused the enemy to abandon its plan to attack. Nevertheless, it is still difficult to understand why the enemy, during the course of its overall land operations, did not once attempt to attack Group Windisch with strong forces from the south-west.

But it is equally mystifying that the Germans continued to ignore the deep southern flank of their entire battle group for so long – in particular, the southern flank of Narvik sector. From Ankenesfjell, on the opposite side of Beisfjord, for instance, the German defence of the entire city and harbour of Narvik could have been fully observed and compromised by the enemy. On 16 April, a reconnaissance operation led by Naval Company Erdmenger was finally sent to Ankenes. A reconnaissance troop was also sent to Beisfjord, a village of little consequence, which harboured refugees from Narvik and shipwrecked workers from sunken commercial ships.

Although the commander of Narvik Sector believed it was very important to take possession of the high terrain south of Beisfjord in order to broaden and secure that critical front area, this failed to take place in a prompt and timely fashion. Further, the occupation of the high peak, Ankenesfjell, was carried out with forces that were much too weak (on 18 April, with one ski platoon from Naval Company Erdmenger) (see Bibliography, 16). The ensuing developments, with the enemy's strong attack on Ankenesfjell, only underscored the Germans' original view that this peak was of some significance. Because security measures were taken too late, the newly improved southern flank suffered an extremely fierce, static battle with high casualties.

After its successful battle to expand the area of occupied ground, Battle Group Narvik was then increasingly pressured into a defensive posture.

The big question: should Narvik be held?

The main enemy in the second half of April turned out to be the weather, which became worse by the day. The storms created deep snowdrifts, and the mass of snow continued to accumulate with the continued snowfall.

At this point it appeared that the enemy planned to begin its landing immediately, and then quickly move to a large-scale attack against Narvik itself. On the evening of 21 April, division headquarters received a radio message from Naval Command West: 'Heavy British naval forces approaching on a north-west course' (see Bibliography, 39). On the next day, in fact, one battleship, one cruiser, and three destroyers were positioned in Ofotenfjord and shelled the German positions around Narvik from about 0930–1100 hrs. This shelling appeared to be preparation fire, as in the previous days the British had already landed troops in Bogen Bay, and there was a growing sense of an imminent attack. At 0800 hrs on 22 April, the Tromso radio station issued a warning to the citizens of Narvik to leave the town as quickly as possible, as the commander of the British naval forces in northern Norway intended to shell and bomb the city in an attempt to throw the Germans out of Narvik. On 23 April, the wire-tapped evening news from Paris and London also predicted a large attack on Narvik.

Dietl faced a difficult decision (see Bibliography, 40). Should he try to hold out against a major enemy attack? This would the leave 2nd Battalion/139th in its coastal positions, with no access to coastal fortifications and heavy artillery (a situation similar to that previously of the Norwegian Oberst Sundlo). Or should he give up Narvik in favour of a defensive position in the mountains? After long reflection, in which 'rationality and heart battled it out against one another', the general decided to hang onto the town and harbour of Narvik. While this certainly had something to do with prestige, it was more a matter of the large quantity of valuable provisions and munitions – essentials of battle – that were still stored in Narvik, which it had not yet been possible to move. However, the Narvik Sector Command received instructions that in the event of a major enemy landing, a hopeless situation, or if in danger of being threatened by enemy landings to the rear (for instance at the Stromnen Strait in Rombakenfjord or in Beisfjord), they were to make a fighting retreat along the ore railway and take a delaying position at the Sildvik–Hundalen line. As a preventive measure, Naval Company von Diest would be transferred to Straumsnes to secure against enemy landing operations at the flank and rear.

After a series of imprecise instructions had come in, finally a specific order from Hitler arrived, flown in by courier on 22 April at 1050 hrs.[19] [20] Accompanying the courier was combat engineer and demolition expert Pionär Hauptmann Oberndorfer. In the event of a mass enemy landing, which would be a devastating blow, the harbour was to be demolished. Nothing was to be left. On 22 April, under Oberndorfer's supervision, the demolition began and lasted until the evening of the following day, cut short only by the scarcity of explosives.

At 0700 hrs on 24 April, the most powerful naval forces so far arrived in Ofotenfjord. In front of Narvik now were arrayed two battleships, three cruisers, and seven destroyers (see Bibliography, 39), which proceeded to bombard Narvik and the surrounding area until 1100 hrs. Fortunately, as before, no casualties were sustained. The enemy landing, fully expected by early afternoon, still did not occur.

Although this landing did not happen, it would have been most practical for the enemy had it been done along the east shore of Herjangenfjord, followed by a link-up with the Norwegians. Then they could have gone on to destroy the German Group North. The only explanation for the lack of a landing is that British high commander, Major-General Mackesy – reputed to be a great ditherer – was being overly cautious and failed to seize his opportunity, despite the immense superiority of his forces.[21]

Even during these first days, with the entry of the powerful fleet in front of Narvik, it was becoming apparent that the Allies were not capable of conducting a coordinated, joint battle. The arrival of the enemy fleet ultimately proved to be nothing more than an exhibition, while in the meantime the Norwegians were fighting on their own in the north and would suffer their first heavy defeat.

The counterstrike by 1st Battalion/139th

The bad weather conditions in mid-April affected mostly the 1st Battalion/139th, which was located far to the north, and whose provisions and supplies were seriously endangered. The main route leading from Bjerkvik via Elvenes to the Oallge Pass had become a narrow path through the snow. Trying to keep it open was a futile effort; snowploughs were no more effective than constant shovelling snow by hand. The troops began to starve. The daily ration was one single package of *Zwieback* (hard toast) split between 10 men, meaning that each man received no more than five small pieces per day. The snow caves hollowed out by the troops as shelters would constantly become covered over with [fresh] snow, and equipment and weapons sank into the deep, white drifts. Visibility was sometimes barely 10 metres, and due to the lack of winter equipment, every forward movement was a struggle.

While the Germans struggled with these harsh weather conditions, the Norwegians made the first strike of their counter-attack. At around noon on 24 April, during a powerful snow storm, 2nd Company/139th (under Oberleutnant Bauer), having been fired on by artillery, was surrounded by a Norwegian battalion on the Oallge Pass to the north. The 2nd Company managed to break out unobserved (leaving behind their wounded, however, with two medium trench mortars), and after a 12-hour march, sometimes up to their hips and chests in snowdrifts, were able to link up again with friendly forces at Elvenes. The enemy pursued them as far as the Fjordbotnmark valley, where, after the strenuous march, the Norwegian soldiers rested overnight in the farmsteads, gathering strength to continue their attack next day. Due to the storms and the deep snow, the Norwegians were not expecting a German counter-attack, and heedlessly neglected to post guards outside their sleeping area. From their positions at Elvenes, the Germans got word of this, and the commander of the 1st Battalion/139th decided to surprise the sleeping enemy soldiers. He pulled together all of his own weakened forces, called in the 13th Company/139th from Storv Lake, and at 0400 hrs on 25 April, with only about 230 men, ambushed the Norwegians in the Fjordbotnmark valley. The Norwegians, torn from their sleep, defended themselves fiercely. After a six-hour battle, however, they were thrown back with heavy losses of 83 dead, including three company commanders, nearly 100 wounded, and 208 captured. German losses came to nine dead and 17 wounded (see Bibliography, 51). It later became known [to the Germans] that the defeated Norwegian 1st Battalion/12th Infantry Regiment – an elite ski unit – comprised an intimidating force of about 600 men.

While this was taking place, further north on the mountain of the Fiordbotnmark valley was the entire Norwegian Alta Battalion, and on the Oallge Pass was one battalion from the 15th Infantry Regiment. Both Norwegian battalions looked idly upon the destruction of the 1st Battalion/12th Infantry Regiment.[22] The Alta Battalion, due to unfamiliarity with the situation and poor visibility, assumed that the Germans themselves were under attack. The other battalion watching the battle had just captured Oallge Pass and was awaiting the arrival of its artillery, which was stuck in the snow.

At the time of this writing, there has been no other known mention of this assemblage of enemy battalions in Elvenes – all three in the same place at the same time. With one vigorous stroke, they could have seriously wounded the entire Group Windisch and opened the route to Bjerkvik to the other enemy forces. But thanks to the decisive attack by 1st Battalion/139th Mountain Infantry Regiment, under its commander Major Stautner, this did not happen. After this surprise assault, the Norwegians began using more cautious tactics, which continued as long as the fighting lasted. Thus, after his early successes, the enemy slowed down and was always able to be thwarted by new defensive measures, which benefitted all of Battle Group Narvik.

As weather conditions improved, division headquarters expected enemy attacks to continue. The predominating view was that the enemy would retain its point of main effort, or *Schwerpunkt*, in the north, against Group Windisch. Meanwhile, the increasingly unfavourable situation on the southern flank of the Narvik Sector, and the southern flank of the overall battle group, continued to receive less attention from division headquarters. This was evidenced by the fact that the Narvik Sector was given no reinforcements, but instead, had forces taken away.[23]

These units, spread as they were over such a wide area, would need steadfast leadership, which, with the insufficient and sometimes lacking communication with Narvik, could not be guaranteed. For this reason, Generalleutnant Dietl decided to move the command posts. On the evening of 24 April, the division headquarters were transferred to Sildvik, with Hauptmann Bach remaining in Narvik as division liaison officer.

CHAPTER 3

The Battle for the
Southern Flank

Attacks by both the enemy and the Germans (Map 7)

In mid-April, as the Norwegians pushed slowly down from the north, the enemy (initially the British) was trying to move overland from the south toward Narvik. The staging area for enemy operations became Bogen Bay, approximately 18km away on the north shore of Ofotenfjord.

The enemy's approach from the south suggested that he did not intend to attack Narvik immediately and directly, presumably aware that this would be only a localised victory. The Allies knew they could expect fierce resistance from the Germans, who could be expected to simply move back into new positions in the mountains, with their rear open toward the Swedish border. Should the Germans quickly recapture Narvik, the enemy no doubt realised the way to dislodge all the German battle groups would be to surround and attack on both flanks of his horseshoe formation. If enemy forces were to move from the south, in coordination with the Norwegian movement down from the north, they could create a pincer movement and cut off the German combat units from the rear (somewhere in the area of Hundalen–Bjornfjell). This clearly would have been the correct approach for the enemy.

Regardless of whether such an operation plan ever existed, thanks to the Allies' lack of cooperation and poor, indecisive leadership, nothing of the sort was ever put into action. Instead of following the more expansive, circuitous direction of attack that was available to them, the enemy bit fiercely into individual defensive positions and exhausted himself in frontal attacks. Any time the enemy did choose a more circuitous, indirect route, it became a slow, plodding process that took up a great deal of time, which the German commanders put to good use in building new defensive lines.

The spring season, with its constant inclement weather, and the challenging terrain ought not have, and should not have, been allowed to stand in the Allies' way. Furthermore, the enemy's fumbling battle commanders, who knew nothing of flank attacks, rapid evasion, large breaches, rapid pursuit, and so forth, only abetted the German defence again and again by providing pauses, during which they could dig in new defensive positions. In the hard battles to follow, Battle Group Narvik was always given the gifts of time and opportunity to rearrange its existing weak manpower, switch out forces, regroup, and concentrate on the current main effort.

In late April, the enemy readied himself for the jump across Ofotenfjord, seeking to acquire his foothold on the fjord's southern coast and commence with plans to attack Narvik. Between 25 and 28 April, under the protection of two cruisers and three destroyers, a steady stream of fishing cutters sailed from Bogen Bay to Haakvik Bay, which lay directly opposite. Approximately two British battalions were put ashore, which slowly advanced into the Haakvikelven valley and onto the coastal road toward Ankenes, expanding the occupied beachhead and the developing blocking positions. The weak German naval security forces (ski reconnaissance) fell back to Beisfjord, abandoning the coastal village of Ankenes which lay opposite Narvik harbour. In order to reinforce the strength of the security force that remained on the southern shore, as the enemy entered Ankenes, he was fired on by combined firepower from Narvik (medium mortars and a light infantry gun platoon from 2nd Company/139th Mountain Infantry, along with the two mountain guns). Under this shelling, the British vanished into cover and remained quiet.

Having entered Beisfjord, the enemy was easily able to make the leap across the 400-metre fjord toward Narvik under the protection of its battleships, gain a foothold in the harbour area, and roll up on the German defence around the town from the south.

The sector commander (Major Haussels) saw a second, greater danger with the entry of the enemy into the Haakvikelven valley. Here, with just one deep flank attack around the southern end of Beisfjord and on through the Molnelven valley in the direction of Sildvik, the Allies could cut off the entire German front at Narvik, and even attack the rear of Battle Group Narvik.

The sector commander now recognised that on the southern flank, the neglected defence line ought to have been expanded, and occupying this forward area also meant having control of its dominating peaks.

During the period that followed, however, the enemy presumably did not take into account that this deep flank attack was an option, or that it was even possible, and therefore made no attempt to attack there.

The Germans ought to have taken quick counter-measures to prevent the potential danger from the south, starting with blocking the enemy in the Haakvikelven valley.

On 28 April, a small combat ready-ready section was formed under Leutnant Mungai from troops pulled from the coastal front (one mountain infantry ski group, approximately 20 sailors, and 20 anti-aircraft artillerymen with two Norwegian heavy machine guns). Their first task was to seize the mountain saddle at Peak 606 (south of the Beisfjord settlement) and occupy the important pass into the Haakvikelven valley. They were also instructed to put on a great display of force, blocking the enemy's advance by means of an attack.

The very next day, Section Mungai started out from Peak 606 toward the Haakvikelven valley. Well-supported by heavy machine-gun fire, the few skiers drove back the enemy security outposts along the road at Storv Lake and pushed on amid continued resistance for some 5km until forced to stop at a strongly constructed emplacement at Mattisjorden. While a handful of skiers stayed to provide cover and keep the enemy occupied, the section retreated back to the mountain saddle at Peak 606. For their part in this advance, which was well-executed and without casualties, the anti-aircraft soldiers deserve particular credit. It was they who hauled the heavy, cumbersome Norwegian heavy machine guns down into the valley for continuous protective fire, closely following the attack through snow several metres deep on carriages with neither snow tyres nor sled runners. Afterwards, they hauled the weapons back up the steep slopes under the protective fire of the infantry.

Meanwhile, the enemy landings in Haakvik Bay continued unabated, and 1 May saw cutter after cutter crossing over from Bogen Bay. Heavy fire from the battleships in front of Narvik struck the shore, in the harbour area, and on the mountain slopes around Narvik, holding the defenders at bay. On the southern flank, the threat appeared to increase hour by hour (see Bibliography, 16).

In response to the enemy landing, the sector commander decided to counterattack the same day, 1 May. The plan, once the enemy was on land, was to push back his left flank, and if possible, either eliminate the beachhead at Haakvik or halt the advance with firepower. This could only be done by using the forces available to him from the coastal front around Narvik, but whose weakness would have to be accounted for. Once on land, the Germans would encircle the enemy in a pincer movement, with Section Mungai advancing through the Haakvikelven valley and one company of mountain infantry moving toward Haakvik via the line Ankenes–Emmenes.

The release of the infantry company from the coastal front was considerably delayed when, on the morning of 30 April, due to threatening developments in the north, division headquarters ordered two companies immediately be sent to them from Narvik Sector. This meant reorganising the existing defence and losing precious time, but on the night of 1 May, 6th Company/139th (led by Oberleutnant Obersteiner) was finally pulled from the coastal front. Moving stealthily, the company was able to reach the heavily shelled harbour road as far as Fagernes without casualties. Unnoticed, they crossed Beisfjord in row boats. In a quick surprise attack, the company threw the British out of Ankenes and Baatberget, but then, because of the closely spaced adjacent mountain slopes and deep snow, the German advance was compressed into an increasingly confined area along the narrow coastal road. Just before Emmenes, 6th Company/139th encountered another strongly occupied enemy position. Suddenly, as the company was about to storm the position, three destroyers opened fire on them from about 800 metres. Under constant shelling and heavy losses, the company worked its way back to Ankenes, one person at a time. By 6 May, after various stragglers found their way back, the whole of 6th Company/139th, whose company commander had been killed in action, numbered only about 50 men.

The now weakened Section Mungai, having advanced once more from Peak 606, was also denied victory on the ill-fated day of 2 May. It too failed to break through the enemy position at Mattisjorden, which was manned by an approximately battalion-strength force. Retreating to its previous position, the section then slipped away with the ski reconnaissance troops deeper into the Haakvikelven valley.

From its start, the operation to clear out the enemy beachhead forming around Haakvik had been undertaken with too few forces, but the primary reason it failed was that the main attack, which was conducted directly along the coast, fell apart under fire from British destroyers.

Against expectations, the enemy did not immediately advance on Ankenes again. Within the next few days, the British, who were fighting on land around Narvik for the first and only time, were relieved and replaced by Polish mountain battalions.[1] With the time won during this replacement process, the hard-hit 6th Company/139th was ordered to a defensive position above Ankenes on the Ankenesfjell, and to spread out over an area of about 3.5km in a series of outposts. In addition, Section Mungai was sent to Peak 668 (known as Harhaugen) as a security force. Between Section Mungai and 6th Company, rotating reconnaissance troops took over the badly needed security and surveillance of the whole of Ankenesfjell.

In the coming days, fierce battles raged over the newly created southern front. Slowly, but relentlessly, the Poles pushed on up the southern slope of Ankenesfjell with increasingly powerful forces. Dispensing with attacks along the coastal road toward Ankenes, they moved into mountain positions, set up their heavy weapons, and stepped up efforts to seize more and more high, dominating terrain. In their attempt to push the German defenders further back and shatter their blocking positions south of Narvik, however, the enemy exhausted himself in frontal attacks on short-range objectives. The question as to why the enemy, who in the days ahead would prove to have far superior and generously equipped forces, did not immediately (as was mentioned previously) set out on a wide sweeping movement southward around Beisfjord, where he could have broken through the entire deep, left flank of Battle Group Narvik with one strong thrust, remains a mystery.

The commander of Narvik Sector, fearing just such an attack, reluctantly decided to pull another mountain infantry company from the coastal front as reinforcement for the left flank of the southern front. On 10 May, nine German fighters appeared over Ofotenfjord, their howling bombs creating mayhem among the ever-present British battleships, and scoring several hits. For 7th Company/139th, this chaos provided an unexpected opportunity to slip away from its positions on the Framnes Peninsula almost unhindered.[2] Arriving at Beisfjord by lorry transport, the company immediately climbed up to the saddle at Peak 606, where it relieved Section Mungai. Section Mungai now headed east, where it was to provide security to Skamdalen near Peak 34. The 7th Company/139th, numbering about 100 men, moved into position along the line Peak 606–Peak 773 (Hestefjell)–Peak 650 (Skavtuva). The backbone of this position consisted of heavy weapons: on Skavtuva were one heavy machine-gun group and one Norwegian heavy machine-gun group, on Hestefjell was one Norwegian heavy machine gun, and on Peak 606 were two Norwegian heavy machine guns, with two medium mortars behind them. One group of sailors was assigned as the resupply echelon from Beisfjord to the mountain positions.

Meanwhile, the attacking Polish mountain riflemen were achieving considerable success. On 6 May, as the enemy closed in, the fatigued 6th Company/139th had to to fend them off in counter-attacks. On 8 May, after having been thrown back, the enemy nevertheless captured the high Peak 295 and pushed 6th Company further back to the high mountain rim around Beisfjord. On the steep mountainside, 6th Company desperately struggled to resist and keep from being altogether thrown down the slope and into the fjord.

Having captured Peak 295, the Poles had gained excellent observation posts with the best views of Narvik. On 8 May, an enemy battery located in Haakvik began shooting into the town and continually fired hard into the flank and rear of the German coastal defence, which had been set up to cover an attack from the direction of Ofotenfjord.[3] Of particular concern was that this enemy battery could also reach beyond the peninsula of land where Fagernes lay, which previously lay out of reach of the enemy destroyers. Now the entire ferry route to Ankenes came under fire. German counter-fire from the two mountain guns at Narvik remained weak and ineffective due to the shortage of ammunition.[4]

The 6th Company, despite its extremely precarious position, had been able to keep the enemy, who were positioned everywhere above them, from climbing down to the ferry crossing point at Beisfjord. Therefore, the enemy headed to Ankenesfjell, with some of the troops moving south-east, intending to capture more dominating high ground. In the night, the enemy, with an approximately company-sized force, captured Peaks 405, 677, and 734, and then ambushed the German 10-man outpost at Peak 668 (Harhaugen). The few infantrymen at Harhaugen inflicted heavy casualties on the attackers and managed to elude capture at the last moment by entering Beisfjord via the steep rocky cliff. But they had to leave their wounded commander behind, along with all of their equipment and baggage. All communications between 6th Company/139th at Ankenes and 7th Company/139th at the southern end of Beisfjord were now broken off. Communications could not be re-established, and from then on each company remained isolated, positioned at the right and left flanks of the southern front, each fighting on its own.

By mid-May, although suffering heavy losses, the enemy occupied almost the entire Ankenesfjell at a strength of about one to one-and-a-half battalions. Only slowly did he get around to sending out scouts and tentative reconnaissance towards 7th Company/139th. From their high terrain and mountain peaks they had captured, the Poles had a complete view not only of Narvik, but also of the entire Beisfjord and the roads that ran along its shores. With heavy machine guns and high-angle fire weapons, they were able to effectively disrupt all traffic. With the Allies and their warships dominating Beisfjord, German sea planes (Wal) with supplies could not land safely. Even at the first sign of a landing approach into Rombakenfjord, vigorous anti-aircraft fire broke out from Ankenesfjell.

It still appeared that the main goal of the enemy was to seize Ankenes and thereby capture the route through Beisfjord to Fagernes and Narvik.

On 16 May, without preparation fire from the ships' guns, the Allies attempted a surprise midnight landing to the rear of 6th Company/139th at Ankenes. But when the eight fully occupied cutters approached from the direction of the Framnes Peninsula at about 0130 hrs, they were spotted and stopped by fire from a 2cm anti-aircraft gun at Fagernes. Between this and the heavy machine guns firing from the mountainside position at Ankenes, the approaching enemy now came under crossfire, suffered brutal losses, and was forced to turn around. At approximately 0240 hrs, the ships sailed off into the direction of Haakvik under the cover of a destroyer that had come to their aid. Meanwhile, another 17 ships had gathered at the entrance of Narvik harbour.

In the daytime, the enemy tried to attack 6th Company/139th again, but with a frontal assault. On this day alone, 6th Company had to fight off three consecutive attacks, partly with close combat and counter-attacks.

To restabilise the situation at the southern front of Narvik, and most importantly, to re-establish communication between the two companies deployed there, the Germans would have to counterattack, with the specific goal of retaking Ankenes. With the recapture of this important high ground, they would have a continuous, more easily defended front. The main thrust was to be led by 7th Company/139th, this time attacking from the south-east in a north-west direction, with the goal of forcing all enemy emplacements off the mountain (see Bibliography, 16).

Yet the attack on 16 May failed as well. The enemy had a deeply dug-in battalion-strength force with a wealth of heavy weapons, while German forces were weak and without artillery support. But the failure was for other reasons: first, a German assault force of mountain climbers was sent from Beisfjord to climb across an almost vertical rock wall to recapture the dominating Peak 668 (Harhaugen), but just below the peak, they were sighted and fought off. Further, 7th Company/139th, which had advanced approximately 2km, suffered losses of six killed in action and five wounded, and had to return to its starting position. And then a simultaneous foray by 6th Company/139th against the enemy-held Peak 405 was supposed to link up with the attack by 7th Company, but this did not take place.

After this new failed attempt, any further plans from the section commander to clean out the area at the southern front had to be abandoned for lack of resources. Now, it could only be a question of maintaining this forward sector with all resources despite the unfavourable situation that had arisen, and to prevent the enemy from further penetrating into the south.

Static battles on the mountains south of Beisfjord

In the weeks to follow, a hard and bitter static battle developed around the southern front, which still consisted only of the two separated flank positions. As the two companies remained firmly tied to their positions, and there was no longer any communication between them, there was no continuous battle line within the sector. There was only enough manpower to field individual outposts made up of groups of five to six men, who were separated by a large gap of 500–600 metres. Tactical depth, as in all of the front sectors around Narvik, was absolutely non-existent. This contradicted the basic principle that if the area in front of the main battle line can be largely dominated by fire, the defence has no hope of success. In addition, the enemy still had the high ground and was able to cover all of the strongpoints with fire. The rugged spine of the Ankenesfjell, with its individual peaks, its many cut-outs, ravines, clifftops, gullies, and troughs offered the enemy constant opportunity for surprise attacks, but for the German mountain infantrymen this terrain made sightings and observation very difficult. In this instance, the defence was conducted as a purely infantry fight, and the mainstay of the entire battle was the single combatant at his most elemental level.

Over the four weeks during which the southern front was held, the troops deployed in the deserted, rocky mountain terrain suffered extreme winter conditions, for the most part out in the open, without adequate shelter or the much-needed warmth of a fire, exposed and vulnerable to the mercy of the lingering arctic winter. The men quartered themselves in snow caves or made small shelters of stones covered over with tarpaulins. In the shelters of Ankenes and Beisfjord, days off and relief shifts were impossible due to the lack of manpower.

The static battle continued during every hour of every day and night under extreme physical and psychological pressure. Due to the steep slopes, the positions occupied by 6th Company/139th in the Ankenes sector were under extreme tension. Literally every machine gun and rifle nest there had to be defended to the utmost and held until the last breath, as there was no extra space in which to retreat, or the entire company could have been thrown down into Beisfjord. This battle demanded acute awareness from every single man, constant observation of the enemy, and double the usual degree of attentiveness due to the wide gaps between the neighbouring rifle nests. Amid constant frontal bombardment from the many heavy enemy weapons, the guns on the cruisers and destroyers lying in Ofotenfjord fired incessantly into the defenders' flank and rear, hoping to crush and break the Germans' will to resist.

Because the thinly occupied lines of 7th Company/139th at the southern end of Beisfjord had to be ready at all times, sleep and rest were out of the question. Always on alert, the individual small groups had to be already in position in case of an alarm. They had to keep their few weapons aimed in and ready to quickly nip in the bud any enemy attack or possible breach, which could not otherwise have been contained by these weak forces.

While the enemy, with its far superior numbers and weapons and a nearly inexhaustible supply of munitions, could fire away incessantly, the German supply situation demanded great frugality. Only a limited ration of ammunition could be allowed per weapon, available only for immediate defence against an attack, which meant it would not be possible to stage an offensive on an identified enemy assembly area or observation post.

The sparse ammunition resupply to the southern flank could only be carried out with great difficulty and in constant threat of enemy fire. For 6th Company/139th, it had to be brought via the harbour road to Fagernes, which usually lay under bombardment from ships, and from there in row boats across Beisfjord under the eyes of the Allies on the Ankenesfjell, then up the mountain slope up to the positions, while still under constant visibility of the enemy. For 7th Company/139th, supplies were brought in by lorry on the roads along the fjords toward Beisfjord, constantly in sight of the enemy, and from there they were lugged up to the saddle at Peak 606 in a five-hour climb and brought forward to the individual positions. Because of threat of fire from the ships and the heavy weaponry lying in wait, movement along this stretch meant a constant race with death. Assigned to these resupply units were naval personnel, who bravely and tirelessly served their comrades of the mountain infantry.

It was under these conditions that the defenders of the southern front fought a protracted static war which went on day and night, and whose individual, small, but fiercely fought battles were lost and won mostly in close combat.

The most critical point of the defensive battle grew to be the right corner position at Ankenes, where the Poles repeatedly and eagerly stormed in, in persistent attempts to gain a victory.[5] On the morning of 17 May, 6th Company/139th fought off an attack by two Polish companies, and on the following night, had to defend against another strong advance. Weakened and battle-fatigued, the company could barely hold on, and during the night of 18/19 May they were pulled out and relieved by 8th Company/139th (under Hauptmann Salzer). On 19 May, this freshly deployed company had to fight off the forceful advances of two enemy companies. The enemy reinforced its frontal efforts and, at around 2200 hrs, attacked 8th Company several times, now in battalion strength. This attack was also fought off in a hard battle, and the positions were held. Although the enemy's preparations had been observed and promptly reported, and urgent air support had been ordered, no help appeared.

Although since 10 May the section commander had repeatedly requested help for the hard-pressed southern front, it was not until 20 May that the defending companies received air support. Amid cries of relief from the mountain soldiers and sailors, German warplanes attacked Polish positions on Ankenesfjell in low-altitude flights with on-board weapons, and then bombed larger targets outside of Ankenes and at Emmenes. But the planes had barely disappeared when the enemy again attacked 8th Company/139th, in more intensified, but unsuccessful thrusts. Then mortars came hammering down on the German positions from the higher enemy positions, while mortars from the land battery at Haakvik and the heavy projectiles of ships' guns simultaneously came crashing in on the rocky slopes.

On 23 and 24 May, the pressure against the Ankenes position intensified. Strong mortar fire plunged down from Peaks 295 and 405, and all day long the firing from the Haakvik battery and the destroyers in Ofotenfjord went on without end. A new German air attack came on 23

May around 1400 hrs, during which enemy staff, weapon emplacements, and camps were bombarded, but without lasting effect.

As described in the following battle report from 8th Company/139th, the fight at Ankenes was carried out in fierce, constant close combat:

> In the early morning hours of 24 May, the enemy conducted constant attacks and advances in the attempt to capture the left flank position of Group K. When the fog lifted at around 0400 hrs, the enemy abruptly started firing at the strong point, two heavy machine guns and several light machine guns fired frontally from their high mountain position, three medium mortars and several light mortars, through their well-placed shots constantly forced us to cover. Suddenly, from the left flank, where the enemy had worked its way close enough to make their assault, several machine guns fired. Then an entire enemy company attacked the nine men at the strong point, who defended themselves fiercely. Taking cover behind boulders, the enemy slowly crept closer and detonated his first-hand grenades right in front of our foxholes. Realizing that [our] group was now weakened and not able to hang on much longer on its own, a runner was sent to the neighbouring group for help, 600 metres away. Meanwhile, with well-aimed shots and machine gun bursts, the remaining enemy soldiers were pinned down and prevented from making a break through. But then the first infantryman was fatally shot and rolled down the mountain. Immediately afterwards a second infantryman was badly wounded by a shot in the neck. The two light machine guns fired in short, choppy bursts until the fire from the [enemy] machine guns stopped. The first infantryman took a chest shot and sank back. The man closest to him now lay ready at his light machine gun and once more held off the enemy. The enemy readied itself for an assault. Then the fourth of our infantrymen was killed, by a head shot. The enemy had now moved into the dead zone, and the group commander Oberjäger K. jumped up to attack them with hand grenades. Just then he was fatally shot, collapsed, and rolled down the steep slope. In the meantime, the second machine gunner was also wounded. Out of the whole group, just two men were still able to fight. The first machine gunner, although seriously wounded, crawled back behind his weapon. Gunfire rattled once more toward the enemy. The message runner, having returned from his mission, now joined the attack. Most of the way to the other group's position, he had been under enemy fire and had run for his life, but then rushed back, knowing that every last weapon was needed at the outpost. The enemy still did not succeed in that last attempt at a breach.
>
> At last the much wished for help and support came. With seven infantrymen, Leutnant P. rushed in and attacked the enemy in the flank, amid a loud 'hurra,' as the few remaining enemy soldiers turned to flee.

Although the enemy on Ankenesfjell did not advance one step farther against the Germans' determined defence, the battle became more strenuous and more heated from day to day. It brought bloody, gaping holes that the enemy could replenish, but which the German defenders could not easily do. The two remaining German companies were increasingly worn-down by their unrelenting struggle against the much stronger enemy force.[6] This was especially so for 8th Company/139th, which, since its deployment, had faced bitter fighting of long duration and with heavy losses. To remain steadfast, it had to be provided with continual, small numbers of reinforcements. Without help from the division, these had to be released by the sector commander, and only from the coastal front around Narvik. Almost every day, single groups and heavy weapons were brought to Ankenes, including portions of the Pioneer and Signal Platoon of 2nd Battalion/139th, and various groups of sailors, including the proven naval shock troop of Leutnant zur See Rauch, to help balance out the casualties to some extent. The naval groups were each assigned mountain infantrymen as instructors for the mountain battle. This finally brought the strength of 8th Company up to about 160–180 men, with four heavy machine guns, one Norwegian heavy machine gun, three medium mortars, and one 3.7cm anti-tank gun.[7] Nevertheless, the company still faced an enemy that was five times larger, with an absolute superiority in heavy weapons and artillery.

The Narvik Sector commander was confident in fulfilling requests to release all these reinforcement troops, more so at this point than at the beginning of May, as a direct enemy landing at Narvik was no longer expected or feared (see Bibliography, 16). As the original main defence position around Narvik and the coastal front was stripped and weakened, more and more fighters and weapons were thrown against Ankenes. It now became clear that the *Schwerpunkt* (main effort) of the defence of the overall sector had shifted to the mountains south of Beisfjord.

Where 7th Company/139th stood at the southern end of Beisfjord, the enemy – apparently much impressed by the counter-attacks of 17 May – remained relatively quiet except for active reconnaissance. It was not until 27 May, after the enemy forces in front of 7th Company had been reinforced to the strength of about two battalions, with triple its number of heavy weapons, that they entered the field as part of a major attack on Narvik.

In the last days of May, the sector commander came to the conclusion that a decisive attack against the southern front was imminent, primarily against Ankenes, but also against Narvik. According to intelligence reports on 23 May, the enemy was planning a landing from the direction of Rombakenfjord between Tunnel 3 and 4 (see Bibliography, 49). Then on 26 May, several prisoners were brought in from a Polish motorised shock troop, which had suddenly tried to break through on the road from Emmenes but had been shot up and forced into a quick retreat. According to their statements, the German position at Ankenes was to be seized in the next few days at any cost, and Narvik itself was to be taken at the same time in an amphibious attack.

These points were confirmed by intelligence conveyed to Group XXI in reports from the Luftwaffe.[8] Upon this, division headquarters gave Narvik Sector command of two additional fully combat-ready mountain infantry companies (1st Company/137th Mountain Infantry, with 108 men under Oberleutnant Schweiger, and 2nd Company/137th Mountain Infantry, with 118 men under Oberleutnant Riegler), who had just recently parachuted in.[9] According to instructions from division, both companies were supposed to be held ready as reinforcing reserves (*Eingreiffreserven*) for deployment in the weakened coastal sector around Narvik, with one company on its right at Fagernes and one on the left wing at Forsneset.

After jumping in to Bjornfell, the 2nd Company/137th set off quickly, singing and marching as quickly as possible along the ore railway, sparing no effort to come quickly to the aid of their comrades in their sister regiment at Narvik, arriving on 27 May at 0500 hrs. Unlike 1st Company/137th, which was held ready in the area assigned to them by the division, 2nd Company/137th was ordered to Ankenes by the sector commander, where they were to remain in reserve behind 8th Company/139th. This action had been expressly disapproved by Generalleutnant Dietl, and in fact, it would not turn out well (see Bibliography, 39).

By the end of May, the division's primary focus was to the north, toward the Norwegians who were bearing down on Group Windisch. But Dietl was also carefully watching the events as they unfolded at the southern front. He therefore strengthened the defensive line that had been built up at Beisfjord with a naval company from Regiment Berger, deployed at depth on the left flank. On 2 May, the regiment was ordered to move a security line forward along the line of Peak 660–Peak 639 (3km south-west of Sildvik). Beginning on the night of 2 May, they occupied this line along with the 3rd Naval Company. The general had become concerned with the massive movement of ships in Bogen Bay (German air attacks of 2, 3, and 5 May had apparently again been without success), and all the more so when reports arrived on 9 May citing the constant movement of enemy ships in Skjomenfjord, as well as landings along its southern end at Elvegaard, and Sorskjomen, further to the south. From Elvegaard, a road led inland and connected in Norddalen to a summer trail, which ran parallel to the Swedish border in a broad, eastward arch, and then on up toward Hundalen. This offered the enemy the opportunity to make the secretly feared, broad-ranging detour with an outflanking manoeuvre against the defensive line at Beisfjord. On 10 May, the division therefore requested constant air reconnaissance over the Skjomenfjord area. The very next day, intelligence reached Group XXI that Skjomenfjord and the surrounding region were clear of enemy. This report initially caused the division headquarters great concern, and therefore continuous observation was maintained in all directions and constant reconnaissance was ordered in the direction of Skjomenfjord. The ski reconnaissance troops travelled up to 50km into the no man's land of jagged, snowy mountain peaks. Their information, confirmed by aircraft reconnaissance, was always the same: no enemy movement.

The enemy had in fact the failed to take advantage of the opportunity at hand, although he could have put the entire Battle Group Narvik in a difficult situation (for the structure of the battle group as of 13 May, see Appendix 2). Admittedly, at this time, the mountains still lay in deep winter conditions, making travel difficult, but this was not impossible to overcome. The 2nd Mountain Division proved this, having marched some parts of the division along the same road on its way to rescue Battle Group Narvik. Why the enemy did not take the opportunity to attack remained unclear. It may have been some sort of 'terrain-avoidance' in combination with fear of resupply problems. Thus, the enemy forces that landed in Skjomenfjord seemed to have wanted to settle for forward-deployed security measures toward the east, pitting a company-strength force against the advancing forces of the 2nd Mountain Division.

CHAPTER 4

The Defensive Battles of Group Windisch in the North

Enemy breakthrough attempt in the east at Graes Lake (Map 8)

By early May, Group Windisch had fought heavy defensive battles in the north, with most of the burden on the 1st Battalion/139th (under Major Stautner). The initial phase began at the end of April, with powerful shelling from the ships in the nearby fjords.

In the early morning of 27 April, the regiment relocated its command post from Bjerkvik to Elvegaardsmoen. But that morning, at 0530 hrs, an enemy cruiser sailed into Herjangenfjord, and with 15cm shells, bombarded the regimental staff out of these new quarters, killing seven and wounding six. Two large barracks were also burned to the ground, destroying large stores of food, equipment, and valuable signal instruments. The ship's guns also targeted the resupply route from the line of Bjerkvik–Elvenes to 1st Battalion/139th. Over the following days, Bjerkvik, Elvegaardsmoen, the roads to Elvenes, and those along Hartvik Lake came under continuous fire from the ships' guns. By 28 April, the Germans had to evacuate Elvegaardsmoen, leaving behind only the field hospital, identifiable by its large Red Cross flag. Because of the constant shelling of the few roads in the regimental sector, travel on these roads was obstructed. Any attempts to travel on side routes, or off-road, meant struggling through the deep snow, which for transport vehicles was nearly impossible.

At this point, the shelling from enemy ships presumably meant one of two things; either the enemy was preparing to land troops in

Herjangenfjord, or they were destroying rear area installations, food stores, and other resources in preparation for a major attack from the north.

The second assumption proved correct. In the north, the Norwegians had recovered from their tough loss at Elvenes against 1st Battalion/139th, and now, after having been given reinforcements, they pushed forward once more – this time with considerably more care. Knowing that the road from Elvenes to Bjerkvik was especially well secured by the Germans, they made their first thrust against the poorly protected right flank of Group Windisch, intending to cut into the German line, or at least to tie down the strong forces at that location. They advanced eastwards in increasing strength, and by moving through Graesdalen, they attempted to attack the Germans on their flank. Here it must be pointed out that the Norwegians were extremely mobile on the tough mountain terrain in these winter conditions. With this advantage and fresh reinforcements, they could have simply come in with a wide, sweeping approach and won some easy victories. What was lacking there, however, was the necessary decisive leadership and combat experience.

At the time of the major Norwegian attack, which soon developed along a broad front, Group Windisch (consisting of 1st and 3rd Battalions/139th Mountain Infantry Regiment) was in the following defensive positions:

The majority of 1st Battalion (2nd, 4th, 5th, and 13th Companies with the attached Ski Platoon Trautner of 1st Company/139th) were still positioned at Elvenes, and covered the major Nordland road that ran through Bjerkvik. The battalion's ski reconnaissance troops monitored and conducted reconnaissance toward the east across an area 8km in width, as far as the area between Lort Lake and Hoitind (1,167m). The rest of 3rd Battalion/139th (12th Company, and parts of the 14th and 15th Companies) were positioned as regimental reserves along with the regimental staff in the area north of Hartvik Lake. Due to expected enemy landings in Herjangenfjord, 11th Company/139th had gone into positions at Peak 98 near Bjerkvik. Adjoining 11th Company on its south was the Naval Battalion Kother (3rd Naval Company), and at the south end of the fjord, at Ojord, was 3rd Company/139th. The far eastern flank of the entire Group Windisch was secured only very weakly, as any movement of major Allied forces was thought impossible in the deep snow and wild, jagged mountain terrain. Thus, the important entrance into the Graesdalen, on the mountain saddle south of Graes Lake, was secured only by a picket (Picket Smolle), with just 16 men, one heavy machine gun, and a group deployed to the left front on the Stortind. Further, the main road from Haarstad that led far into the west, was, as before, secured by only one platoon.

The defence on the northern front had a general advantage over that on the southern front, in that after expansion of the occupied area, the northern front contained dominating mountains and hills that could be exploited as outpost positions.

In the correct understanding that the defensive line at Graes Lake was a key point of the German northern front, the Allies at first attempted to break through there. After having broken through, and with a continued attack toward the west through Vasdalen, they would also have been able to push the rearmost positioned units of the German regiment toward Herjangenfjord. There they could have staged a landing, confronted the German units, cut off the whole of 1st Battalion/139th which was still positioned far to the north, and with this blow, could have shattered the entire northern front. At the same time, with one push from Bukkedalen toward the south to the ore train, possibly in conjunction with a wide, sweeping attack by the Poles who were positioned along the southern front, it would have been possible to cut off and surround the entire Battle Group Narvik.

On 28 April, reconnaissance troops of 1st Battalion/139th in the north-east sighted a Norwegian company on skis, which over the course of the afternoon had moved across the Durmalsfjell toward Lort Lake and dug in there.[1] On the same evening, enemy troops had also taken the small village of Hotaas, on the right flank of 1st Battalion/139th. In the early morning of 29 April, about 200–300 Norwegian troops on skis and snowshoes were observed moving eastwards.

These reports, which were unsettling news for the right flank of Group Windisch, led to two differing assessments of the situation by division and regimental headquarters. The latter remained focused, as always, on Herjangenfjord, where an imminent enemy landing was feared, but it was unwilling to hand over control of its carefully guarded reserves to adequately cover the right flank. Generalleutnant Dietl, in seeing the enemy's approach from the north to Graes Lake, recognised that an initial thrust by the Norwegians was imminent. But from his perspective, the enemy still appeared to shy away from landings for the moment. In order to adequately oppose the expected advance in the north-east, division headquarters felt compelled to provide Group Windisch with additional forces. At 1300 hrs on 30 April, 1st Company/139th (under Major von Schleebrügge) was sent marching toward Graes Lake.[2][3] Because no other troops were available, the division decided to take them from the apparently less threatened Narvik sector, to be held ready for Group Windisch for future needs (under an order given at 1000 hrs on 30 April).[4]

Meanwhile, in the middle of the night of 28/29 April, between 2300 and 0015 hrs, the Norwegians attacked Picket Smolle several times with about 100 men on the mountain saddle south of Graes Lake. The enemy attacked several times, but was fought back with losses. Next day, even from a great distance, the crew at the outpost could see new enemy attack preparations being made, such as the arrival of ski columns and sled platoons, and the positioning of heavy weapons. Calls to regiment for help remained fruitless.

On 1 May, the Norwegians arrived in battalion strength and planned to break through at Graes Lake and force the Germans off the mountain, through Graesdalen and into Bukkedalen and Vasdalen. In mid-morning, after two enemy aircraft had bombarded a handful of German positions, one Norwegian company attacked on the west shore, followed by a second company echeloned at their rear, above the frozen lake. A third company went from the north-west to capture the towering Stortind. The enemy's advance was backed by both heavy weapons and artillery.

Up on Stortind, at just under 1,150 metres, a brief engagement of hard, close fighting erupted. The Germans, weakened and few in number, were nearly encircled, but at the last moment managed to fight their way out and retreat to Britatind (1,009m), 1km to the south. This too had to be abandoned to the pursuing Norwegians.

Down at Graes Lake, the Norwegians were slowly working their way closer in wide skirmish lines through the deep snow, when, from 2,500 metres away, the Germans opened fire. By afternoon, the small number of German defenders, five of whom had been wounded, ran out of ammunition and were forced to retreat and abandon the mountain saddle they had held for three days.[5]

With this, the enemy, with its furthest forward units, was able to capture the important saddle and pass leading down into Graesdalen. Yet he failed to exploit this situation quickly enough. He made only tentative reconnaissance efforts further to the south, instead of immediately occupying the mountain saddle and then pushing further into the right flank of Group Windisch. This negligence cost the Norwegians not only a victory, but more heavy casualties as well.

Then, in a forced march, the weak 1st Company/139th quickly closed in. At 0400 hrs on 1 May, after an extremely arduous march through the pathless and featureless wasteland of snow and rock, the 1st Company/139th arrived at Hartvik Lake. On the same day, at about 1000 hrs, the ski platoon and troop moved forward. The plan was to reach the plateau of Britatind above Graes Lake via the eastern rim of Leigas Lake, and attack the enemy, who was still in the midst of a fight, in his flank. The remainder of the company was to move on through Graesdalen to reinforce Picket Smolle.

While still in sight of enemy ships in Herjangenfjord, the ski platoon advanced and arrived on Peak 697 at around 1600 hrs. Under fire from ships' guns, the platoon took cover in the rocky terrain, and was then attacked by bombs and machine-gun fire from enemy aircraft which were attempting to halt its advance further up the mountain. Still, the platoon managed to reach the east slope of Britatind without casualties. From there, it saw Picket Smolle had already retreated and was headed south through the Graesdalen, and that the mountain saddle was now occupied by the enemy and swarming with Norwegian troops. The enemy troops were out in the open, and the ski platoon immediately fired on them. The rest of the company then ascended the slope of Graesdalen valley; panting and at the end of their strength, they attempted to retake the important mountain saddle by storm. The Norwegians, probably fearing a major German counter-attack and an outflanking [manoeuvre], abandoned the mountain saddle at the southern end of Graes Lake without much of a defence, and retreated across the lake. There, outside of the range of the German weapons, they took positions and dug in. Thus, the situation on the right flank of Group Windisch was restored, primarily by the decisive attack by the 1st Company/139th.

Now it became a matter of back-and-forth battles over the ownership of the western mountain peaks of Graes Lake, where the enemy had meanwhile taken control and dug in. In the night hours of 2 May, members of the German ski platoon climbed forward in a wide sweep toward the north-west, and attacked the units on the Stortind from the rear. Between 40 and 50 men of the Norwegian units were smashed, and the rest disappeared to the north. During the same sunlit arctic night, the German forward-deployed reconnaissance could see enemy units to the west, near Peak 559, consisting of two companies that had dug into the snow. These two companies should have been under observation by the ski security troops from 1st Battalion/139th (2nd Company/139th) in the north-west, and their supply route to Holtaas blocked.

Toward the mountain plateau of Britatind, which had previously been lost, a small group from 3rd Battalion/139th had been deployed, who also threw the enemy out of his mountain position. But over the course of 3 May, this small group was unable to hold out, as the stronger enemy assaulted and surrounded them. While the Norwegians assaulted them from all sides of the mountain, the company, still fighting, had to retreat south to an area below the summit of Britatind. The Stortind was also lost again.

Meanwhile, the Norwegians carried out more preparations for attack. With a favourable line of sight and occasional decent visibility, the Germans could observe the entire enemy approach north of Graes Lake. Footpaths and sledge tracks were laid out, bivouacs and tent camps cropped up in the wintery whiteness, and battery emplacements were built. The enemy was able to move about freely because at more than 3km away, they were out of range of German infantry weapons, and no artillery was available.

On 3 May, at about 0400 hrs, after bombing the positions of 1st Company/139th and preparing the area with fire from their heavy weapons and artillery, the battalion-strength enemy force proceeded to attack both sides of the Graes Lake.[6] Despite their great superiority, their frontal attack gained no ground amid the Germans' strong defensive fire; after two unsuccessful assaults, and after being fired on by the two

German heavy machine guns – each of which fired off 20,000 rounds on that one day – the Norwegians began digging positions in the snow.[7]

Next day, at 0400 hrs, the enemy attacked with increased force in an attempt to finally break up the defensive line in the right flank, but was also defeated this time, taking many casualties. Toward midday, the battle slowly wound down. The 1st Company/139th had one more essentially offensive success, and by repeated advances was once more able to occupy the peak of Britatind. A strong reconnaissance troop deployed further forward, toward Stortind peak, however, was caught in a Norwegian ambush and, after a hard defence, was overpowered and captured.

Although this had been a victory, and the German losses to this point had been small, it was obvious that the position at the southern end of Graes Lake was gradually becoming impossible to hold. The enemy, in company strength, had already dug in with heavy weapons, eastwards into the rocky slopes of Bukkefjell (1,146m), and from there posed a considerable threat to the German flank which could not be neutralised. (A further issue was that the wounded men had to lie for up to six hours in snow before they could be rescued and evacuated.) Moreover, a gathering of enemy forces appeared north of Graes Lake, in numbers much larger than ever before. After the previous futile frontal assault, it appeared that they intended to relocate further eastwards in preparation for a wide encirclement from the east. Even regimental HQ, whose attention had always remained fastened on Herjangenfjord, could no longer deny the possibility of a dangerous, threatening outflanking movement. The regiment now decided to return to its original positions and give up the important mountain saddle with its entrance to Graesdalen. As a cover toward the east, a new reinforced front was to be constructed, running along the line of Britatind–Peak 256–Storebalak. The addition of the two companies that had been released from the coastal front at Narvik, plus some restructuring, provided the forces necessary.

Apart from all else, the advance undertaken by these two companies demonstrates the high degree of commitment overall among the troops. Due to the difficult terrain, division HQ allowed for a time frame of three days for the march, but Company Müller (Oberleutnant Müller had taken over the company from Hauptmann Brucker, who was ill) left on 1 May at 1600 hrs and, after an arduous forced march, arrived at Hartwick

Lake early next morning, 2 May, at 0330 hrs. Navy Kapitän Erdmenger's company also made excellent time, departing Hundalen at 2330 hrs and arriving at the regiment on 3 May at 0700 hrs. The accomplishments of both companies are all the more impressive considering that only a few had skis or self-improvised snowshoes, while the majority had to complete the long march through the wild mountain terrain in soft snow that was several metres deep and which was only passable in the night hours when the snow froze and hardened enough to support their weight, heavily loaded with weapons, ammunition, equipment, and baggage. In a 29-hour march, almost without pause, the mountain infantrymen trudged alongside their navy comrades through a desert of snow and rock to bring relief to their battling comrades. Although the men were on the verge of collapse, the commanders kept pulling them forward and upward. Only a very few remained back on the trail. Exhausted and breathless, but battle-ready, they reached regimental command post.

At about midday on 3 May, as ordered, Navy Kapitän Erdmenger released 11th Company/139th from its coastal defence position at Bjerkvik. The company was to extend from the end position of 1st Company/139th (which was now located on the line from the summit of Britatind to the eastern slope of Leigastind) all the way to Peak 265. During the night of 4 May, Company Müller captured Storebalak along with positions to the north-east, and had to push reconnaissance forward toward the Naeverfjell. The 12th Company/139th remained as regimental reserve.

With this, Group Windisch now faced the approaching Norwegians with two battle groups which were widely separated from one another, with 1st Battalion/139th up to the north at Elvenes and three companies standing at the right flank, west of Graesdalen.

Missed chance for a flank attack against 1st Battalion/139th in the west

While the enemy advanced against the right flank of Group Windisch, the situation for 1st Battalion/139th grew more serious by the hour. From their mountain positions high on Fjordbotnheidet, the Norwegians continued to hold down the battalion at Elvenes with their heavy weapons, artillery, and constant aircraft attacks, firing at the slightest sign of movement. Simultaneously, on the night of 26 April, British destroyers appeared in Gratangsbotn for the first time, and under their fire the 25-man security force of 13th Company at Laberget was driven from its shelters. The arrival of the enemy warships could have signalled that a landing was imminent, or could also have simply meant that the enemy was trying to destroy the battalion's positions and weapons nests on the left flank by means of the ships' artillery.

The battalion commander did not consider his positions strong enough for a sustainable defence against an attack. Based on the enemy's sustained fire and the arrival of reinforcements, it was clear that an attack was coming, so he decided to pull further back; on the night of 27/28 April, 1st Battalion moved in stages, unhindered, into a new position along the southern rim of Reise Lake, with outposts positioned 2km forward to the north.[8] That day, six more destroyers arrived in Gratangsbotn fjord and again opened fire on the security force at Laberget.[9]

The 29th of April passed quietly, its only engagement consisting of firing with the sole mountain gun against the enemy troops that continued to gather at the village of Holtaas. But next day, a messenger arrived from Laberget, reporting that in the early morning hours, in Gratangsbotn, at Laberget, and to the west of Laberget, four warships and four transports had put in and unloaded troops.

On 1 May and the days following, the skies were clear and sunny. Now, 1st Battalion/139th also had tough defensive battles to face. The weak security force had settled in near Laberget, about 3km into Labergdalen as far as Peak 141. At Laberget, the troop landing came to an end, with approximately 1,500 French alpine infantry troops coming ashore. Including the Norwegians, this constituted a strength six to eight times greater than 1st Battalion/139th. On the same afternoon, the security force (Ski Platoon Trautner, 1st Company/139th) on Snaufjelde (694m) observed increased enemy movement from Elvenes into Labergdalen, on the left flank of the battalion. Several German Heinkel bombers, in their first deployment on the northern front, circled above the mountainous area, with the enemy disappearing under cover. After bombing the area from Elvenes to Oallge Pass, the aircraft took heavy machine-gun fire from hidden mountain rifle nests along with severe anti-aircraft fire from the British cruisers and destroyers lying in Herjangenfjord. Then all communications from the security force, which was protecting the left flank in Labergdalen at Peak 141, ceased. As it later turned out, it had become caught in an encircling attack by the much larger enemy force, and captured. Between 2000 and 2300 hrs, an enemy company attacked the German combat outposts along the road southwards from Elvenes, but was beaten back.

On 2 May, the Norwegians gradually began their attempt to outflank the battalion from the right. In midmorning, under the cover of thick fog, they advanced from Holtaas towards the south. Faced with the enemy's superior numbers, the German security force on Peaks 559 and 785 was forced to retreat. The enemy operation was accompanied by one aircraft, which either directed the artillery fire or scouted mountain terrain which was to be seized. Especially striking that day was the agility of the enemy artillery fire, which indicated that it was under French control. German mountain artillery was completely out of ammunition and was taken back to Elvegaardsmoen.

Fearing a deep flank attack from left and right (Peak 785 and Labergdalen), the battalion commander [Major Stautner] considered calling in his units from as far as the peak at Storv Lake. Dietl, however, prevented this measure from being carried out, at least for the time being. He emphatically insisted that a threat to the flank was not sufficient reason to abandon a position or to sacrifice any ground associated with it.

On 3 May, air operations were carried out by both sides. Toward evening, the enemy artillery, which had already advanced with its battery as far as north of the Reise Lake, also became very active and kept up its shelling until about midnight.[10] After firing constantly all day long, the enemy troops attacked the road once more, but were again fought off by the combat outpost.

Over the following days, the battles in 1st Battalion's sector grew more intense, both on the ground and in the air, as the enemy tried to break through along the road south toward Bjerkvik and knock out the defensive positions from the direction of the flanks.[11] On 4 May, all afternoon and into the night hours, there was heavy aircraft activity from both sides, during which the Luftwaffe tried to support the hard-fighting 1st Battalion wherever possible. Toward 2300 hrs, after heavy artillery and air preparations, the enemy again advanced toward the positions of 13th Company/139th on the left and 2nd Company/139th on the right at Reise Lake, but then stopped short and dug in. The enemy also unsuccessfully attempted to use their mortars to shoot the German units out of their position on the Snaufjeldet. Ski Platoon Trautner, guarding the left mountain flank, used deception tactics to head off an attack on the left flank of 1st Battalion: time and again, small numbers of troops, or individual soldiers, would suddenly appear at the flank and rear of the enemy, shoot fast from three or four different positions, and then quickly disappear, thus feigning more troops than there actually were.

In order to counter the pressure from the enemy on the right flank of 1st Battalion, the regiment decided to deploy part of its last reserves (12th Company/139th) to recapture the commanding Peak 785. During the night of 4/5 May, a platoon (Leutnant Neubacher with 19 men) advanced on the mountain position, which was defended by seven enemy machine guns. The platoon reached a point nearly 200 metres up the mountain, but due to their lack of mobility in the snow were ambushed and captured by the much faster Norwegian ski troops. Thus, along with pure numerical inferiority in both men and weapons, the lack of winter equipment also made itself felt. Skies, snowshoes, sleds, winter camouflage clothing, snow glasses, and so forth were scarce. Some of the men had already become snow-blind.

On 5 May, the Luftwaffe began to engage more and more. Time and again, the aircraft appeared with their German insignia, primarily to attack and neutralise the enemy artillery. But with its excellent camouflage against the deep snow of the mountain terrain, the enemy artillery could not be identified. Communication with the ground troops below was not available.

These battles, too, revealed the enemy's lack of ability to work together, their poor leadership, the inflexibility of the non-commissioned officers, and insufficient battle experience on the part of the troops. Even with their superior numbers in troops and weapons, they did not succeed in knocking the German battalion out of its position. Through flank attacks from left and right, there was ample opportunity to actually destroy the entire 1st Battalion/139th, but attempted outflanking manoeuvres either came to a standstill (as at Labergdalen) or were carried out slowly and hesitantly. Due to poor tactical movement, their advances were easy to detect, enabling counter-measures to be taken. Ultimately, these advances ended in a frontal charge. No envelopment attack involving the coordination of individual units ever took place.

Enemy breach in the centre

On 5 May, the situation for Group Windisch became extremely critical when enemy forces appeared widely spread out on their deep open right flank. At the same time, however, division leaders found the enemy's long-term plans and intentions quite difficult to identify. The enemy's direction of attack, in particular, was a mystery. Would it come from the road to Bjerkvik, from Graesdalen toward Hartvik Lake, or farther north-east toward the ore railway? All possibilities were still open.

In any case, Dietl decided to counter further enemy encroachment in the north by shortening and restructuring the front. He would simply allow the looming main attack to die out in the snow and mountain terrain, regardless of which direction it came from. Above all, for the sake of a continuous front, the dangerous gap between the two right and left battle groups would be closed up. Reserves, pulled from nearby units, would be held ready behind the most endangered sections, and the right deep flank would be sufficiently secured. But since neither reserves nor fresh units were available, they would have to draw on their own resources.

The 1st Battalion/139th was ordered to pull back to the southern line between Storv Lake and Roasme, while still leaving security in the previous positions. That the battalion would now come into the line of fire of enemy ships would have to be an accepted risk. During the night of 6/7 May, the new positions were occupied in organised shifts, and after the retreat, 13th Company/139th became available as regimental reserve. The 1st Company/139th was to immediately move into security positions in the Kuberget area to the north-east. On 8 May, Naval Company Erdmenger was positioned between Company Müller and 11th Company/139th; this meant that the 11th Company, which covered Leigastind, would link up with 1st Battalion; this allowed 1st Company

/139th to be released. The division also ordered 3rd Company/139th, from the former coastal front at Herjangenfjord, to be relieved by parts of Naval Battalion Kothe. The fresh and fully battle-ready mountain infantry company could now be sent to the 1st Battalion, to be deployed on its right flank as part of 3rd Battalion (11th Company/139th).

Now, however, the Norwegian attack broke loose with force, its main thrust unexpectedly aimed into Group Windisch at its centre and front, on the juncture between the 1st and 3rd Battalions. As the Norwegians continued to assault the forward bastions with more force, it became clear that these exit and control points were a high priority for them. During the night of 5/6 May and into the following morning, they attempted several, although unsuccessful, attacks against the occupiers of Britatind. The 1st Battalion was also confronted with a hard battle for Peak 842, occupied by only the platoon of Leutnant Schwab, which had been reinforced with one heavy machine gun. At 0100 hrs on 6 May, after a two-hour artillery preparation, the enemy attacked Peak 842 and Roasme from both sides, but was repulsed after a battle lasting several hours, with losses of 40 dead and wounded.

The weather once more turned cloudy, foggy, and cold, which aided the enemy's movements. They carried out multiple advances on both sides of the road to Bjerkvik, but were stopped at Reise Lake by the combat outposts. Suddenly, on 7 May, they succeeded in breaking through. Coming from the direction of Peak 785, during the early morning hours, with support from artillery and aircraft, the Norwegians attacked Peak 843. After multiple assaults, this peak finally had to be abandoned to the enemy.[12]

On Roasme Peak (856m), which was the extreme right outpost of 1st Battalion, a fresh platoon from 3rd Company/139th had recently taken over. Again on 7 May, under cover of fog, the Norwegians immediately pressed forward and quickly captured Roasme. By exploiting this breach, it was possible to separate 1st Battalion from its neighbour to the right, effectively splitting apart the thin front line of Group Windisch.

This splitting of forces made the situation for Group Windisch appear increasingly critical, and demanded the immediate recapture of Roasme (see Bibliography, 40). The attack was to be carried out at night, when the snow was frozen and had formed a hard surface, instead of during daytime, when the snow was too soft and difficult to push through.

But this counter-attack never took place. In the early morning of 7 May, problems developed on the right flank. The enemy had captured Leigastind (1,335m), which pushed 11th Company/139th back eastwards of the high mountain. Then, on that same afternoon, the far-forward Britatind peak was also lost to the enemy. Now, an enemy battalion was on the advance from that direction with strong artillery support. The entire front threatened to collapse.

The deterioration of the situation forced the division headquarters to order an immediate retreat of the northern front.[13] In order to facilitate the release and retreat of Group Windisch to the new line, which ran on the line of Peak 416–Peak 676–south of Leigas Lake, a radio message was sent out at 1700 hrs requesting urgently needed support from the Luftwaffe.

The relocation to the new front line was much hampered by the snow, which was as much as 2 metres deep, and by the looming advance of the Norwegians, who were mobile in the snow.

On the morning of 8 May, the units of 1st Battalion retreated along the road toward Bjerkvik under heavy artillery fire and continual enemy contact. In midmorning, the enemy also attacked the east slope of Leigastind once more, and steadily kept pushing 11th Company back. At 0930 hrs, the regiment had to request air attacks on the eastern slope of Leigastind and Roasme peak to aid the process of settling into the new positions.

Advancing into the German lines of retreat, the enemy finally tried to break through the centre of its front, and to split Group Windisch's forces. In late afternoon of a stormy, rainy 8 May, a Norwegian company on skis charged at high speed from the south-western slope of Leigastind all the way to the area of Peaks 852 and 676. Their thrust was intercepted by members of 12th Company/139th (regimental reserve), preventing a breakthrough on the road along Hartvik Lake.

With a temporary easing of enemy attacks, the following days brought the Germans a moment to catch their breath and the opportunity to settle into their positions. All day long, the heavy fire and aircraft activity went on, during which a British aircraft was shot down and a French plane made a forced landing.

All of these battles, in the back and forth struggle for mountain peaks, crests, and hills, carried out by individual weak platoons, or often even just small groups of soldiers against a much superior enemy, demanded – along with the constant psychological pressure – a physical endurance seldom asked of a soldier in wartime. In terms of emplacements, there were only a few trenches and holes dug into the deep snow on the broad high plateaus, or on ridges and slopes of mountains armoured in ice and snow. Often cut off, completely dependent on themselves, the men lay shaking with cold behind their scant covers of snow and rock. There were no warming shelters, no warm clothing, and no warm rations. There was no artillery support, no communication with the rear or with widely separated neighbouring units. Each round of ammunition had to be rationed. The days were filled with storm, snow, fog and cold, and beyond that, just the constantly attacking enemy.

In his personal journal, a lieutenant from 2nd Company/139th described these days:

> 3 May: Since the night before 1 May, we have not emerged from our ice-covered field guard emplacement. Last night more very heavy artillery fire. Aside from this, four Norwegian aircraft appeared and dropped their bombs. I am receiving more reports of deaths by freezing. The few tents, the uniforms are frozen as stiff as boards.
>
> 4 May: A frost-chattering, sleepless night. Awareness of day versus night has begun to completely disappear. We doze away. Only because of the division of the meagre portions of meat and *Zwieback* are the men still alive. We are endlessly exhausted, endlessly tired.
>
> 5 May: In the afternoon, heavy artillery fire begins. For eight hours, there is droning and howling without pause. Round after round, hit after hit.
>
> Having observed several transports of wounded through the snowy, jagged mountains, only one wish lives in me: not to be badly wounded!
>
> 6 May: Members of the 2nd Company marched to reinforce 3rd Company on the Peak 856, where strong enemy attacks have taken place. The peak is covered with only a small amount of snow, as it is swept by cold winds. We must spend days and nights outside without even the slight protection of snow dugouts. We stomp, scamper, and jump around to warm ourselves. But we never get warm, after the wind and cold have sapped away any warmth we gained during our climb.

8 May: Shaken by cold chills, we await the day. The enemy shoots its artillery and machine guns. With effort, over the course of the night, we have created some rock cover. Here the men lie abandoned on bare stone, defenceless against the wind that increases in strength and cold. Off and on the enemy troops try to advance, but are fought off with machine-gun fire. In the course of the day, the sky grows dark. Snow begins to fall. Once more a horrible night awaits.

9 May: More cold, snow, and wet rock. There is no wood to light a fire with. There are no covers and other means of protective warmth. The enemy artillery fire is never quiet, but rumbles constantly. At our back, about 10km away, the enemy ships' guns speak incessantly. The fire from their muzzles can be clearly seen.

In the course of the day, a column of transports from Elvegaardsmoen arrive here, consisting of Norwegian prisoners of war. These people were underway for 12 to 20 hours in this terrible weather. They bring just enough rations that now, every two days, a small can of pork and a packet of captured Norwegian *Zwieback* can be distributed per man. The coming night will bring more prolonged artillery fire and more snow.

Added to the concern about hard, determined enemy attacks, the regiment now realised that, under clear visual conditions, the entire front could be fired on from the rear by the enemy warships in Herjangenfjord.[14] Just as concerning, however, was the strength and fighting power of the companies. They had only about 50 men each, so that only some of the machine guns could be manned. The troops were exhausted, especially those from 1st Battalion, who had been fighting since the first days of the landing and were worn down by weather and constant deployment (see Bibliography, 39).

On 10 May, the enemy resumed his advances. A running attack began at 0300 hrs from Roasme toward Peak 676, which could not be defeated until 1200 hrs. The following days brought active reciprocal reconnaissance activity, amid heavy fire, during which the Germans studied the enemy's intentions, and the enemy tested out the new front.

On 11 May, as was long feared, the battleship *Warspite*, with its 38cm guns, entered the battle with the intention of pounding the German positions to pieces. With gigantic, echoing, loud crashing sounds, its heavy shells burst into the mountains, yet because of the well-camouflaged German positions, and apparently due to the unknown location of the front, the shots missed badly. For the most part overshooting the German positions, the heavy ships' guns fell too far out and reached the Norwegians deployed opposite them.

Up until 12 May, the enemy opposite Group Windisch was estimated to consist of about 7,000 Norwegians from the Norwegian 6th Division, with one mountain artillery section, plus about 1,500 French alpine infantrymen. The German strength was about 800–900 men (without the 1st Company/139th). The group was now structured for defence as follows:

On the right stood 3rd Battalion, with Naval Company Erdmenger at Storebalak and both sides of Vasdal (Peak 265); 11th Company was located on Peak 697; 12th Company was on Peak 852 south of Leigas Lake, at the end of 1st Battalion's position; 5th and 3rd Companies were south of Roasme, on Peak 676; and 2nd Company and Ski Platoon Trautner were on Peak 409 and both sides of the road to Bjerkvik.[15] The 13th Company/139th was pulled out of the left flank of 1st Battalion and now formed the regimental reserve behind 1st Battalion; the released Company Müller was also regimental reserve, stationed behind 3rd Battalion in the area north of Hartvik Lake. With this, Group Windisch had created a continuous front for the first time. At the same time, however, those at the end of the line were tasked with securing the important supplies and materials at Hartvik Lake. Were this to fail, Group Windisch would be completely dependent on the difficult-to-deliver supplies from Bjornfjell (see Bibliography, 40).

Although 12 May passed very quietly, 3rd Battalion reported a mustering of strong enemy forces in Graesdal, as well as movement in front of 1st Battalion, raising suspicions of new and larger plans to attack. Moreover, on that day Herjangenfjord also filled with enemy ships of all kinds and sizes. From their mountain positions, the men were able to observe unaided the approach of the powerful fleet to their rear. Although the scene played out in a completely calm manner, it sparked fears of a new, major threat to the rear. Up until now, despite the enemy's vastly superior land power in a mobile battle, their attacks had fallen apart, thanks to the leadership and the great endurance and determination of the defending troops in the mountain battle. This fleet's advance, however, which signalled a major enemy landing, threatened to put an end to the entire Group Windisch.

CHAPTER 5

The Narvik Sector and Ore Railway at the End of May

Although the German units and the security troops deployed along the coastal front at Narvik (the remainders of 2nd Battalion/139th Mountain Infantry Regiment and the Naval Company) had not come into direct enemy contact for some time, they were nevertheless pinned down by fire from the ships out in the fjords. British destroyers and cruisers passed one another while sailing back and forth in Ofotenfjord, often close to land. Due to the scarcity of artillery and ammunition, German forces could rarely, if ever, engage with them.[1] The enemy warships also sailed into Rombakenfjord, but at that point still did not push further through the narrow Stromnen Strait. Another particularly favourite target was the ore railway and its structures which lay on a 20km stretch within range of the British ships' guns, and whose tunnels, bridges, and tracks were repeatedly fired on, damaged, and obstructed.

The activity of the British naval forces in the waters around Narvik is illustrated in detail in the following excerpts from the war journal of Battle Group Narvik and the daily reports by Narvik Sector (see Bibliography, 39, 41):

> 17 April: 1750 hrs, three British destroyers fire on 7th Company/139th Mountain Infantry. No casualties.
>
> 20 April: Four destroyers and two cruisers fire on defensive positions around Narvik. A cruiser in Rombakenfjord fires on the railway track and damages the small railway bridge at Forsneset. The ferry across Rombakenfjord at Vassvik, which had previously been in service, was shot to flames and destroyed, with three deaths and two seriously wounded.

21 April: At 1425 hrs, a British cruiser and one destroyer sail into Rombakenfjord. Cruiser opens fire on the ore railway. Overhead wire contacts destroyed. The railway connection to Hundalen is now disrupted.

2100 hrs. A destroyer conducts continuous blockade of Ofotenfjord, Herjangenfjord, and Rombakenfjord.

22 April: At 1000 hrs, two British cruisers open fire on the infantry positions and the ore railway.

23 April: At approximately 1100 hrs, destroyers began shelling the railway and individual positions. Casualties at Tunnel 1 – Naval Company – five dead, 18 wounded.

25 April: During shelling of a tunnel in the sector of Naval Company von Gaartzen, one man was killed and one seriously wounded. Shortly before this, houses in Djupvik were fired on. Because the shelling happened very suddenly, there was not enough time to evacuate the buildings, resulting in four deaths and eight wounded in the company.

At around 1700 hrs, around 50 mortars [sic – possibly mortar rounds] in the area of the Narvik train station.

26 April: More fire attacks by two cruisers and two destroyers on defensive positions. At 1130 hrs, enemy destroyer sails into Rombakenfjord and 15 minutes later begins bombarding the Sildvik – Hundalen railway sector.

27 April: Daily ships' artillery fire in Narvik.

29 April: The Troeldal power plant on the northern shore of Rombakenfjord shelled at 1145 hrs by an enemy destroyer and burst into flames.

30 April: At 1215 hrs, one cruiser and two destroyers sail into Rombakenfjord as far as Stromnen strait and from 1245–1445 hrs, shell the strait and the Sildvik train station.

3 May: Moderate shelling in Narvik throughout the day. In the morning, extreme high-angle fire from battleship which was being observed by aircraft [at] Beisfjord. Several buildings destroyed. Losses in Narvik: four dead and one wounded.

3/4 May: Enemy destroyers on intense patrol in Rombakenfjord. Harassing fire toward the entire railway.

7 May: Intermittent shelling from Narvik by cruisers and destroyers. At 0700 and 1200 hrs, short fire attacks on the ore railway. Tunnel 1 shelled.

8 May: Intermittent shelling, also during the night, from Narvik, by one light cruiser and four destroyers.

10 May: Two dead from 10th Company/139th from shelling in Narvik.

11 May: Narvik, 1540 hrs, more shelling by warships.

14 May: In front of Narvik, four destroyers, harassing fire.

15 May: At 0042 hrs, Narvik is shelled during vigorous enemy warship activity.'

To avoid standing idly by and having to simply endure the constant shelling, the coastal front defenders returned fire whenever possible, although any opposition with their few, weak weapons was naturally hopeless. Thus, for instance, during the night of 28/29 April, both of the captured British guns, two mountain guns, and two anti-tank guns suddenly opened fire on a British destroyer from up in the area around Tunnel 1. The destroyer immediately turned away, but returned with three more destroyers, which then retaliated harshly. Even with just infantry weapons, the mountain infantrymen attempted to confront the large, heavily armoured ships. When crew members, seen out in the open on the ships' decks, were fired on by 2cm anti-tank weapons and heavy machine guns, the ships would veer off. Even snipers took part in the battle against the ships and their constant bombardments, as described by Stabsfeldwebel Herzog of 8th Company/139th Mountain Infantry:

> Early in May, two British destroyers cruised for hours just 600 metres off shore and fired on the defenders, forcing them to take cover. The staff sergeant suddenly jumped up, pulled himself to full height and said: 'Now I will show them.' With this he aimed his rifle at the bridge of one of the destroyers, right where the light shone on the white caps of the unwary and self-assured British naval officers. Having struck its target or not, the shot definitely caused the destroyer to turn away (see Bibliography, 3).
>
> The esprit of soldiers' in the coastal positions is also exemplified by the deed of one of the privates. As of 1 May, the battle flag of the Reich had flown from highest mountain ridge of Fagernesfjell, overlooking Narvik. It was destroyed after being shot 60 times by 15cm gun rounds from a British destroyer. Next day, the soldier climbed up the snow-covered mountain slope on skis, carrying a 5m-long pole and a flag. Nearing the summit of the 1,270m peak, he clambered up the rocks and hoisted the new flag.

On 30 April the division headquarters had to relocate once more. The ore railway was under constant shelling, telephone communications from Sildvik were frequently interrupted, and clear radio communications necessary for conducting the battle had become impossible. Thus, in the midmorning of 1 May, the division staff moved to its new command post on Spionkop.

For the first time, at 2400hrs on 3 May, radio communication was successfully established between the transmitting station in Bjornfjell and Germany. Next day, at 1950 hrs, a radio message came in from OKW [Oberkommando der Wehrmacht – the Armed Forces High Command]. According to the message, as of 5 May, Battle Group

Narvik was once again to be placed under the command of Group XXI. At 1115hrs on 8 May, Group XXI (General der Infanterie von Falkenhorst) in Oslo sent a radio message with a new order from Hitler that read as follows:

> The forces of Generalleutnant Dietl must hold the area of Narvik as long as possible, and in the case of a forced retreat, and by permanent destruction of the ore railway, render it useless to the enemy for a long time. If the territory forward of the Swedish border cannot be held, efforts should be made for an elite, experienced mountain unit, provisioned and supplied by air, to retreat in the direction of Bodo, while in case of emergency, the rest can be ordered across the Swedish border. (see Bibliography, 41)

In midmorning of 17 May, a new radio message was received from Group XXI:

> Führer (Hitler) also holds that in case of the possible loss of the town of Narvik, the formation of a bridgehead at the ore railway is urgently desired. Efforts will be made for increased deployment of the Luftwaffe from new airfields.

Revealed here, as in previous orders and guidance from the highest leadership (see Chapter II), is a certain sense of insecurity. While this allowed Dietl some degree of freedom of action, the directive itself expressed the Führer's desire to hold tenaciously onto the area around Narvik. Once placed in this position, Dietl strove to fulfil [the Führer's intent] with all resources available to him. For him, there would be no half measures.

But as energetic, tough, and tireless as he was, the general felt increasingly pressured and burdened with worry. During the month of May, the enemy grew stronger and kept pressing in from north and south. Resupply problems, especially for Group Windisch, became ever greater. His troops suffered bitter casualties, were worn down, and still lacked the basic needs, not just for battle, but for existence.

On 8 May, Dietl wrote in his personal journal:

> Our people do all they can to hold the present positions, but they are very exhausted. Ammunition is scarce. The enemy is superior in weapons, men, and equipment. Everything depends, therefore, on bringing in new forces. It is possible, however, that the enemy attacks will be stopped dead in the difficult snowy terrain.

I am firmly convinced that I can endure my difficult situation only if:

(a) I receive fresh forces, even only a few, as soon as possible;
(b) provisions for Group Windisch could be further managed on overland routes;
(c) the necessary resupplying were to be done by air.

In his so-called 'wish-list' of 29 May, sent to the OKW, Dietl further detailed all concerns, needs, and desires for the battle group (see Appendix 10).

CHAPTER 6

The Situation in the North Becomes Critical

Enemy landings at Bjerkvik in the flank and rear of Group Windisch

There was inclement weather on 12 May, the first day of the Pentecost. It was cold and windy, and rain showers mingled with the fog and driving snow. Down in the valleys and even along the shorelines of the fjords, a fresh snowfall had left a blanket of snow 25–30cm deep. During recent weeks, British warships had increased their shelling in the area of Bjerkvik each day, sending all calibre of shells thundering down on Narvik and Group Windisch's positions. Now they were seen cruising in the fjords more actively than usual. At midmorning, Ofotenfjord began to fill with ships, some of which had previously been anchored in Bogen Bay. Eventually there were reportedly 14 vessels, among them one battleship, one anti-aircraft cruiser, three cruisers, six destroyers, and four sizeable merchant steamers (see Bibliography, 39).[1] Towards midday, a cruiser, accompanied by several destroyers, sailed slowly along the coastal front at Narvik, only to turn and head towards the east shore of Herjangenfjord in the direction of Bjerkvik, continue along the western shore, and return to Bogen Bay. On the cruiser's mast flew the admiralty flag. Its journey along the shoreline could only mean that the British high commander was making an on-site inspection of the area in preparation for an imminent landing.

From the large number of warships in the waters around Narvik, it was obvious that a landing assault was about to take place. The only question was, where? Division headquarters strongly expected it to be in Herjangenfjord, to bolster an Allied advance from the north and an attack on the left flank of Group Windisch. But an enemy attack on Narvik itself could not be completely discounted. The town of Narvik had become a symbol, and if the Allies were to capture it, they would not only gain prestige, but also divert attention from their less than favourable situation on the European mainland (see Bibliography, 39).

All coastal sectors were placed on high alert, but because the division had so few standing reserves available, the individual sectors could not be reinforced. Thus, the defence of the east coast of Herjangenfjord had to be left to the three companies of Naval Battalion Kothe. All other units of Group Windisch were positioned facing north in heavy defensive battles against constant attacks from the superior Norwegian forces. For the moment, 13th Company/139th Mountain Infantry Regiment was held in reserve, as the regiment believed an enemy breach was possible at any time and reserves would be needed behind the thinly manned defence lines.

At around 2200 hrs, the powerful enemy fleet began advancing. The warships, interspersed with some 30 rather large cutters and small fishing steamers, now sailed a north-westerly course at slow speed out of Bogen Bay. The constant poor visibility prevented German observers from identifying the precise landing point. Not until just before midnight, when the ships steered into Herjangenfjord, did it become clear that they were about to land at Bjerkvik (see Bibliography, 39).

In the midmorning of 12 May, the division sent a radio message asking for Luftwaffe bombardment of the assemblage of ships. In the evening, another request for help went out for help from the Luftwaffe, but the weather conditions were so bad that an air deployment was deemed unlikely, if not impossible.[2]

Meanwhile, the fleet's advance came to an end. The forward-most British destroyers came within a few hundred metres of the north end of Herjangenfjord, formed a semi-circle, and with their guns, dominated the entire bay. The heavy ships arrayed themselves in a staggered line, with bows facing eastwards. On the far right stood the battleship *Resolution*.

Precisely at midnight, a red signal flare went up. At that moment, the warships opened fire all at once, with all guns focussed toward the whole coastline west of Bjerkvik to as far as Gjeisvik. The depot at Elvegaardsmoen also came under fire. The thunder of heavy guns rolled across the water and echoed hundreds of times against the rocky walls of the fjord. From the ships came flashes of light; the heavy shells howled and screeched into the pale, luminous night; in the devastating explosions, the coastline became submerged in fire and billowing smoke. Many of the wooden structures in the small towns and fishermen's villages quickly burst into flames, their fires festooning the water's edge. Salvo after salvo burst onto land in hellish blasts, while the German defenders – sailors and a number of mountain infantrymen – huddled behind the cover of the rocky terrain.

This massive artillery preparation lasted until 0200 hrs. Then, under the cover of intensified enemy fire, with the entire coastline shrouded in smoke, fog, and fumes, the Allied forces finally came ashore. The first landing attempt failed when the German defenders fired on six of the approaching ships, causing 20 of them to turn away (see Bibliography, 10). But from on board the ships, the German defensive positions were identified and systematically knocked out by carefully aimed fire. The German naval men, unaccustomed to ground battle and unable to shoot back, could not cope with the shelling; instead of standing fast under cover or falling back to alternate positions, they began to desert their posts and head eastwards, clambering up the mountains, suffering heavy losses as they went.

The second enemy landing attempt did succeed, however, and in that first wave some 30 craft landed at various points between Bjerkvik and Gjeisvik. The disembarked enemy troops (French alpine infantrymen) quickly finished off some remaining individual defence nests, then advanced under the cover of heavy weapons that had been quickly rushed ashore. The rest of Naval Battalion Kothe, badly shaken up from the previous shelling, was only able to manage a small amount of counter-fire before retreating into the mountains toward the east.[3] Only some scattered troops still held their ground south of Gjeisvik until 0600 hrs that morning, but they later retreated as well.

The Allies' landing had succeeded fully, and the German coastal front was now in ruins. The enemy, with continuously strengthening force, was now at the left flank and rear of Group Windisch, whose situation became untenable. It was now a question of retreating from the positions that had been constructed to the north, and the construction of new lines of resistance. This would take a major miracle. The entire northern front, now under enemy threat from three directions, would have to be rotated 90 degrees.

Along with this mounting crisis for Group Windisch, another unfavourable situation arose for Narvik Sector which had resulted from the premature relinquishing of the coastal area. Narvik Sector was now vulnerable to possible shelling from a third side, that is from Ojord, which would enable the enemy to make a dangerous leap, not only from the south across Beisfjord, but also from the north across Rombakenfjord.

The French forces, having landed in intervals, attacked with two battalions toward Elvegaardsmoen and Hartvik Lake, with one battalion attacking the road leading north in the direction of Elvenes. Their goals were obvious: by attacking eastward, the enemy hoped to roll up on the German mountain positions at their flank; by attacking toward the north, they would open up the route that was now blocked by 1st Battalion/139th Mountain Infantry Regiment, which would allow the Norwegian forces through. At the time of the landings, the Norwegian forces, with heavy artillery support from their land batteries, also attacked from the north, targeting both sides of the road leading to Bjerkvik. Overall, the enemy's plan was for Norwegian and French forces to form a pincer movement that would overwhelm and crush all of Group Windisch.

Group Windisch, having been partly restructured at an earlier point (see Chapter IV, in the third section "Enemy breakthrough at centre"), now suddenly found itself in a vortex of heavy fighting on three sides.

Exhausted, but still able to fight, with the enemy at their rear, the mountain infantrymen put up a strong resistance. But tactically speaking this was an extremely tough situation, one that called for quick decisions and immediate action from regimental headquarters. In order to escape from the impending encirclement from three sides (strong enemy units were also in Graesdalen), there was only one solution, which was to set up the necessary security and cover, and retreat eastwards! The regiment had initially intended to solve the issue by counter-attacking on the left flank, but given the scarce resources and the fact that the enemy was now on land, this plan appeared doomed to failure.

At 0500 hrs on 13 May, the regiment issued orders to recapture the very vulnerable north front behind Hartvik Lake and to construct a new defensive front along the line Storebalak–Lillebalak–Fiskloes Lake. All heavy weapons, equipment, and provisions that could not be taken along were to be destroyed (see Bibliography, 53). There was no doubt that this movement rearwards, which meant pivoting the front, flank, and rear by 90 degrees, while under constant pressure from a greatly superior enemy force, would pose an extraordinary challenge. To the division headquarters, which under the given conditions had to approve the regiment's retreat, success was very doubtful. With the enemy attacking at the left flank and rear, and given the state of the troops' resources, it could not succeed without Luftwaffe support. All Generalleutnant Dietl could do for Group Windisch at that point was to send in the last available reserves, a pioneer platoon from the 83rd Mountain Pioneer Battalion (under Leutnant Brandt) for support.[4]

In order to even begin disengaging from the heavy ongoing battles with the Norwegians and enable the relocation of the northern front in an orderly process, the enemy would have to be pushed back. The French troops that had landed on the German flank and rear had brought several tanks with them, but luckily, they moved haltingly, feeling their way from Bjerkvik toward the basin of Elvegaardsmoen, which was filled with smoke and fumes, toward Hartvik Lake, and along the road north. This provided enough time to send German forces to stop them.

Toward 0400 hrs, a platoon from 2nd Company/139th Mountain Infantry Regiment (Leutnant Bauer with 30 men) was ordered to halt the enemy advance on the road leading to Hartvik Lake. The small platoon did not hesitate to engage the much superior enemy force, hoping to at least intercept their advance and win precious time. They did, in fact, successfully halt the French advance.

Next, Ski Platoon Trautner and parts of the available reserve unit, 13th Company/139th Mountain Infantry Regiment, were ordered to rendezvous with Section Bauer, and together they were to attack toward the south and force the enemy back to the coast. Despite repeated attempts, this counter-attack also fell through, having come under heavy fire and incurring casualties even during their advance. The ski platoon was also unable to link up with Section Bauer, and advanced [on its own] under heavy fire, taking casualties. This counter-attack failed to push the enemy back, even after repeated attempts. Both 13th Company/139th and

Ski Platoon Trautner took positions in the steep mountain slopes with their front facing west and were then able to cover by fire the roads to Hartvik Lake and to Elvenes, preventing a further enemy advance. They also witnessed the continued enemy landings at Bjerkvik and the French capture of the camp at Elvegaardsmoen, which was badly torn up. Several enemy tanks, attempting to advance along the road north into the rear of 1st Battalion/139th, were taken out with precision fire aimed into vision slits and optics. As the tanks turned away, they became mired in deep snow on the roadside, and their escaping crews were finished off.

It was now 0700 hrs, and still no one had heard from Section Bauer and 2nd Company. It was later learned that the platoon had been almost completely wiped out. Leutnant Bauer, like most of his men, had been killed, and the rest were wounded and captured. After a fierce battle, only a few men had escaped the enemy encirclement.

But from the high mountain position at Peak 220, on the other side of the road towards Hartvik Lake, German machine guns chattered away. This fire was from a small section of 11th Company/139th (led by Oberleutnant Tollschein, with 20 men and three heavy machine guns), tasked with covering the retreat of 3rd Battalion. Under this fire, the enemy, who was advancing eastwards with little apparent concern, now came to a stop. The furthest forward line of riflemen collapsed under the machine-gun fire, and the next line quickly took cover, attempting to work their way forward in single jumps, still continuing their defensive fire. Neither the constant fire from ships' guns nor the two Norwegian aircraft, which were supporting the expansion of the beachhead, were of any further help. The enemy then made a powerful assault with a mass of troops, attempting to overrun the German positions. Unable to break through the heavily defended barrier, they were turned back, incurring brutal casualties.

After two hours, however, the enemy once again stormed Peak 220 and, this time with support from tanks, attempted to break through on the road heading east. On the deeply snow-covered road, three medium tanks approached the area of Hartvik Lake. Although the tanks moved carefully, they soon hit a minefield and their tracks were blown off. The simultaneous attempt at a breakthrough by the enemy infantry was brought to a halt by the combined fire of the 13th and 11th Companies.

For almost 24 hours, these two small companies held the enemy back, locking up the front and preventing a breach. Attempting to soften their target, the enemy hammered down on the thinly manned positions with artillery, mortars, and even with anti-aircraft guns from their ships in the fjord. Despite the casualties they inflicted, however, they could not break the will of the few German mountain infantrymen. Through their long combat experience, the German soldiers had developed a masterful use of terrain, cover, and camouflage, and were able to evade the heavy enemy fire.

The weak companies of Group Windisch that had been thrown to the west failed to halt the establishment of the enemy's bridgehead as originally ordered, but they did keep them from impacting the majority of the regiment as it continued its relocation process, providing time to retreat in safety. Just in time, before the worn-out security troops were finally forced to give way to the steady onslaught of French forces, the retreat was completed.

This was how [the French] fought:

> In the night of 13 May, after repeated defeats, the French attempted a surprise assault to capture the Peak 220, which blocked their way. In leaps, crouching down, the French alpine infantry work their way toward the occupied hilltop on their left, with one Norwegian heavy machine gun and one light machine gun. Their flat helmets and grey anoraks pop in and out of view as they creep up the three sides of the slope. They move in lightning quick leaps and then throw themselves prone, constantly working their way closer. Many of the bounding figures are hit by precision rifle shots, plunge backward, and roll down the slope. As the enemy comes closer and enters the dead zone between depressions and holes, the machine guns can no longer be used. Now the French have reached a point close beneath the peak, and are within close combat distance. Their hand grenades fly like dark balls. As they break through on the black funnel-shaped peak, they are still met by machine gun sheaves and shots at just a few metres – then the last of the defenders must retreat. Five mountain infantrymen are left, and they have only one single point of exit not blocked by enemy – a high, rocky cliff, which the French have not climbed up on. Without thinking long, the five men jump off. Flying through the air in a rush, they hit a snow drift and after a 60-metre fall they land in deep snow. Battered, scratched, and raw, the last five men leave the left summit of Peak 220 and stumble their way east, toward the new position. [No reference in German original]

As difficult as it may be to comprehend how these weak troops west of Hartvik Lake, only the size of a company at the most, could, for such a long time, withstand an enemy force approximately 10 times superior to them, supported by tanks, aircraft, and heavy ships' guns, it is even more difficult to understand why the enemy did not attempt to advance south from Hartvik Lake. Initially, there were no German forces at all at this spot. The 3rd Company/138th (under Oberleutnant Ploder) had been pulled forward as division reserve at Outpost IV in the early morning of 13 May, where they were placed on alert. They were to appear on the hill at Mebyfjeldet (on the line of Peaks 482–548) south of Hartvik Lake and provide cover for the retreat of Group Windisch.[5] Prior to 0600 hrs, Peak 482 was secured by only two units, and 3rd Company/138th returned, unaware of the situation until they encountered the regimental commander at Outpost IV, who then reassigned them.

The enemy force, which was carrying out reconnaissance from its area at Gjeisvik, initially met with absolutely no problems south of Hartvik Lake. But instead of immediately advancing further, they remained firmly in position at the Mebyfjeldet. There, during the daytime of 13 May, they were beaten back again by 3rd Company/138th, which had been sent to Mebyfjeldet to provide cover for the retreat of the regiment.

Although during its retreat the regiment needed to be protected from the enemy at the bridgehead, more importantly the bridge across the Vasdalselven [the Vasdal valley river] at the end of the road into the mountains eastward of Hartvik Lake at Gamberg needed be kept open and guarded against quick access by enemy tanks. The wide river had already thawed and now gushed torrents of white water, which without the bridge would be impossible to cross.[6]

As security for the bridge, and as a rearguard position, the regiment placed the regimental pioneer platoon and one platoon from Naval Company Erdmenger under the direct command of the regiment. They were ordered to halt any tanks that broke through. The rest of Naval Company Erdmenger was tasked with covering the right flank against the large enemy force in Graesdalen.

The most difficult part of the relocation fell to 1st Battalion/139th, which was on the left flank. While still engaged in battle with the Norwegian troops, and under the careful and unflinching guidance of the commander, the battalion began to disengage. The rest of 2nd, 4th, 5th, and 3rd Companies were pulled back in stages. Upon receiving their orders, the light machine gunners and riflemen retreated from Peaks 416 and 676 individually, in a leapfrog movement, exploiting terrain features, under cover of heavy machine guns in favourable firing positions. After the 1st Battalion had got through, then 3rd Battalion was also able to break off enemy contact, and through clever concealment and deception, they were able to pass unnoticed in front of the enemy rearguard positioned on the Leigastind opposite them. At approximately 0900 hrs, the regimental staff made its retreat and set up its new command post at Outpost IV. The overall relocation process was supported by two mountain guns from the area east of Hartvik Lake, which now fired off the last of their rounds.

The retreating companies all followed the route leading across the south-west slope of the Vasdalfjell (on the line of Peaks 852–894), which was covered with brittle snow, and was fully visible from both Herjangenfjord and the dominating Leigastind. On this dangerous stretch, undisturbed by enemy fire, the troops moved at a distance from one another down the steep slope to the road along Hartvik Lake, where the companies were assembled. They were able to cross the only bridge across the Vasdalselven at Bamberg without being fired on, and once on the other side, the battalions began their ascent into the mountains. The bridge was covered by the heavy machine gun platoon of 1st Battalion and one platoon from Naval Company Erdmenger until the last rearguard and security personnel had crossed over. In the early hours of 14 May, the bridge was detonated by a platoon from Naval Company Erdmenger.

The enemy intended to strike the German flank, and together with the Norwegian forces, defeat the regiment in a devastating pincer movement. In the attempt, the enemy suffered a high number of casualties, and did not immediately continue in pursuit. During the night of 13 May, they ceased their futile attacks. During the retreat across the Vasdalsfjell, the German units were within enemy sight, but no shots were fired. This revealed the lack of cooperation and communication that existed between the enemy fleet, the Norwegians, and the newly landed French troops. Subsequent prisoner-of-war accounts were in agreement that while the French and Norwegians had both observed the Germans coming down the open slope, both mistook them for Allied troops.

The almost unbelievable success of the relocation was due in great measure to the efforts of Naval Company Erdmenger. Alone on the right flank on both sides of Peak 265, they were tasked with security against the strong enemy force in Graesdalen. After the company had to sacrifice a second platoon to the regiment, it totalled only 25 men with two heavy and four light machine guns. Norwegian attempts to attack from Graesdalen were immediately halted from long distance by the sailors' machine-gun fire. Heavy enemy mortar fire buried individual nests, requiring the company to change local positions, but without losing even a metre of ground. During the night of 13 May, after the Norwegians in the east were seen moving in an encirclement, and the high peak of Naeverfjell (contrary to what the regiment had believed) was no longer in German hands, Naval Company Erdmenger pulled back to the south.

The losses in men and matériel incurred by Group Windisch during their difficult retreat movement meant a considerable, painful forfeiture of defensive power. Along with the blocking units, the security forces far to the west along the road to Haarstad were also lost. On 12 May, a messenger was sent to bring back the platoon that remained at Herjangenfjeld before its line of retreat was cut off. He was too late, as the road that ran to Bjerkvik was already occupied by the enemy.

The platoon moved west through the mountains, and on 16 May, exhausted and unaware of the situation, reached Gratangsbotn, where it was captured by the French.[7] Especially painful was that three physicians and 45 non-transportable seriously wounded had to be left behind in the Elvegaardsmoen field clinic when the camp was evacuated on 13 May. Because no vehicles or sleds were available for transport at the time of the retreat, the depot at Hartvik Lake, with large supplies of ammunition and rations, had to be set ablaze. A large number of heavy weapons, which because of their heavy weight, could not be transported across the mountains at that time, also had to be destroyed. Thus, 1st Battalion lost five medium grenade launchers, and the two light infantry guns and its two mountain guns were blown up. Only a few worthwhile goods were saved, carried by Norwegian prisoners of war, who willingly adapted to the role of carriers in this hour of need. The troops themselves hauled their entire infantry weapons and equipment down the mountain and up over the steep, bare slopes in the cutting east wind.

Filled with deep sorrow, Generalleutnant Dietl feared for all of Group Windisch. The group's situation remained unknown until the following morning, 14 May. Since 2145 hrs on 12 May, regular communication had been blocked due to radio signal interference, and messengers needed too much time to cover the long distance. But according to accounts by the flood of companies of Naval Battalion Kothe on their retreat, enemy forces had shown up in Ojord on the evening of 13 May and the entire east shore of Herjangenfjord was in enemy hands. The division leaders were aware that even in the case of a successful retreat, further defensive measures by Group Windisch could only be carried out with a strong intervention by the Luftwaffe as quickly as possible. Repeated urgent radio messages went out to Group XXI, [who responded that] according to Air Command Trondheim, the persistent bad weather rendered this nearly impossible for the time being.

During their massively planned landing on 13 May, the enemy could only count one single victory, which was that all road connections within their bridgehead area in the north were now in their hands. But their obvious goal, that of defeating Group Windisch and destroying the northern front at Narvik, had not succeeded. This reflected poorly on the superior enemy, whose leadership after the landing appeared hesitant, indecisive, and even without a plan. Their troops lacked offensive spirit, and the ability to recognise and exploit the advantages of their respective situations. Moreover, there was a lack of cooperation between the Allies, i.e., the British fleet, the French who landed in the west, and the Norwegians who were attacking in the north and north-east. In terms of missed opportunities, the following is but a brief outline:

The French allowed themselves to be held back for much too long a time by the weak German security troops. They did not attempt a decisive breakthrough at Hartvik Lake, made no attempt to cut off the German retreat south of the lake, and on the night of 13 May they did not attempt to pursue to the end.

The Norwegians, for whom it would have been possible to intercept the entire German retreat, not only from the north but also the north-east through Vasdalen, undertook no vigorous attacks, and they too allowed themselves to be put off by only small security units.

The fire from the British fleet in Herjangenfjord was so poorly conducted and so lethargic (from barely 8,000 metres) that it had little effect on the retreating Germans.

All in all, there was the distinct impression that each of the Allies was waiting for the success of the other, hoping to attach itself to the victory and take all of the credit.

In the following days, there would have been opportunities to knock out all of the weakened Group Windisch. It had shed much blood, lost much weaponry and equipment, had no positions ready on their new front line, and its men were badly worn down by the constant fighting (see Bibliography, 16). But the enemy forces simply continued to slowly fumble their way forward.

Defence in a new position

The troops of Group Windisch, in a state of confusion after all the fighting, now found themselves in retreat, and it was with only the greatest effort that they managed to regroup, reorganise, and move into their newly designated positions. By 0400 hrs on 14 May, the last security units had arrived at the eastern edge of Hartvik Lake and crossed the bridge at Gamberg [before it was destroyed]. All elements of the group gathered at Outpost IV.

The fighters from the northern front arrived in ragged, unkempt condition, their faces gaunt and eyes deeply hollowed. Here was 2nd Company, still 49-men strong. Over there was 4th Company, which had lost almost all of its heavy weapons and was now divided up into two platoons for infantry battle, one platoon with rifles, the other with pistols.[8] From another direction came Naval Company Erdmenger, its men incapable of even occupying a new position. Many suffered nosebleeds and vomiting from physical overexertion.[9] For high-angle fire weapons, the entire 1st Battalion had only three medium mortars.

In the midmorning of 14 May, not one man was in position on the new main battle line (see Bibliography, 44). After weeks of constant battle and bivouac in rock and snow, the worn-down troops, especially those of the 'Black 13th', had experienced enormous psychological and physical demands, and immediately on arrival were too exhausted and apathetic to manage the climb up to their new mountain positions. Had the enemy pursued them with just a little energy, the 'front' would have been overrun before it was even manned, and Group Windisch would surely have been scattered. But the enemy only tried to pursue on both sides of Hartvik Lake and from Graesdalen, doing so in a cautious manner, giving the German units the chance to reorganise and build up their new defence over 14 and 15 May. Their defence line was intended to connect with the positions of the reinforced 1st Company/139th (Group von Schleebrügge) on Kuberget, initially running along the north slope of the Kobberfjell (914m), the north flank post of the Storebalak (763m), and from there once more jumping back to climb over Peak 648, toward the south to Peak Lillebalak (572m) and through the depression of the Fiskloes Lake to Peaks 482, 548, and 509 at Mebyfjeldet.

Over the course 14 May, the new front line saw its first battles. Not until then did the French attempt to advance south of Hartvik Lake. Their repeated attacks were repulsed by the 13th Company/139th on Peak 482 and by Company Müller on Peak 548, at which time the enemy dug in at Peak 401. The 3rd Company/138th Mountain Infantry Regiment had advanced further south on both sides of Peak 509, and here they could considerably mitigate the enemy pressure against the left flank, which was open at the time, as the continuous front line was still not firmly in place. More dangerous than this was a strong forward push by the Norwegians from the Bukkedalen, who now closed in with force once more. During the midmorning of 15 May, they were able capture the high Storebalak and Peak 717 which lay to its east. But in a counter-strike by parts of 12th Company/139th, Storebalak was recaptured. At the same time, the small number of German defenders was so exhausted that the men slouched limply over their weapons, and it was clear that they could no longer put up serious resistance (see Bibliography, 16).

On 15 May, the enemy attacked on a broad front south of Hartvik Lake. Enemy forces attempted to advance toward Peak 509, and in the afternoon stronger troops pushed into the saddle between Peaks 548 and

482. Both companies positioned there were pulled back because they were threatened with encirclement.

With that, the high plateau of Mebyfjeldet, which had changed hands repeatedly in a back-and-forth battle, was now occupied by the enemy. Eastwards of Hartvik Lake, some rather weak enemy forces attempted to cross the Vasdalselven bridge over Gamberg to the south-east.

In the evening, toward 2000 hrs, after artillery preparation by the Norwegians, the enemy finally captured Storebalak once more – a hard blow, as this commanding peak provided a wide view from all sides.

On 16 May, the Norwegians, who gradually brought up the majority of their 16th Infantry Regiment, attempted to capture Kobberfjell (914m) and Peak 648 in a furious assault. By 2200 hrs, after a hard battle in which two enemy ski companies were repulsed and thrown back, and after many casualties, the situation on Kobberfjell was restored.

On 17 May, the weather was foggy and the visibility poor – the sort of weather the Norwegians seemed to favour. In the evening, toward the eastern side of the Kobberfjell, a new attack from the north was underway. It led to breakthroughs at certain positions, and after a two-hour battle the attack was brought to a halt and the mountain was once again completely in German hands. On the same day, there were weaker advances toward Fiskloes Lake, which were fended off.

In order to break through at Kobberfjell, which was now the new north flank post, and Storebalak, the Norwegians tried coming in from the north. It was a futile attempt, and afterwards they approached it from the north-west, primarily intent on the recapture of Peak 648. During the night of 18 May, an attack from two sides was beaten back. With the French in the west, all was quiet, although sometimes trench work could be observed.

In order to prevent the enemy encirclement of the left flank, the German lines had to be extended further toward the south. By 17 May, Group Windisch's front ran from the mountains of Kobberfjell – Peak 648 – and Lillebalak, to the jagged, high terrain scattered with lakes and valleys at the eastern end of the line from Fiskloes Lake–Holm Lake. With separation lines south of Lillebalak between the 3rd Battalion on the right and 1st Battalion on the left, the units were deployed as follows:

12th Company on Kobberfjell, 11th Company on Peak 648, parts of 14th Company and 15th Company on Lillebalak.

3rd Company at Fiskloes Lake, 4th and 5th Company south of there, and 2nd Company at Holm Lake.

Close nearby, at Outpost III south of Lillebalak, Company Müller was positioned as regimental reserve, later as reserve of 1st Battalion.

Because of the threatening situation, on the evening of 16 May, 13th Company was temporarily deployed in the sector of Group von Schleebrügge, and was held ready on 19 May south of Kobberfjell as reserve for 3rd Battalion.

On 15 May, 3rd Company/138th was released from the front, initially as division reserve, which as of 17 May was provided to Group von Schleebrügge for support (see following section). On 20 May, the regiment received a platoon from the newly reassembled Naval Section Kothe. Naval Company Erdmenger was not yet fit for deployment.

Conditions were the same as they had been for days and weeks. The troops may have believed they had already endured and suffered the worst of it, but their misery was far from over. The battle locations had changed, but not the fear of the terrain and the weather conditions. The battle knew no end. Increasingly, the defensive battle was carried on by only very small groups that constantly shrank in strength – troops of few men, lone machine guns, and individual fighters with rifles and hand grenades. Most often they were located 100 metres, or even as far as 0.5–1km, from one another, with only themselves to depend upon. At all times they had to prepare to defend on all sides, constantly alert and on sharp watch, so that in the dimly lit nights, or during suddenly occurring fog, they would not be bypassed or cut off. For weeks they had been in this wasteland of rocks, mountain peaks, and high plateaus without a roof overhead, and without the life-saving warmth of a fire. The rations could not be increased because there was no one available to bring them in – almost every available man was in the fight. During the day, there were some slices of bread and one small can of meat per five men. Increasingly, deaths occurred where men simply collapsed on their weapons from utter exhaustion.

Then spring finally came, and with it the weather began to change. By 13 May, the sun shone fully and warmly for several days. Yet with the warm temperatures also came the thaw, and ice and snow in the deeper areas now turned to mud, water, and snow bogs. The melting snow ran from the mountains, splashing and flowing into countless streams and rivulets. Now there was hardly a dry place to be found. By 19 May, frost settled in again, and thick clouds of fog covered the hills and valleys, hampering visibility. And then came the rains, bringing moisture from above this time. Soaked through from top to bottom, the men crouched and shivered in the gradually collapsing snow caves, which were the only positions or shelter available. They were now sat drenched in icy water, or simply lay on bare rock, where icy winds ripped through the soaked, thin, ragged uniforms and scarce tents. Even the wounded had to lay out in the open until they were lucky enough to be carried back, which was a day-long trip. Many froze to death, while others died of exhaustion before they could be brought to the military hospital in Bjornfjell.

It was futile to try using explosive charges to hollow out shelters and defensive nests in the rocks. Therefore, the soldiers built walls and nests with loose rock, which were constantly knocked down in the shelling and laboriously rebuilt afterwards. Finally, the men improvised shelter in small ravines, *bergschrunds* (ice split from the rock), and clefts in the rocks, which were eternally damp.

The days of storm, fog, cold, and rain devastated the strength of the troops. And the troops were everything! The officers took shelter in the same way as the men, in bare rocks. The command posts were gaps between the rocks that dripped with moisture, where the commanders wrote their reports and orders on their knees with frost-stiffened fingers. Even the division command post on Spionkop was nothing more than a tiny board hut, where Generalleutnant Dietl could less often be found than outside at the fronts. He was on the move for hours and days, rucksack on his back, covering dozens of kilometres on skis or on foot, visiting his men, making on-site situation assessments. Everyone was equal at the fronts around Narvik, from the general down to the last man – sailors, mountain infantrymen, and anti-aircraft artillerymen – one single battle community in the truest sense of the word. They had only one mission and saw only one goal: they had to and wanted to defend and hold Narvik!

The high level of comradeship found at Narvik is illustrated in the following passage:

> On 18 May the commander of 3rd Battalion, Major Hagemann and two officers succeeded in retrieving Lieutenant Trautner, who had been killed on 16 May. The fallen officer had to be brought back from the forward slope directly under the enemy's line of sight and fire, during which Hauptmann Schönbeck provided covering fire with his machine pistol while his commander crawled forward. (see Bibliography, 16)

This comradeship was also present on the southern front at Ankenes, on the Framnes Peninsula, along the ore railway, and with Group von Schleebrügge. Along the entire German front, still some 50km long, were barely more than 1,500 men, fighting in continual battle and gasping for breath. In contrast, the forces on the enemy already had about 12,000 men, not counting the powerful enemy fleet (see Bibliography, 3, and Appendix 5). And the enemy had weapons, matériel, equipment, machinery, plenty of rations, excellent care, were equipped and dressed for wind and weather, and could house their troops in heated, sturdy tent camps and warm bivouacs, which could actually be seen from a long distance, but could not be attacked due to a lack of artillery.

With burning eyes, the soaked, freezing defenders stared down from their positions on the mountain, at the wide, extended chain of great open bivouac fires.

But during these melancholy days, there also came a ray of light and hope. When the weather cleared up, the Luftwaffe finally stepped in with some strong sorties. On 17 and 18 May, their Stukas appeared for the first time. Now, German air activity went on all through the day. The planes zoomed low and close over mountain crests and ridges, plunged down, made reckless curves into the mountain valleys, attacked depots, batteries, supply columns, and gatherings. The rattling and hammering of their on-board weapons rang back in multiple echoes from the mountains and rock walls, and fountains of debris from bomb impacts erupted through the harsh, wild mountain landscape.

With the landings at Bjerkvik, the arrival of further strong enemy forces, and the loss of important terrain, the division headquarters saw that the overall situation had become extremely serious. By 13 May, the northern front had been able to hold up against all attempted encirclement movements and attempted breaches. The French forces had gained the ability to communicate and work with the Norwegians in joint land operations, and it was now significantly easier for the enemy to use the roads to bring in supplies to the entire front in the north. With this, they could bring their entire wealth of matériel into play. It should also be kept in mind that from Ojord, the enemy was only one jump away from Narvik.

Dietl could no doubt see that in the long term no amount of toughness and will to resist on the part of the troops, nor any leadership or art of improvisation, would be enough against the expected heavy enemy attacks from all directions – not without reinforcements, weapons and ammunition, and continued assistance from the Luftwaffe. On 14 May, Group XXI received a message concerning the seriousness of the situation on the northern front (see Bibliography, 40). While it would be possible to get by on the small amounts of supplies and reinforcements that were brought in on an irregular basis, this would only be the case if they were to continue fighting the battle in fierce, small defensive-style battles, filling only the most urgent gaps that appeared again and again, doing so without a dense and deep occupation force, and even doing without sufficient reserves to relieve the battle-worn troops. This meant that every man would still be crucial, and every round of ammunition [needed to be] hoarded. Six hundred mountain infantrymen were supposed to arrive on 20 May by glider transport, and 2,000 paratroopers were promised for 4 June, but Dietl's thoughts on where to best utilise them, whether to go behind the enemy lines or to place them at the front for a counter-attack, proved a pointless exercise: neither arrived in those numbers.

On 20 and 21 May, Group Windisch, which between 17 and 19 May alone had 19 dead, 32 wounded, and 18 missing in action, had yet another crisis to contend with. The Germans assumed that the French had about one battalion on the Mebyfjeldet, and perhaps two battalions of alpine troops in front of the German left flank. But major enemy relocations in strength of about one battalion were observed across Daltind (614m) in the direction of Trold Lake, and from Vasdalen came strong Norwegian forces. In order to confront all the enemy action against the deep left flank, the thin front had to be stretched out further toward the south. In addition, Section Brandl was created out of 1st Battalion south of Holm Lake, consisting of parts of 4th Company and Pioneer Platoon Leutnant Brandt on Peak 472, plus an attached platoon of Company Müller (with three light machine guns and one heavy machine gun) on Peak 488. Over the course of 20 May, repeated artillery-supported enemy attacks on various positions of the front were defeated. Nevertheless, the French, who were pushing through north of Daltind toward Peak 488, had been able to take this peak. In order to prevent the positions from being penetrated from the south, the German left flank was curved in eastwards, and Peak 428 was occupied. Toward evening, a new attack from the forces coming from the west toward Peak 428 appeared imminent, and in addition there was the possibility that the enemy would attempt an outflanking manoeuvre across Trold Lake to the east.

A rapid advance by the Norwegians against Lillebalak became dangerous for different reasons.[10] In the early morning, the second (last) platoon of Reserve Company Müller from the area of Lillebalak was pulled from the regiment and ordered to Outpost III (at Peak 3, east of Cirkel Lake). The company had to be held ready behind the apparently endangered south flank, together with 3rd Company/138th, which had meanwhile become the division reserve again. Toward 1030 hrs, the Norwegians, with a strength of one or two ski companies, broke through in the fog on the north peak of Lillebalak. They threw out the weak defenders of 3rd Battalion and, as there were no reserves left for a counter-attack, were able to establish themselves on the peak. From this 200-metre high position, they completely tied down the positions of 1st Battalion (3rd and 5th Companies) with heavy flanking machine-gun fire.

Prior to the expected arrival of additional parts of his battalion, the commander of 1st Company/139th (Major Stautner) quickly assembled about 25–30 men and hurried to the neighbouring sector. With two light machine guns, they climbed up the main peak of Lillebalak (572m), which lay under heavy shelling from enemy artillery.[11] After the artillery fire had let up, Major Stautner and his small number of men led a counter-attack on the north peak, crossing the rocky, jagged plateau that lay between the peaks, while under the heavy fire of enemy machine guns and several snipers. With a 'hurrah', the small group of soldiers broke through on the north peak and pushed the Norwegians back, capturing two heavy machine guns. In their hasty retreat, the enemy suffered heavy losses.

During this successful counter-attack, two Norwegian companies led a continuing attack on both sides of Peak 648 from the north-east. These attackers were fended off and were seen moving close by, but in the opposite direction. Lillebalak was now recaptured and occupied, and with four heavy machine guns and one medium mortar, it became the most important flank bastion of the entire front. The recapture of this mountain was of great consequence. Without it, any necessary retreat later on by 1st and 3rd Battalions would have been impossible in an ordered procedure. Evacuating the positions would have exacted heavy losses, and the battalions would have taken intense enemy fire while retreating (see Bibliography, 52).

Toward 2330 hrs on 20 May, the Norwegians led a strong renewed attack. Exploiting the weather-related poor visibility, the far superior enemy forces stormed and captured Peak 648. The entire occupying force of nearly 50 men were either killed, wounded, or captured. At the same time, two precious heavy machine guns were lost.

Next day, after the loss of this important high-elevation terrain, the situation escalated further. A concentration of enemy forces in the depression between the north peak and Peak 648, apparently preparing for an attack on Kobberfjell, was fired on from Lillebalak and destroyed.

In the early morning, between 0400 and 0500 hrs, an enemy force of about company strength, under the cover of [fire from] one cruiser and two destroyers in Rombakenfjord, landed at Troeldal, proceeded north-east, and by mid-morning had taken possession of Hergotten. This landing caused great concern for division headquarters, as it was feared that the enemy might roll up on the newly planned German positions even before the division had finished relocating from the south, and then be able to capture its key peaks (see Bibliography, 40).

Therefore, at 1000 hrs on 21 May, Dietl ordered more parts of 3rd Company/138th (Leutnant Raabe with 15 men and 36 attached naval personnel), who had arrived in the meantime, to cross Rombakenfjord to the north of the Stromnen Strait and secure the south-west flank of Group Windisch until their retreat was completed.[12] On the evening of

21 May, with a British destroyer lying in the fjord just 1,000 metres away, the small section rowed across twice, unnoticed, and fulfilled their mission.

The situation for the entire northern front had become increasingly threatening. The enemy had captured one dominating peak after the other out on the main battle line, and could be expected to attempt a complete encirclement by moving from the south-west and north-east. Therefore, the division headquarters ordered the front to be moved back further. Dietl summed up the situation in the north: 'The Bogen is overtaxed, no shelter, nothing warm to eat, many cases of frostbite, several people have drowned in the snow bogs. The regiment appears on the brink of collapse' (see Bibliography, 40). With the front line in its unfavourable location at that moment, the constant frontal attack by the enemy, and the ever-increasing pressure against the open deep flanks, an enemy breach was possible at any time. Given that the manpower on the front line was sparse and reserves insufficient, it became crucial to fall back and move to a sector more favourable in terms of terrain, and in doing so, to shorten, and at the same time strengthen, the front.

Group von Schleebrügge, a subordinate element of Group Windisch, was to hold a line from the Swedish border above the line of Peak 620–Homelven–along the southern edge of the higher and lower Jern Lakes and into the Storelven Valley, where Peaks 303 and 79 stood, with the so-called lake belt on the high plateau of Haugfjeldet as a natural barricade.

In order to effectively secure their retreat against enemy ambush, Group Windisch formed West Sector (under Hauptmann Brandl, with the attached Pioneer Platoon Leutnant Brandt, Company Müller, 3rd Company/138th – which had been reassigned to them – Heavy Machine Gun Demi-Platoon 4th Company, and Demi-Battery 2nd/112th Mountain Artillery Regiment, without guns). The mission required the previous positions still be held in case of an enemy breakthrough, allowing the regiment time set up a long-term defence in its new position.

At 2100 hrs on 21 May, 1st and 3rd Battalions, under the cover of West Sector, began to disengage and head for Outpost III. Tired out, with the ranks of their companies badly depleted, they retreated. Heads down, unshaven and emaciated, uniforms soaked, weapons shouldered, machine gun harnesses slung, they marched through the night for nearly 12 hours, hauling along their equipment.

At 0500 hrs on 22 May, parts of West Sector also disengaged without incident.

The securing of the north-eastern flank by the new Group von Schleebrügge

By 5 May, after the battles at Graes Lake (see Chapter IV), the overall situation for Group Windisch had become extremely critical. On the same day, at about 2200 hrs, a pioneer troop reported very strong enemy forces advancing far off in the east through Raudalen. The enemy reportedly had already taken Peak 910 and now occupied the area to its west. The long-unspoken fear of a wide flanking movement through the inhospitable mountain terrain in the east now appeared to be a reality. This enemy advance and the simultaneous, continuing pressure from the enemy at the south-western front of Narvik Sector apparently signalled the start of a pincer movement against the rear of the entire battle group in the direction of the ore railway. With a breakthrough on both sides, moving across the mountains from the south and north – where not a single defender was positioned – Battle Group Narvik could become encircled.

Because of the recent arrival of the enemy in the north-east, which had prompted the Germans to immediately create a new front sector as a counter-measure, heavy fighting broke out later all the way to the Swedish border.

But the specific details of the situation were not yet clear. Despite the division's repeated requests of 6 May for air reconnaissance on the right flank, no information had come in. To secure the far right flank, division headquarters ordered Group Windisch to immediately release 1st Battalion/139th from its position west of Graes Lake and relocate it to Kuberget (820m).

So once again, the quick, battle-proven 1st Company/139th engaged in heavy fighting, and over the following weeks prevented an encirclement and breakthrough on the northern flank toward the south-east in the direction of Bjornfjell.

At 0400 hrs on 6 May, the company marched from Hartvik Lake, the ski platoon in the lead, crossed Fiskloes and Cirkel Lakes and arrived at the dreary, rocky area of Kuberget on 7 May. The company carried with them a supply of reserve ammunition, warm clothing, and canned rations. They set up an outpost in a hut at the upper Jern Lake as a valley base station to supply the coming battle in the mountains.

The 1st Company/139th started by building a defensive front that faced north-east, improvising their defensive positions in snow caves and nests in the rocks. The largest group was positioned on the Kuberget (Company Trupp, 3rd Platoon, one heavy machine gun, and two medium mortars), and they spread out further to the north on 9 May.[13] With this, two groups from 3rd Platoon and one light mortar occupied Peak 860, and the newly formed ski platoon (28 men, mostly from the 13th/139th under Feldwebel Bussmer), with one heavy machine gun, was positioned forward on the Naeverfjell (985m).[14] From there, the ski platoon, together with reconnaissance troops, found that the Naevertind (1424m) area from Peak 977 north-eastwards and Peak 1067 to the south-east was still free of enemy troops, so sent only a small group there to secure the high peak of Naevertind. On the eastward end of Bukkedalen, heavy enemy concentrations and movement from the Raudalen toward the south-west were observed, as well as some heavy traffic in that valley, where columns of horse-drawn sleds approached along the cleared roads.

Over the following days, the enemy slowly moved closer, trying to seize advantageous positions for an attack against the hastily erected German outposts in the north-east, an assault they now felt compelled to carry out. They occupied Peaks 977 and 910, and under the cover of thick fog, their ski troops quickly dug in on the west slope of the Naevertind.

On the mountains, the weather was cold, foggy, and windy, with recurring snowfalls. Shivering from the cold, the German soldiers crouched in their snow caves. Rations remained scarce, and the company was frozen and hungry (see Bibliography, 45).

It was this sort of foul weather and poor visibility that the Norwegians were able to use well to their advantage in their first strike. In the fog and snowstorm, the weakly defended Naevertind fell into the hands of the superior enemy forces. The Norwegians had worked their way closer from all sides and lay in wait all day, hidden in the snow, camouflaged in their thick, white fur jackets, while supplies were brought up from Bukkedalen. Above them, the seven German defenders had taken shelter behind boulders. As the weather raged, fog billowed around them, and the snowstorm whipped across the slopes and flanks of the mountains, the enemy suddenly broke through. The small group continued to defend, even when they ran out of ammunition, until they were finally captured.

But on Peak 860, on the same day, cries of alarm pierced the blustery snowstorm, and the German troops, grown numb from cold and apathy, rushed from their snow caves and tents hidden behind the rocks. At the last moment, as the enemy troops appeared amid the snowdrifts, the German troops were able to fight them off.

On 13 May, enemy movements were observed in Bukkedalen, heading east, and the Norwegians were being resupplied from Raudalen, which pointed to further enemy attacks.

On 14 May, in the fog, under the constant cover of mortars, the Norwegians attacked the unit on the Naeverfjell in an encircling movement from east and west, but were forced back at 2100 hrs. Then, after the commander of the only heavy machine gun was killed, and the munitions used up, the fate of the surrounded ski platoon was sealed. Fighting to the last, surrounded and pressed together, 18 men were taken prisoner. Three of the men tried to reach the company on the Kuberget, but finally crossed into Swedish territory and were interned.

Because of the prevailing fog, nothing was known of the actual situation of 1st Company/139th on the Naeverfjell, and the Norwegians, now free from danger of a counter-attack, were able to establish themselves on this second important peak.

On 15 May, under heavy mortar and machine-gun fire from the west, north, and east, the enemy attempted to penetrate the position of 1st Company/139th on the Kuberget and, by means of a local encirclement, to capture this main outpost.

Continual enemy attacks were carried out until 1400 hrs from the north and the east, i.e., from the direction of Naeverfjell and Naevertind, placing heavy pressure on the weakened 1st Company. From Naevertind, a strong force of enemy troops worked their way nearer, initially occupying

Peak 1067. From there, in the late afternoon, the enemy, who were advancing in company strength against the German groups on Peak 860, were repulsed. Also in the late afternoon, the Norwegians attempted a surprise attack against the handful of defenders on Peak 860. About one company of Norwegians sped down the Naevertind on skis. From both Peak 860 and the left flank on Kuberget, the German infantry fired on them from covered positions behind rocks, inflicting severe casualties. Disregarding this, the Norwegians, well camouflaged in their white coats, abandoned their skis and continued their advance up the slope on foot. Beaten back, the Norwegians hurried back to their skis and fled down the valley toward the east. Then came heavy mortar fire, and the enemy began to close in again from three sides. By 1800 hrs, the situation for the two groups on Peak 860 was untenable, and they had to be pulled back in order to avoid being cut off. The advances continued until 2200 hrs, but were defeated before they reached the last outpost of Kuberget. Among losses on the German side was the commander of the last heavy machine gun on Kuberget.

On the same day, when the weather cleared, the valley south-west of Naeverfjell was seen to be heavily occupied by the enemy. It appeared here that they were planning to break through between 3rd Battalion on Kobberfjell and the adjoining force on Peak 794, which in the meantime had been occupied by a small group from 1st Company/139th. The enemy's intent was to come in from the west and take Kuberget, the last obstacle in the north-east on the way to the ore railway,

Leutnant Trautner's ski troop (previously with 1st Battalion), which had been provided to 1st Company/139th on 15 May, was immediately deployed on the endangered Peak 794. This included its remaining 14 men and the last heavy machine gun belonging to 1st Company. These were to hold this peak and maintain communication with 3rd Battalion, which had been established for the first time on the previous night.

At around 0100 hrs on the night of 15/16 May, after a day and a half of marching through deep slushy snow in the valleys, some additional, very welcome reinforcements arrived on the Kuberget. They were the first part of the 1st Company/1st Airborne Infantry Regiment under Leutnant Becker, totalling three officers and 63 men, with four light machine guns and five heavy machine guns. They had parachuted in north of Bjornfjell at 1145 hrs on 14 May, and only six hours later, on orders from Generalleutnant Dietl, had marched to the threatened sector of the front.[15] Major von Schleebrügge had two heavy machine guns from the paratroopers placed on Peak 794. The majority of the paratroopers were deployed as security on the right flank, eastwards of Kuberget, with a concave-shaped front.

The reinforcements for 1st Company/139th had arrived just in time, as 16 May would be a day of major fighting. In the early morning, the Norwegians broke into the entire sector to the east of Kuberget (Peak 1067), as far as Kobberfjell. With a force the strength of two battalions, they made a powerful thrust southwards, intending to overrun the blocking positions of the reinforced 1st Company. The terrain of the high plateaus was hilly and strewn with huge boulders and crevasses, which the approaching enemy expertly used as cover, effectively backed by many heavy weapons. From the high peaks of Naevertind, Naeverfjell, and Peak 1067, which they had captured, the enemy now dominated all German positions. As mortars struck the snow nests and rocky defences, the German defenders soon suffered increasing losses; the effects of the bombardment worsened when shots detonated in the rocks, sending out sharp splinters. Enemy snipers, well camouflaged and unseen, took precise aim on individual men, shooting from long distances through their rifle scopes.

The Kuberget was under attack from three sides until 1100 hrs. Two attacks accompanied by heavy fire were fended off by the paratroopers and the sailors. The enemy also failed to break through frontally, from the north. But on the left, to the west, a crisis arose. From the valley toward the south-west of Naeverfjell, the Norwegians were slowly working closer to Peak 794 and Naeverfjell Lake, which lay further to the west at 1,200 metres elevation. Here, some 80–100 Norwegians proceeded toward the small Ski Group Lindner on the left shore of the lake and attempted to surround it. The only light machine gun in the group jammed just at the most crucial moment. As the fight continued, the machine gun was made ready to shoot again, but during the pause in fire, the group leader used his own machine pistol and the three riflemen against the enemy force, that was nearly 12 times larger [than his own]. After resisting for several hours, the group was finally able to retreat before the enemy had the chance to surround them completely.

In the meantime, on Hill 794, Ski Platoon Leutnant Trautner was repeatedly attacked by more than one company. At about 2200 hrs, after surrounding the ski platoon, the enemy broke through its position. Every defensive nest and boulder shelter was fiercely defended. After emptying his sub-machine gun, Leutnant Trautner was killed. Two of his men died with him, and three were wounded and taken prisoner along with two unwounded infantrymen. By 2215 hrs, Peak 794 was taken, the enemy having succeeded in a deep breakthrough.

In the sunlit arctic night, the battle for Peak 794 continued. Oberfeldwebel Rohr had taken over the remaining men of the ski platoon, and, reinforced by two paratrooper groups who had been quickly sent to him, counter-attacked. The Norwegians who had successfully broken through were thrown back out of their nests in the rocks and the Germans recaptured their former positions. Then, after a 12-hour battle, things slowly quietened down. That day, the reinforced 1st Company/139th had taken many casualties.

During the midmorning of 17 May, 13th Company/139th appeared. They had been pulled out of Group Windisch and still numbered just 50 men. Together with the remaining members of Ski Platoon Rohr, they made ready for a counter-attack in the direction of Peak 794, planning to reverse the enemy breakthrough and recapture the lost terrain.

With heavy losses on both sides (including Leutnant Müller), several enemy positions were captured and some ground was retaken in a hard battle. Finally, due to scarce ammunition, some of the captured terrain had to be partially given up, and the defence limited to Peak 794. At 1200 hrs, the enemy attacked Peak 794 in force again, and shortly afterwards [also attacked] Kuberget. All positions remained in German hands, but then came under heavy machine-gun and mortar fire.

Just how bloody the battles were over these three days is apparent from the casualty report of the reinforced 1st Company/139th, which during this period had 13 dead, 25 wounded, 27 missing, and seven losses from frostbite (see Bibliography, 39). This came to a total of 72 men, or almost half the company strength.

On 18 May, with improved weather, the tireless attacks on Kuberget continued. Toward 0700 hrs, a strong advance was defeated in a fight to the last man. Heavy fire from mortars and heavy machine guns held the defenders behind a small cover of rocks until the advancing enemy was close enough for an assault, which the Germans then pushed back. After this futile attempt to overrun the German positions from the north, the enemy left on their skis, crossing the terrain a few at a time, attempting to go around and approach the Kuberget from the west and east. This time they brought their heavy weapons into position at advantageous points wherever possible, and by the afternoon, heavy machine guns were able to fire into the rear of the occupiers of Kuberget until they were defeated by the paratroopers' heavy machine guns. With all of these fluid movements, the enemy could not be engaged as they remained outside the limited range of the German heavy weapons. And, due to lack of artillery, the enemy could not be touched from long distances.

In the north-east, things did not look good. The enemy now stood with a force of about two battalions on Peak 860, at the northern edge of Homelven valley and south of the Naeverfjell Lake. A large number of heavy weapons were in a semi-circle around the main outpost at Kuberget. While 1st Company/139th had previously been able to hold this last bastion, the situation remained serious. It was all the more so, as confirmed enemy movements further eastwards brought fear of a broad outflanking movement along the Swedish border.

Although the challenges of the terrain were equally tough for both sides, during the battles in the north-east the enemy made the mistake of constantly latching onto individual German outposts, when they would have been better served by moving on past them. By pushing through to the Swedish border in the north-east, the enemy would have had the opportunity to cut off all of the remaining German troops. But instead, their deployment developed very slowly and cautiously.

For the time being, because of how the situation developed for 1st Company/139th, the division headquarters was forced to focus primarily on the threatened north-east flank of Battle Group Narvik as a whole. In the expectation of renewed, imminent, and intensified enemy attacks, and an expansion of enemy forces to the east, 1st Company/139th now urgently had to be provided with all available reserves and incoming reinforcements. It was the same old song: again, something had to be improvised out of nothing; a defensive cover had to be created at the front while all available units were disengaged and removed. To overcome this challenge, every last reserve was scraped together and thrown into battle. Now, although additional parts of 1st Company/1st Airborne Infantry Regiment had arrived, no more division reserves could be created; any troops coming in had to be immediately deployed. Thus, from all sides came small groups of miscellaneous mountain infantrymen, sailors, and paratroopers to the rescue of 1st Company/139th, which was in danger of being surrounded.

To start with, 3rd Company/138th Mountain Infantry Regiment, which as of 16 May was positioned on the upper Jern Lake as division reserve, was ordered at 0100 hrs on 17 May to deploy toward the open right flank of 1st Company/139th. The 3rd Company found the Homelven valley was still free of the enemy. At around 1500 hrs on 17 May, the company engaged and defeated some small enemy units at Peak 529, and pushed forward to Peak 620 near the Swedish border and occupied it. At 0100 hrs on 19 May, additional parts of 1st Company/1st Airborne Infantry Regiment (74 men with 12 light machine guns under Leutnant Mösinger) arrived at Kuberget.[16] In addition, at 2100 hrs on 18 May, Naval Company Erdmenger, now ready for deployment, received division orders to move immediately to Peak 794, where parts of a strong enemy force had advanced to within about 30 metres of the German positions.

Looking forward, the plan was to provide support and security for the deep right flank until the morning of 6 May [sic], when the reinforcement troops would arrive behind the right flank of the 1st Company/139th. For this, Naval Company Steinecker was deployed on Rundfjeldet (771m) and Naval Company Weinlich on Haugfjeldet (660m), under the command of Hauptmann Brucker.[17]

With the reinforcements provided to the commander of 1st Company, Major von Schleebrügge, they now built a lengthened defensive front toward the south-east to prevent the enemy from an outflanking manoeuvre on the right. On the evening of 18 May, the Norwegians could be seen making preparations for an attack with ski troops and heavy weapons; they also relocated units of near-battalion size from Peak 1,067 further south-eastwards.

On 18 May, a naval platoon from Section Brucker (Leutnant Brauns with 30 men and two light machine guns) was deployed on Peak 529, which created a continuous front extending to Peak 620, where 3rd Company/138th was located. Then, during the daytime on 19 May, 3rd Company/138th was replaced by Naval Company Steinecker on Peak 620. This naval company had been pulled from Section Brucker on orders from division headquarters. The 3rd Company/138th was now freed up to serve as division reserve. Ski Platoon Rohr (previously Trautner), now at full strength, once again became the reserve for south of Kuberget.

During the night of 18/19 May, the division announced that in the interest of unified leadership and clear issuance of orders, 1st Company/139th, now grown much larger, was to be consolidated under the designation of Group von Schleebrügge. Its assigned section was the west slope of the line Kuberget–Swedish border. The 13th Company/139th on Peak 794 was placed under the command of Group Windisch. The rest of Section Brucker (Navy) was ordered to oversee the construction of a rear position on the line of Rundfjeldet–Haugfjeldet (see Bibliography, 40).

The new Group von Schleebrügge was to manage its front so that the furthest forward line was occupied only as an outpost; the mountain infantry groups were to be kept together in readiness 500 metres to the rear as strike troops. Thus, as of the morning of 19 May, 1st Company/1st Airborne Infantry Regiment (Leutnant Becker) took over the main defence of the Kuberget. The 1st Company/139th was held in reserve behind the group's sector, which included the line of Peaks 529–620.

On the afternoon of 19 May, the enemy began making continuous attacks on Kuberget, which led to the first breach there. As the eastward slope lay under very heavy enemy fire and heavy fog, the Norwegians slipped past two groups of German paratroopers. When the fog lifted, the Norwegians suddenly appeared at their rear. After the commander [Leutnant Becker] was wounded, the German positions were evacuated. In a counter-strike, however, with a group of German mountain infantry, the positions were retaken. Small attacks on 20 May were easily repulsed. On the following day, all was quiet.

During the night of 22 May, in the process of a general retreat and relocation of the northern front, even the hotly contended Kuberget was abandoned with no pressure from the enemy. The retreat took place under thick fog, and was secured by 1st Company/139th and the ski platoon. At Peak 529, on the right flank, the order to retreat was delayed for hours when a messenger was wounded. Only this part of the retreat took place to some extent under enemy fire.

It was 12 hours before the Norwegians retook Kuberget, but not without a preliminary heavily shelling.

CHAPTER 7

The Major Attack on Narvik Sector

Enemy landing leading to the giving up of Narvik city and harbour (Map 7)

Toward the end of May, the commander of Narvik Sector (Major Haussels) faced the daily possibility of major enemy landings in the city and harbour areas. To the south, on the other side of Beisfjord, the front was facing the Poles, who were putting up a furious battle (see Chapter III). The situation north of Narvik Sector had also become critical; after landing in Bjerkvik, the enemy had penetrated as far as Ojord, where they had positioned land artillery. This was also just a short distance from Narvik, separated only by Rombakenfjord.

The coastal front around Narvik was structured as follows:

On the right was Naval Company von Freytag, lined up at the end of Naval Regiment Berger (Naval Company von Diest from Naval Battalion Holtorf) around Tunnel 3.

Then came Naval Artillery Section (Leutnant Nöller) at Orneset, followed by 6th Company/139th Mountain Infantry Regiment and the Pioneer Platoon from 2nd Battalion on the Framnes Peninsula, whose positions adjoined those of Naval Company Möllman and Naval Company von Gaartzen in the harbour area.

Sector reserves were the so-called Train Station Company (about 40 men with two light machine guns) and 1st Company/137th Mountain Infantry Regiment, which was placed under command of the division on 26 May (Oberleutnant Schweiger with 108 men, one light machine gun, and one medium mortar), which was positioned at Tunnels 3 and 4.[1]

The strength of each company averaged about 70 men and about six light machine guns (this according to the previously mentioned data on the south front and Group Windisch). The heavy weapons available and deployed were as follows:

- Naval Company von Freytag: two 3.7cm anti-aircraft cannons and one light machine gun.
- Naval Artillery Section: one light machine gun.
- 6th Company/139th Mountain Infantry Regiment: two light machine guns.
- Naval Company Möllman: two Norwegian heavy machine guns.
- Naval Company von Gaartzen: two Norwegian heavy machine guns.

On the Framnes Peninsula, there were also three medium mortars intended to cover the bay of Vassvik and Taraldsvik, and two light infantry guns positioned in the harbour and along the entire north coast.[2] In depth, along the mountain slopes some 150 metres above the city, was the Light Machine Gun Platoon from 2nd Battalion/139th Mountain Infantry Regiment, with four light machine guns aimed at the harbour, and two more light machine guns on the slope of Fagernesfjell for support for 8th Company at Ankenes.

The artillery consisted of half of a mountain battery, whose two guns had been moved some 700 metres north-eastwards of the Narvik railway station, and two captured 10.5cm guns, which were ineffective due to their makeshift construction. In terms of anti-aircraft weapons, there were seven 2cm guns and one 3.7cm gun on hand, which were deployed both for anti-aircraft defence as well as defending against possible landing attempts in the harbour and the bays of Vassvik and Taraldsvik.[3]

The sector command post and the main observation post were located at Peak 79, some 200 metres north-west of the railway station.

As of 27 May, the strength of the entire sector including the south front (not counting the two newly assigned 1st and 2nd Companies of the 137th Mountain Infantry Regiment) consisted of nearly 900 men, which at that time included only about 350 mountain infantrymen (see Bibliography, 42). In this very thin coastal front, with its few men and insufficient weapons, the entire defence front could only be constructed in a linear fashion, with outposts. All depth structure had to be sacrificed.

At this time, Lieutenant-General C. J. E. Auchinleck took command of the Allied land forces at Narvik. General Auchinleck attacked with more vigour than his predecessor. In addition to destroying the German battle group, a further important [aim was] the actual recapture of the town of Narvik. For the enemy, the taking of Narvik would be highly symbolic, bringing favourable world-wide publicity and visible proof of the Allied victory in the far north.[4]

It was a beautiful, sunny, and generally quiet day on 27 May. Suddenly, at around 2030 hrs, a powerful enemy fleet was reported in Ofotenfjord, sailing in the direction of Narvik. The sector commander immediately passed the report to division headquarters in Bjornfjell, with the urgent request for air support against what was certain to be an imminent enemy landing operation.

At about 2300 hrs, the enemy warships arrived at Narvik. At the same time, aircraft from the carrier *Glorious* circled over the town. Four destroyers entered Rombakenfjord, the furthest forward of these about in line with the mountain area where Tunnel 4 stood. In the bay of Taraldsvik, two cruisers and a destroyer came about, and one cruiser took up its firing position at Ankenes.[5] [6] The ships were positioned at a distance of between 1,000 and 2,000 metres from land. Behind the warships, at the entrance to Herjangenfjord, were transport ships and more auxiliary ships.

Under the eerie calm of the arctic midnight sun, the enemy fleet completed its display and, gun turrets rotated out, lay ready and in wait. The threatening silence lay heavy on the defenders, who had been hopelessly outnumbered from the beginning. No weapon was allowed to fire, so that precise positions would not be detected and bombarded by the ships' guns. Only the men in their observation posts peeked out over their shelters, trying to track any movement out on the water.

At 2310 hrs, the division reported the enemy landing to Group XXI and asked Trondheim for air support. But just at this critical moment, direct radio contact was interrupted, which meant that the radio message had to be routed through Wilhelmshaven.

At 2340 hrs, under the midnight sun, the approaching enemy fleet came to a stop in a tight semi-circle in front of Narvik. At the same moment, a red signal flare went up, just as it had in Bjerkvik, and then all guns, some as large as 15cm calibre, burst forth in a devastating bombardment of the German coastal front around Narvik. In continuous sequence, hundreds of shells roared in the direction of the ore railway, detonated in front of the tunnel entrances, howled against the rocky shore of Framnes, and burst between the buildings in Vassvik. With a primeval rumble, fragments from the large, heavy shells thundered into the slopes of Fagernesfjell. Shots rained noisily on Ankenes and Nyborg as well, and volcano-like fires burst out on Ankenesfjell. Everywhere in the town and harbour, in Fagernes, and on the shore of Ankenes, wooden buildings burst into fire like blazing torches. With booming and thundering, the ships' shells blasted into the rocky terrain, sending out thousands of whistling, splintering fragments, spraying rock all around.

Within just 10 minutes, several telephone lines in the sector were shot up. Crouched down and bathed in sweat, the men of the signal platoon from 2nd Battalion/139th ran through the hellish scene attempting to [repair the lines], but despite their self-sacrifice, the communication network could not be maintained.

By 0015 hrs, the shelling from the many ships' weapons increased to an unimagined ferocity, density, and speed. For the defenders, it was possible to communicate only through gestures, as every word shouted was swallowed up by gunfire. Meanwhile, three howitzer batteries fired from Ojord, their rounds exploding with a sharp, punishing crash over all streets and town squares, especially in the area of the rail station.[7] They also targeted any suspected mountain infantry positions, as well as the sector command post.

Gradually, it became possible to identify certain enemy *Schwerpunkte*, or points of main of effort. These were the headland at Orneset with its rock plateau, the ore railway at Tunnel 1, Peak 79 in Taraldsvik, the southern end of the harbour at Fagernes, and Ankenes. Across the entire rocky coast eastwards of Orneset as far as Taraldsvik hung thick clouds of gunpowder and stone particles that glowed in the lightning flashes of each new impact. All signs pointed to an imminent landing, but before it began, the enemy seemed intent on pulverising the coastal defences and destroying the German supplies, which they apparently assumed were in Fagernes.

But even this last and more intensive shelling could not frighten the defenders. Though they were completely defenceless, at no time were the positions abandoned and given up. Despite being in the vortex of the shelling, the men held out with determination. Having taken cover in the rocks, casualties were few.

At 0015 hrs, the enemy began to disembark. From the north, a large motor boat rounded the spit of land at Orneset, presumably having come from one of the transport ships, quickly followed by more of the same. Soon there were 10 fully occupied boats speeding toward the spit at Orneset. As they moved close along the shoreline, their crews were able to unload easily in the small bay eastwards of the land spit, out of sight of the German main observation post. At the same time, enemy fire in the area of Orneset increased to its utmost intensity, and the shelling from the four destroyers in Rombakenfjord along with that of the land batteries of Ojord concentrated on a selected breakthrough point on the right flank.

This first enemy landing with its accompanying preparation fire struck the weakest spot in the entire coastal front – Naval Artillery Section Möller, which had only 50 men, six light machine guns, and one heavy machine gun. The ships' shells continued to strike at the sailors' positions, forcing them to take complete cover and leaving them unable to fire on the enemy until the last moments of the landing. This fire, along with the flanking machine-gun fire from the scattered nests of Naval Company von Freytag, inflicted some of the earliest casualties, which were on the uncovered, fully occupied boats as they approached.[8] Toward 0030 hrs, however, as the first wave of the landing arrived and the men waded through the shallow water and approached [the shore], the fire curtain that had so far largely crippled the German resistance, now lifted. But as the surviving defenders dashed from their covered positions, they were met by the enemy's hand grenades. A short, close-quarters battle arose, which cost heavy casualties on both sides, one of whom was Naval Leutnant Nöller, who suffered a severe head wound. The last of the naval artillerymen were soon forced to vacate their positions to the more powerful enemy, retreat, and head for the slope south of the railway line in the area of Tunnel 1, to link up with other troops.

Just 10 minutes after the successful landing, the protective fire resumed, shielding the new arrivals and debarkations.

During this first landing, all the other positions between Taraldsvik and Vassvik continued to be shelled hard. One of the hardest hit was Naval Company von Freytag, positioned to the right, as far as Tunnel 4, which was pinned down at the ore railway. Another was 1st Company/137th Mountain Infantry Regiment, standing by as reserves under the protective cover of the tunnels, and now pinned down by heavy ships' shells striking the tunnel entrances.

In the meantime, at the sector headquarters, even amid the roar of enemy fire came the sound of the short fire bursts by the German light machine guns and the boom of hand grenades from Orneset. But then the battle noise faded away, and the enemy's rolling barrage leaped onto the rocky plateau at Orneset, flared up at the entrance to Tunnel 1, and then moved along the ore railway. It seemed obvious that at Orneset's weak defence was destroyed and the enemy landing had succeeded. Now the German counter-attack led by 1st Company/137th began, coming in from the right, that is, from the area of the tunnels. Everyone at the command post listened intensely for a new round of destructive shelling, announcing the attack into the flank of the enemy. But still, there was nothing to be heard.

The sector commander was filled with deep concern. When would the counter-attack break loose? Everything now counted on throwing the enemy back into the water as fast as possible, before they could get further reinforcements. Counting the number of boats, the enemy must already have had about 500 men ashore.

Due to weakness on the German side, a counter-attack against additional landing groups, or even a blockade of the constantly expanding bridgehead, was becoming increasingly hopeless. Therefore, a messenger was sent to the ore railway with the order for the company to head immediately for Orneset. Then a second one was sent. In addition, at 0050 hrs, a radio message went to the division with a situation report, and a request that more air support be sent quickly.

Still, nothing pointed to a coming attack on the right flank. Instead, toward 0100 hrs, in the arctic twilight, the first brown-clad enemy troops appeared high on the rocky peak near Orneset. There was no other option now than to promptly release the last of the sector's reserves (the so-called Train Station Company). On alert for some time, the Rail Station Company was only about platoon-sized and inexperienced in combat. It was now ordered to leave the train station and deploy along the railway toward Orneset, and to push the enemy back, or at least hold them back long enough for the counter-attack that was planned from the area of the tunnels on the right. Fifteen minutes later, the weak company was reinforced by eight more pioneers from the division demolition squad under the command of the ordinance officer from 2nd Battalion/139th (Leutnant Fink). The advance led by these sailors, most of them inexperienced in infantry combat, was a complete failure. Because even the commander failed, almost every man fled toward the slopes of the Taraldsvikfjell at first sight of the enemy. Only the small group of pioneers stayed and fought ferociously against the superior enemy, attempting, however ineffectively, to disrupt the continuing attack on the railway. Finally, this small band of troops worked its way to Tunnel 1, where they were able to reinforce the artillerymen who were still there with their two makeshift guns.

A counter-attack by 1st Company/137th Mountain Infantry Regiment was still anxiously awaited. An enemy infantry unit was spotted climbing up on the railway roadbed and crossing the tracks toward the south. In expanding the area they occupied, it appeared that the enemy had been able to advance further than Tunnel 1. The loud sounds of a battle could be heard coming from that area.

At 0130 hrs, to finally get the attack order to the companies along the ore railway, a third messenger was dispatched. This messenger, too, did not arrive. The enemy's ever-expanding and reinforced vanguard threatened to cut off these companies, and in order to maintain at least basic communication with them, at 0145 hrs, the last available radioman was dispatched as a messenger. He was to follow a route across the Taraldsvikfjell, and like the others, he carried with him the order to counter-attack. But the radioman arrived at the ore railway much too late.[9]

Shortly after 0200 hrs., the sector command post saw that more strong enemy forces were advancing across the railway to the south. And not one troop was available to stop them!

Between 0200 and 0230 hrs, about 10 motor boats made another landing at the previous breach point. With this, about 1,000 enemy troops had come ashore (as it was later was learned, these were two battalions of the 13th Demi-Brigade of the French Foreign Legion).

The situation was becoming critical. Now, heavy machine-gun fire lashed out from the strongly occupied rock plateau at Orneset, flanking the German positions at Taraldsvik. Two light machine guns were pulled from an extra deep sector of 6th Company/139th on both sides of Vassvik, which then were deployed at Taraldsvik with their front facing east. These would have been able to effectively suppress the enemy machine guns. But towards 0350 hrs, the enemy appeared to be trying to expand the landing zone toward the west as well with an advance toward Taraldsvik, which they apparently intended to capture for further landings. Under cover of fire, they brought in large quantities of heavy weapons across the open meadows and fields of the local farms. It was only with great effort on the part of German machine guns (including those of the sector command) that they were forced either into cover or to turn back. The enemy's onslaught was halted in its early stages, but only after deploying half of 6th Company/139th.

The German defence increasingly began to splinter into individual battles that could no longer be carried out in a coordinated manner. Everywhere, separate groups and individual troops put up tough resistance. Even though they had been separated from one another and had to fight with no communication between them, they were able to slow the progress of the far superior enemy. Leutnant Seibt, together with his few artillerymen, a small group of pioneers, and some scattered soldiers fiercely defended Tunnel 1 with rifles and hand grenades, stalling the enemy's advance along the ore railway and preventing them from rolling up on the German positions there. At around 0400 hrs, after a long fight and after suffering casualties (Leutnant Seibt went missing in action), the rest of the small band retreated along the railway. To prevent a rapid enemy pursuit, the pioneers blew up the tunnel.

Eastwards of the train station, the two mountain guns fired persistently, but with long pauses due to the scarcity of ammunition. Constantly under fire themselves, they still continued to fire on the enemy batteries at Ojord, whose high-angle weapons aimed behind the Germans in an effort to destroy their cover and rock nests. One enemy battery was taken out. By around 0330 hrs, out of ammunition, the two German mountain guns were useless. When the Foreign Legionnaires pushed forward and closed in on the German positions, the mountain artillerymen fought them off with rifles and fixed bayonets in infantry-style combat, and then pushed on in the direction of Tunnel 2.

In the meantime, from the north slope of Fagernesfjell, the heavy machine gun platoon leader of 10th Company/139th also spotted the strong enemy force advancing toward the south. On his own initiative, he sent a pair of heavy machine guns across the Taraldsvik creek, very close to the bottom of a ski jump. The two guns effectively opened steady fire both on the enemy troops as they retreated across the railway line and on the troops attacking at Taraldsvik. Shortly after 0400 hrs, however, after the heavy machine-gun crew had climbed up the slopes of Taraldviksfjell, the enemy's vanguard ambushed them from the concealment of the birch forest. Those of the crew who survived were taken prisoner.

The crisis now reached boiling point. More enemy landed, and now came fishing cutters with troops and equipment to Orneset, so that by 0500 hrs, there were about 1,500 men on land there – against a German force of just small, isolated groups. Initially careful and hesitant, the enemy pushed further eastward to the ore railway, constantly and in increasing numbers. Their goal was to move inland to the south, to the mountain slopes near Fagernes, obviously hoping to cut off the entire remaining defence of Narvik from the rear.

A third situation report went out from the sector command to the division with another request for support from the direction of the ore railway. In order to initiate the push toward the south even halfway, there was no choice but to pull out the last half of 6th Company/139th from its coastal position. Together with the remaining weapons from the heavy machine gun platoon (10th Company/139th), they were to move into a blocking position at the Taraldsvik stream and prevent all further enemy attempts to surround them from across the Fagernesfjell. Unfortunately, this meant that the coastal front on both sides of the landing point at Vassvik and the road entering the town of Narvik would be totally exposed and jeopardised for the sake of preventing danger to the rear.

By 0420 hrs, the Allies had already crossed the Taraldsvik stream 1,500 metres above Narvik, and the three small groups from 6th Company that found themselves climbing the mountain slopes were no longer able to stop him. But by means of delaying tactics and heavy machine guns, the Germans were able to considerably slow the enemy advance in the sparse brush and birch forest.

Because all communication had been disrupted, the more recent calls for help to the division went unheard. Even with the troops along the ore railway, which were essentially splintered, there was no communication, and therefore the much-hoped-for counter-attack did not take place.[10] Now only two weak naval companies stood along the entire long coastal front from Vassvik to the harbour. After 6th Company/139th was pulled out, a 1.5km-wide gap was created, so their already thinly manned lines had to be spread out still more sparsely, and at any second they also needed to be prepared for another enemy landing.

Despite the now untenable situation, the sector commander decided to continue to hold. He had been ordered to evacuate the town of Narvik only under extreme necessity, and to then re-establish the defence line along the ore railway and the mountain slopes south of it. But because the enemy already occupied those slopes, this mission had become overtaken by events.

Yet the commander was still counting on a relief attack from the troops at the ore railway which would finally loosen the enemy stranglehold. He also hoped for help from German aircraft, which would ideally attack the enemy ships in the fjords and force them to stop firing. At around 0445 hrs, two aircraft did appear. Flying through the middle of the anti-aircraft fire, they scored some hits that prompted the ships to manoeuvre and temporarily cease fire.[11] But this was minor support, and only of short duration.[12]

German machine guns still clattered away, shots tore through the mountain forests, hand grenades exploded, and fighters had to deal with empty weapons. Then, between 0400 and 0500 hrs, the fire from the ships' guns increased to its highest intensity. Across the town and over the entire area of Tunnel 4, as far as the Framnes Peninsula, an impenetrable cloud of smoke and fumes enveloped [the defenders], along with the fiery spray of exploding shells.

At 0615 hrs, in Taraldsvik Bay, some 300 metres from the sector command post, the second major landing took place. Here, three tanks were also brought ashore. Although one of them broke down under fire from a 2cm anti-aircraft gun and became stuck in the mud along the shore, the two others reached the shoreline road. At the same moment, heavy fighting broke out against the enemy infantry, which was working its way forward in the area of the train station. From the mountain slopes of Fagernesfjell came the sounds of battle and increasing danger. The command post itself came under well-aimed machine-gun fire from south and east, as well as shell fire from the batteries at Ojord.

The sector commander described the situation as of 0630 hrs:

> Of the forces that landed at Orneset, large numbers (Foreign Legionnaires) found themselves on the slopes of Fagernesfjell, and thus, at the rear of the coastal defensive front. Other strong forces (Norwegians) pushed forward to the ore railway, making the last hopes for a successful counterattack increasingly slim. [no citation]

The debarkations at Taraldsvik stopped, but the possibility of more landings at Vassvik had to be reckoned with. The German coastal defence would no longer be able to stand up to them.[13]

Along with concerns for the tattered coastal front around Narvik, a no-less-concerning issue was the situation on the left flank on the opposite side of Beisfjord, where urgent calls for help were coming from 8th Company/139th at Ankenes, and 7th Company/139th at Skavtuva-Hestefjell. Under attack at the same time, 8th Company would be able to hold out for another five hours at most; 7th Company would not last into the evening hours. With this, after capturing Ankenes and Nyborg, under the fire protection of the ships' guns, the far superior enemy forces now battling 8th Company would be able to cross Beisfjord, closing the circle around Narvik from the south as well. If 7th Company's mountain positions at the south end of Beisfjord were to be captured, this would mean that the last line of retreat would be blocked for all defenders from Narvik. Moreover, the enemy would have an open route in the direction of Sildvik and to the rear of the defence at the ore railway.

Communications to the division headquarters had broken off, and there were no more reserves available.

So far, the enemy had not yet penetrated into the town of Narvik, nor had any landings taken place on the Framnes Peninsula or in the harbour area. The enemy appeared to want to avoid a local battle that promised high casualties, but it was clear that their major attack would aim to completely surround the defence around Narvik, encircle it, shell it from all sides, and pound it into extinction.

Based on this situational assessment, it was clear to the sector commander that with only the 150 mountain infantrymen still available, 250 sailors, and anti-aircraft artillerymen, Narvik could no longer be held. Now, under immediate threat of being completely cut off, and after hours of hard defending, the only option left was to retreat. And it was high time to do so.

Because the enemy was pushing forward toward the ore railway, the road along Beisfjord remained the only route of retreat. All troops would have to be channelled to the rear for use in constructing a new front in the deep southern flank of the overall battle group in the mountains above the Beisfjord settlement.

The time appeared to be very advantageous for the retreat. The enemy had not yet finished their encirclement. The town and harbour area were heavily covered with fires, smoke, and haze, which prevented the enemy from watching from their perch high on the mountain slopes. The enemy ships that cruised in the fjord gradually fell silent, apparently to avoid endangering their troops on the ground.

Despite this, the disengagement and retreat of all troops would be a very difficult manoeuvre. A great deal depended on the two hard-pressed companies on the other side of Beisfjord and the two groups on Fagernsfjell; they would have to hold out long enough to cover both left and right. Just as importantly, the necessary orders would also have to come through in time.

At 0650 hrs, Major Haussels gave the order to evacuate Narvik, abandon the remaining coastal positions, and retreat to the southern end of Beisfjord. He gave this order while still unaware that German troops had actually been leading attacks along the ore railway (see section below, 'The situation along the ore railway, 28 May'). After Narvik was lost, however, such attacks could change nothing at all.

The orders required all baggage and equipment be left behind, and that only hand-held weapons and as much ammunition as possible be brought along (see Bibliography, 42). The first assembly area was to be the protective rocky area at Fagernes.

The retreat order, however, did not reach all the troops. Two groups from Naval Company von Gaartzen, with two heavy machine guns, did not receive the order and remained missing. Naval Company Möllmann later retreated on its own. The naval signal station set up by division headquarters high up on Fagernesfjell likewise did not receive the news.[14] A further problem was that the heavy weapons were not able to be transported immediately. The two mountain guns had already been disabled, and the two light infantry guns and three medium mortars on Framnes had been blown up. One attempt to transport the 2cm anti-aircraft guns on a lorry proved impossible under enemy fire, so one of these also had to be disabled. The munitions and supply depot was also destroyed.

The relocation went in a leapfrog manner, initially secured by the last machine gun of 10th Company/139th, together with the platoon of 6th Company on Fagernesfjell. Firing down onto the harbour road prevented the enemy from a quick pursuit. Unnoticed and without casualties, Narvik itself and all defensive positions were abandoned. This took place under fire from the land batteries at Ojord, which continued shelling the burning city. Hidden from sight under the thick blanket of smoke and fumes, the defenders reached cover behind the rocks of Fagernes. There, enemy machine-gun fire fell on them from the slopes of Ankenesfjell opposite, but did not disrupt the ongoing retreat. The 8th Company/139th still stood fast and continued to secure the retreat, providing crucial protection.

In Fagernes, all arriving troops were received by the sector commander, assembled and taken by five waiting transport lorries to the area around Beisfjord village. They were to man a security line here, behind 7th Company/139th in Lakselven valley, which was under heavy attack. Naval Section Dehnert, with four light machine guns, was to remain behind to await the arrival of scattered troops and to bring up the rear once all troops had left Ankenes and crossed the Beisfjord. The interim security on the road to Beisfjord was undertaken by parts of Naval Company von Gadarene with three light machine guns, 3km south-east of Fagernes, and ordered to hold that position until 2000 hrs. The Demi-6th Company/139th was assigned to the final reception point, located about 1.5km north-west of Beisfjord village, which they were to hold until the arrival of all units from Ankenes and Fagernes (8th Company/139th, 2nd Company/137th, Naval Section Dehnert, and Naval Company von Gaartzen). A mine blockade was placed in the road in case of a possible pursuit by enemy tanks. There was also the fear of an outflanking movement from across the slopes of Fagernesfjell on the open mountain flank on the right, and therefore, at 1000 hrs, the heavy machine gun from 10th Company/139th moved into position on its north-west ridge.

Until 1100 hrs, the command post for the sector commander was located at Fagernes (where the majority of 8th Company/139th and 2nd Company/137th had previously arrived from Ankenes); at 1200 hrs, it was relocated to Beisfjord village.

Course of the battle on the southern front, 28 May

The enemy's armada of ships lying at Narvik also directed their heavy fire against Ankenes, setting fire to some 30 houses in the areas around Ankenes and Nyborg, leaving them in ashes. The 2nd Company/137th suffered particularly heavy casualties at this time. The company was ready as a reserve in the small fishing village of Nyborg (south-west of Ankenes), originally intended to be deployed for the planned attack on the open left mountain flank of 8th Company/139th. Despite explicit orders, the company had sought shelter in the houses there, and shortly after 2300 hrs it came under fire from the enemy ships.

The enemy's storm then burst with full fury over the southern front that had been held for so long. At 23.30 hrs, the enemy began its attack with two battalions against the reinforced 8th Company/139th on the mountain slope above Ankenes.[15] Already in an intense fight with the Poles, the company radioed the Narvik Sector commander, reporting the situation as threatening. Because the coastal front itself was under heavy attack, no help could be provided. Toward 0200 hrs, 8th Company/139th reported new and ongoing heavy attacks from powerful enemy forces, with breaches at several positions, doubting it could hold out. The thin defensive front that clung to the mountain slope, composed only of outposts, had begun to disintegrate and threatened to collapse. The area between the settlement of Ankenes and the Ankenesfjell was manned by sailors, who were unable to cope with the constant enemy pressure; they began abandoning their positions and, at about 0440 hrs, retreated by boat from Nyborg to Fagernes. The scattered reserve company, 2nd Company/137th, was reunited with some difficulty, and at was finally deployed with a strength of two platoons at 0230 hrs. The company commander was then ordered to throw the enemy back to the right and restore the area that was breached when the sailors fled.

A daring counter-attack was led by Oberleutnant Rieger at around 0700 hrs against the Poles, who had pushed through the birch forest above Ankenes from the north-west in an attempt to cut off 8th Company/139th on the high ridge of Ankenesfjell. Rieger's attack pushed far further forward than intended. Rieger himself, with a strike platoon of 15 men, broke through and reached an enemy command post at the top of Peak 295. There the platoon was cut off completely and overpowered by the enemy. Oberleutnant Rieger was wounded and captured, while Leutnant Bollenberger and many members of the company were killed, wounded, or remained missing in action. Ultimately, the attack by 2nd Company/137th brought only temporary relief, at the cost of heavy losses for the Germans.

To the west of its Ankenes position, the enemy stormed down the mountain and twice broke through the German positions, but were thrown back again in a close-quarters fight.

A breach attempt by two enemy tanks on the road toward Ankenes also failed. Here, under the leadership of a naval officer, was a section of 47 sailors, nine mountain infantrymen, and five anti-tank troops with a 3.7cm anti-tank gun. After the furthest-forward tank ran into a minefield and was immobilised, the narrow roadway was blocked and its accompanying infantry pounded to pieces.

The defensive power of the reinforced 8th Company/139th deteriorated. As the fighting grew more and more intense (especially due to the batteries located east of Haakvik that supported enemy advances and the many Polish machine guns and mortars), it suffered heavy losses. Although the dwindling company had been able to consolidate and at times manage to counter-attack, it could not prevent the enemy from breaking in here and there, or climbing down the slopes to Beisfjord and into their rear. At 0420 hrs, the company reported: 'Enemy breach at several positions. Casualties high, close combat at many positions. Retreat appears unavoidable.'

The tenacious struggle lasted for over an hour, then at 0545 hrs, one last radio message went out: 'Due to heavy casualties it appears impossible to hold out any longer!' The company had to give up its positions.

Still in the fight and shooting from all sides, individual platoons and groups retreated step by step. S Platoon, which stood above Nyborg with its front facing south-east, continued to resist against all enemy attacks, with the effective support of the light infantry guns on the Framnes Peninsula.

Under orders, the companies retreated, then reassembled at Beisfjord, occupying one last position. Then at 1100 hrs, under enemy fire, the majority of 8th Company/139th and 2nd Company/137th crossed by boat to Fagernes. The enemy had also become exhausted by their attacks, to the extent that they avoided heavy action and often allowed themselves to be stopped – often by only a few men. This enabled the last guards and scattered troops to row across to Fagernes between 1600 and 1700 hrs. The rowboats, however, became riddled with holes from machine-gun fire by the advancing Poles. It was futile to try to bail out the boats and keep them from sinking. The men had to swim, still under fire and suffering casualties, and bring their wounded men to the safety of the opposite shore. Several severely wounded men, for whom no medical help could be expected, and who could not be taken to Beisfjord, remained near the road under the care of a medic, where they were later picked up by the enemy. Other parts of units who did not receive the retreat order, and for whom crossing the fjord was no longer an option, withdrew from Nyborg along the steep rocky shore, making the daredevil climb toward the end of the fjord in the direction of 7th Company. In addition to the enormous casualties suffered by both 2nd Company/137th and 8th Company/139th, they also lost their heavy high-angle fire weapons. Out of their 19 weapons, they sacrificed seven in battle.

Naval Section Dehnert remained in place to protect the retreating troops from possible enemy pursuit from Narvik while they crossed from

Ankenes (although initially the enemy did not advance on the harbour road toward Fagernes). After gathering the last of the late-arrivals at around 1700 hrs, the section finally retreated under enemy machine-gun fire from Ankenes and Nyborg.

The first, rather weak, enemy attacks took place at the south end of Beisfjord against 7th Company/139th on 27 May, shortly after 2200 hrs. By 2330 hrs, the Poles had strengthened their forays with heavy mortar support, but had been defeated everywhere by around 0200 hrs. A renewed enemy attack on Peak 773 (Hestefjell) at about 0400 hrs was defeated, while about 400 men continued to charge up Peak 650 (Skavtuva). The enemy also began to launch an encirclement of Peak 606. At 0500 hrs, 7th Company reported heavy casualties. A series of direct hits destroyed several heavy weapons. In particular, the heavy machine guns, with their rattling full-automatic fire, lay under the constant whistling of mortar shells. Hestefjell was under repeated attack by some 150 men, and Skavtuva was also strongly attacked. Radio communication with the sector command remained intact, but the sector was unable to send one single fighter or one more machine gun to help them.

Toward 0600 hrs, the enemy attacked 7th Company at the front and on both flanks with about 1,000 men (Polish 1st Mountain Infantry Battalion). The company requested help, but once again in vain. The sector commander's order was: 'Hold out to the last man!' If the planned retreat from the Narvik Sector was to succeed, and if the construction of a new defensive front were to be made possible, 7th Company/139th had to hold its position at the southern end of Beisfjord. As the southern cornerstone, 7th Company held the decisive point for the spread-out sector. Holding that position was crucial for the existence of the southern front, and by implication, for the entire Battle Group Narvik as well.

The situation for 7th Company intensified. As part of his overall operation, the enemy had carried out strong frontal assaults, but now began a sweeping encirclement. To the south, in Haakvikelven, about 600 men were observed, some on skis, proceeding in a sweeping movement around Peak 606 toward the open, deep left flank. The company was forced back in places, but persistently counter-attacked and held their endangered position.

In the meantime, the divisional headquarters and the sector command tried to stabilise the situation and rebuild the crumbling southern front, although due to interrupted communications, they worked independently of one another. Division headquarters now planned a defence of the line of Tottadalen–Rombakstotta–Beisfjordstotta–Lakselven valley. Shortly after midday, they were able to establish communication with 7th Company. At 1310 hrs, Generalleutnant Dietl issued instructions for them to hold their mountain positions as long as possible in order to secure the retreat of parts of companies from Narvik and Ankenes. Due to overpowering enemy pressure, the reception point in the Lakselven valley (at the southern end of Beisfjord) was to be avoided. By 0640 hrs, Naval Company Clemens (Naval Regiment Berger) had already received a mission to proceed from its former security line south of Sildvik to a reception point in the Lakselven valley. Two platoons of airborne infantry under Leutnant Keuchel (4th Company/1st Airborne Infantry Regiment) were sent in to supplement the naval company.[16]

The sector commander (Major Haussels) considered building up a new front on the line Resmaalaksa (970m)–Beisfjord village–Lakselven valley to prevent the enemy from making an ascent into the mountains toward Sildvik. The heavy machine gunners of 10th Company, after providing security on Fagernesfjell, were also ordered to climb Resmaalaksa along the southern slopes and occupy this point. But the terrain south-east of Beisfjord appeared very unfavourable for a defensive position due to the thin birch forest. Furthermore, the enemy was sweeping around 7th Company, advancing with two companies on the eastern shore of Lakselven, making these planned defensive positions ineffective. The decision was then made to move to a position above Beisfjord in the mountains. The defensive line was to run along the line Durmalsfjell (Peak 844)–through the high valley of Molnelven at Peak 401–Resmaalaksa–Beisfjordstotta, occupying Peaks 585 and 639 in the east to secure the open left flank. The 7th Company was to hold on tenaciously until all units had gathered in the area of Beisfjord.

After 7th Company had fought off enemy attacks for the entire afternoon, the situation became untenable. The company had taken heavy losses, and eight of its 18 weapons were destroyed by the constant shelling. Even though individual naval personnel fought excellently, there were also those who retreated and enabled the enemy to break through.[17] Toward 1700 hrs, Peak 606 was no longer tenable due to an enemy enveloping movement; at 1845 hrs, Peak 773 (Hestefjell) also had to be given up. At 1945 hrs, the company commander independently issued the order to retreat to Beisfjord, while disengaging from left to right. The company worked its way back, still fighting and covering one another as they retreated. Skavtuva (650m) was held to the last in order to prevent an enemy breach between the mountain peak and the steep slopes of Beisfjord that would result in the entire company being cut off.

At about 2000 hrs, the first men of 7th Company arrived in Beisfjord with several severely wounded. While the last defenders above, in their mountain nests, disengaged from the superior advancing forces, some men still fought on Skavtuva, providing security for the retreat. On Skavtuva, the mountain peak on the right, enemy shells continued to burst, machine guns chattered, and defensive fire flashed. Here, until about 2100 hrs, three men with one light machine gun under Oberfeldwebel Hausotter held out and beat back the attacking Poles on all sides until the last shot. Literally at the last second, they managed to push through to Beisfjord. With great effort, they carried their staff sergeant, who had been shot in his chest and arm, down into the valley. The severely wounded staff sergeant was distressed at the idea of being taken to the field clinic in Narvik, as it had in the meantime been taken over by the enemy. Therefore, the men of his platoon carried him into the mountains on a 10-hour march, which was just starting out, all the way to Sildvik, where he was delivered to the German reserve medical field hospital.

After gathering all of the guards and security units in Beisfjord and destroying the small depot of provisions and ammunition in the area, Narvik Sector began their march into the mountains to occupy the new defensive line, followed by scattered and straggling troops. The 7th Company covered the retreat while in continuous hostile contact with the enemy, who pressured them from the rear for quite some time. The enemy's sweeping encircling movement at Lakselven had not yet had any effect and ultimately fizzled out.

The men of 2nd Battalion/139th and 2nd Company/137th were worn down and beaten, ravaged by combat, faces blackened by smoke, and soaking wet from swimming in the waters of the fjord – some with blood-soaked field dressings. It was in this condition that the sailors and anti-aircraft soldiers were reunited in Beisfjord during the late evening. They now faced another difficult ordeal of several hours, climbing over slippery rocks and crumbly, wet snowfields, and marching through melting alpine marshlands that could not be bypassed. Heavily loaded down, they waded through mountain streams, where some of the over-tired and breathless men were caught in the roaring current and carried off. Finally, they reached the mountain pass on Peak 660, and at around 0300 hrs on 29 May, they moved into their new positions.

Of all the missions, the most difficult would have to be that of 6th Company. Its completely exhausted infantrymen still had to conquer the 1,443-metre high hanging glacier of Beisfjordstotta, to take over security there. Naval Company Möllmann and 7th Company were deployed on both sides of the Molnelven valley, 8th Company on the Durmalsfjell, and Naval Company von Gaartzen further out on the left flank. The rest of 2nd Company/137th had to remain ready as counter-attacking reserves and was attached to 8th Company/139th. The anti-aircraft gunners, who had lost their 2cm guns, filled in the critical gaps in the companies.

Although down in the valleys the warming rays of springtime sun brought forth the green birch leaves, in higher altitudes there was just more hard rock and broad snowfields. The sky became overcast, fog rolled in, and the wind whistled; constant rain penetrated through to the skin, robbing the last bit of warmth from tired bodies. Bivouacking in snowstorms, the men lay on the mountain peaks under the open sky, footgear torn and clothing frayed. Only a few were equipped with coats, covers, or tarpaulin for tents to shield them from nature's fury. But none of the fighters reported in sick (see Bibliography, 16).

The situation along the ore railway, 28 May

As was later learned, the sorely wished-for counter-attack at Orneset had taken place, although much too late. The heavy enemy shelling from the ships' guns held 1st Company/137th and Naval Company von Freytag in their tunnels and behind their rocky cover for a long time. Only gradually did the troops manage to emerge from cover amid the intense enemy fire in numbers sufficient for a counter-attack. Under the constant boom and crash of heavy fire, they climbed up the steep slope to Taraldsvikfjell to take their positions 800m below the high mountain plateau, on a narrow rock terrace that faced west. Altogether there were the infantrymen of 1st Company/137th, some groups of sailors, the rest of the mountain artillerymen under Leutnant Enzinger, and the two pioneers under Leutnant Fink. Because no communication at all existed with the sector command in Narvik, nor had any orders come through, Oberleutnant Schweiger (commander of 1st Company/137th) decided to attack the advancing enemy in the flank. But while still in the final assembly area, heavy fire broke out, causing the first casualties. It was not until 0700 hrs that the Germans led an attack from that area to about 500 metres south-east of Tunnel 1.[18] This vigorous attack came down on the enemy from above as they were advancing on the slope of Fagernesfjell. Taken by surprise, they became confused, temporarily stopped their advance, and even dropped back. But then the much superior enemy regained their composure and brought their many heavy machine guns and ships' mortars into place. Between their fire and that of the ships in Rombakenfjord, the German counter-attack collapsed. The ships, able to observe the course of the assault, sent over their heavy shells and hammered the German attackers with their light anti-aircraft guns. Fighting alongside their men, almost all the German commanders fell: Oberleutnant Schweiger received a fatal shot in the neck, Leutnant zur See Rath and Leutnant zur See Schroth were killed, and Leutnant Enzinger was severely wounded.

After repeated attempts to move forward, the enemy shifted from attack mode to the defensive, attempting to at least hold the terrain that had been gained. Near midday, Kapitänleutnant von Freytag led the rest of his naval company to halt an enemy foray to the east, across Taraldsvikfjell, above the ore railway. He stood fast with some 70–80 men until just before 1530 hrs, but after an order from the division arrived, he pulled back to Tunnel 3.

At the ore railway, due to the push-back and retreat of the sector command to Beisfjord, there had been a lack of vigorous leadership. Now, a critical situation was developing with respect to the enemy: pushing harder toward the railway, they had gone around the demolished Tunnel 1, and had reached the area behind Tunnel 2 by about 1600 hrs.

Here, the division headquarters was forced to offer up their modest reserves. At 1400 hrs [sic], in response to the urgent request from Naval Battalion Holtorf, a platoon from 6th Company/138th (under Leutnant May) had been sent to Tunnel 3.[19]

At 1800 hrs, Naval Regiment Berger suddenly reported that naval elements had already fallen back as far as Tunnel 7 (toward Stromnen). This retreat, without having offered any sustained resistance, could not be justified. Dietl had to intervene with sharp orders in order to prevent the enemy from gaining the important Stromnen Strait with hardly a fight. Enemy control of this passageway would have allowed their ships to sail all the way to the far end of Rombakenfjord, where they could have staged landings.

At 1930 hrs, Naval Battalion Holtorf once more occupied the area around Tunnel 3 in strength. The enemy did not arrive there until 2045 hrs, when, in response to their increased pressure, the battalion was pushed all the way back to Tunnel 4.

In order to provide forceful leadership at the ore railway, Dietl ordered Hauptmann Walther (commander of the 1st Company/1st Airborne Infantry Regiment) to take over the situation, and placed Naval Battalion Holtorf and all other remaining elements under his command.[20] Holtorf received instructions to organise a permanent defence of the ore railway, and above all, to establish communication with the units of Narvik Sector in the mountains to the left. As a fresh resource, he was sent 3rd Company/1st Airborne Infantry Regiment (two officers with 78 men), which had been tasked as division reserves in Bjornfjell since 26 May. Likewise, 4th Company/1st Airborne Infantry Regiment, which had participated in the retreat as part of Narvik Sector's complement, was ordered to the ore railway, where it arrived on 29 May at 1900 hrs.

In order to have reserves at hand, however small, Dietl sent for Pioneer Platoon Leutnant Brandt from Group Windisch, which arrived at Spionkop on the afternoon of 29 May.

By the late evening of 28 May, no information was still available concerning the sector command. Conveying orders from division headquarters to Major Haussels presented enormous difficulties. There was, in fact, radio communication with 4th Company/1st Airborne Infantry Regiment, which, over the course of the day, was sent to Beisfjord and positioned behind Naval Company Clemens. This was in the vicinity of Major Haussels' command post, so now any orders from the division were given to this radio station to be passed on to Haussels. The airborne infantry company's radio station also confirmed the incoming messages. But the radio operators did not actually have the ever-changing, adaptive code key, so that the radioed orders could not be decoded (see Bibliography, 39). The 1st Ordinance Officer of the division was sent with written orders and verbal instructions to the sector command in Beisfjord, but arrived too late, and therefore Major Haussels continued to work independently until newer orders arrived.

Above all for Narfvik Sector, 28 May was a black day for the entire battle group. Along with the successful enemy landing, there were other bitter losses; one was Narvik itself, which had become a symbol of the overall defence; another was the major sacrifice of terrain. Once again, the gaps left in Group Windisch by fallen troops were painful, and the losses in weapons and equipment weighed heavily. Nearly all deployed units were negatively affected, many missing a good half of their numbers. The total losses were 41 dead, 69 wounded, and 176 missing.[21] The two companies of 137th Mountain Infantry Regiment were nearly wiped out: 1st Company/137th had 12 dead, eight wounded, and 25 missing; 2nd Company/137th at Ankenes had 20 dead, five wounded, and 22 missing. Almost all heavy weapons were lost, for the most part during battle. After the loss of the guns at Narvik, the entire battle group only owned two newly supplied mountain guns.[22] Much equipment, matériel, provisions, and ammunition was left behind and had to be destroyed. Each man had only what he carried himself. Still, despite the utmost demands, both physical and psychological, the spirit, mood, and conduct of the troops remained unbroken (see Bibliography, 16).

The enemy reported the loss of 90 French and 60 Norwegian troops. Their reported number of between 300 and 400 prisoners of war is much overestimated.

As was the case during the landing at Bjerkvik, during the enemy's major attack on the southern front on 28 May, they failed to seize the opportunity to make a decisive strike against the already fragmented

Narvik Sector. They could have struck the entire German battle group as they reassembled after the retreat. At the same time, by means of the large enveloping movement south of Beisfjord, which was already underway, the Allies could have moved on up the mountains toward Sildvik. With an intense push toward the ore railway, they could also have overrun the naval companies positioned there. Neither of these took place at the right time, nor in sufficient mass, and therefore the Germans had time to set up a new front in the south.

Narvik itself, under those circumstances, would not have been able to hold out any longer. As a land force, the enemy could have relatively quickly breached the thin, linear front, with its lack of depth structure. With the right sort of tactical thrust, they could have taken the dominating peaks of Fagernesfjell. The German defenders were helpless and at the mercy of the shelling from naval and land artillery. Moreover, the otherwise tedlling effects of the German heavy machine guns had little impact, as their effective range was much limited due to the thick, leafy birch forests on the slopes; the enemy was able to exploit these brushy undergrowth areas for their advances. A further disadvantage for the Germans was the piecemeal deployment of available reserves (e.g., 2nd Company/137th at Ankenes) and the inability of 1st Company/ 137th and Naval Battalion Holtorf to counter-attack at the ore railway, pinned down as they were by heavy shelling.

However, the enemy was also denied a decisive victory here.

CHAPTER 8

The Final Battles of Group Narvik

Threatening situation due to Polish attacks in the south (Map 9)

After the landing at Narvik, the Allies finally appeared to understand the key to the situation – namely cutting off Battle Group Narvik from the rear and surrounding them by means of deep flank attacks in the direction of Bjornfjell and the Swedish border. Therefore, they began to shift their *Schwerpunkt* toward the north-east and south. But again they failed to coordinate their attacks and failed to swing out their advance in the south to the largely uncovered area in the south-east. By putting their effort into the string of connected attacks by individual small groups, they neglected repeated opportunities to concentrate all of their forces on a final decisive breach.

For an understanding of the complicated development of the situation in the south, some important issues should be brought to light. For the southern front, unlike that of Group Windisch after the landing at Bjerkvik, it was not simply a matter of carrying out an orderly relocation movement and building a new front. On the southern front, the troops that had been separated after the landing at Narvik had to actually find one another and regroup. Furthermore, the units remaining at the ore railway were still small in number, with little strength left to resist, and the only available reinforcements consisted of a few airborne infantrymen here and there, men unfamiliar with the situation, the terrain, and the necessary combat skills. Due to the loss of communication, the former sector command of Narvik could no longer issue orders, and no orders or messages came in or went out from the division headquarters. This prompted Generalleutnant Dietl to release the Narvik sector command from its role as ordering authority, and to form the two battalions – Walther and Haussels – giving Hauptmann Walther command of the ore railway (see Chapter VII). Initially, however, this did not prevent Major Haussels from issuing orders to Walther based on his situational assessment.[1]

As a result, neither battalion had contact with the other, nor was there a continuous front line. Instead, there was a large gap, which could not be closed for the time being. To prevent a dangerous enemy breach, the positions had to be pulled back, however premature it may have seemed.

Early on 29 May, Battalion Walther took position on the line Tunnel 4–Tottalen–Rombakstotta, and formed a reserve in Tunnels 5 and 6. Battalion Haussels held the new front on the line Beisfjordstotta–upper Molelven valley–Durmalsfjell. Between Rombakstotta and Beisfjordstotta, with the high Peak 1,436, was a yawning, unsecured gap of several kilometres. It was not possible to get orders through to close this gap, leaving an opening for an enemy breakthrough in the direction of the Middagsfjell (818) and Sildvik, and therefore, the division ordered Battalion Walther to relocate to the rear. The battalion, which at the same time reported heavy enemy pressure at the ore railway, was now ordered to take position next to Battalion Haussels in a line from the Stromnen railway station to 1km east of Peak 1,436, and to secure that area.

The division headquarters actually expected the enemy's main push to take place along the ore railway, from the west. However, it developed from the south, causing great problems for Battalion Haussels. During the evening of 29 May, the enemy felt his way closer with combat-ready reconnaissance troops. But next day, 30 May, was 'a day of evil tidings', Dietl noted in his personal journal, as strong forces attacked on a broad front from the south.

Due to heavy morning fog, visibility was poor and the start of operations was delayed. One or more enemy companies entered Molnelven, and a Polish company was able to take Durmalsfjell by early afternoon. From 0830 hrs, two more Polish companies began advancing across the 1,303-metre high Blaisen, on the deep south-east flank. They then plunged through fog and snow showers toward the left flank outpost at Aksla (962 m).

Here, on the nearly 1,000-metre high peak, in the cutting cold and wind, 50 sailors under Oberleutnant zur See Sommer manned their machine guns and rifles. Initially, the enemy onslaught broke down, but Aksla was eventually lost, and the enemy headed off in the direction of the ore railway. At 1230 hrs, they were reported to be climbing down Aksla toward the north end of Sildvik Lake.

This enemy foray appeared all the more threatening because only scattered reconnaissance troops were on hand to confront them. In just a short time, the attackers could quite possibly reach the ore railway and cut off the whole of Battalions Walther and Haussels, which were still to the west. Battalion Haussels and the division were both involved in a frontal attack in the Molnelven valley, but were also attempting to intercept this apparently strong enemy breakthrough by means of a security line formed from some quickly assembled parts of units. By midday, Major Haussels deployed a mountain infantry company to recapture Aksla, which met with success. Company von Strachwitz (the remainder of 1st Company/137th, parts of 6th Company/138th, and airborne infantrymen), which had been sent to the division by Battalion Walther, was intercepted at 1715 hrs by Major Haussels and deployed to Durmalsfjell, but was unable to recapture this peak.

Dietl had Pioneer Platoon Leutnant Brandt (one officer and 20 men) on hand, which once again had been pulled from Group Windisch on 29 May. In addition, Naval Company Salzwedel (from Naval Regiment Berger) was made available, and the scattered troops of 3rd Company/1st Airborne Infantry Regiment (two platoons with 60 men under Leutnant Rottke) were put on alert. Because it was reported that the enemy forces already advancing toward Peak 713 had now turned toward the east in an encirclement movement in the direction of Hundalen, the general himself took these elements on the train to Hundalen, and stationed them on the line Hundalen—Sildvik. Naval Section Kothe, which was the last division reserve at Spionkop, was tasked with securing the open south-east flank at Peaks 817 and 930, 3km south-east of Hundalen.

Once again, at the last second, a security front was cobbled together from the final available forces. Toward 2000 hrs, a report came in stating that the area around Sildvik, Peak 713, and the north end of Sildvik Lake were cleared of enemy.

A reconnaissance force that had pushed forward toward the south and south-east was able to identify only somewhat weak enemy forces that had no apparent intention of attacking. Apparently, after having run up against surprising resistance, the Poles had pulled back again. The whereabouts of the enemy that had been definitely spotted north of Sildvik Lake was unclear (see Bibliography, 40). In any case, the Poles had allowed a potential victory to slip prematurely from their hands. With a further, vigorous advance, they would certainly have succeeded in breaking through between Sildvik and Hundalen and gone all the way to the end of Rombakenfjord – one of many missed opportunities. It remains striking that, from then on, the enemy made absolutely no challenges against the south-east flank, although it was clearly demonstrated more than once that a solid opportunity existed for the attacking Norwegians to execute a large pincer movement toward Bjornfjell.

An entry in the division war journal of 30 May described the situation:

> This day is especially marked by numerous threatening reports about the enemy, by the endangerment of Sildvik, by a threat to the left flank, and by the continuing absence of necessary radio and telephone communication to the endangered positions. In addition there is constant enemy pressure on Battalion Walther, which creates a very difficult situation at the ore railway. Because of the time-consuming communications and the lack of sufficient reserves, leadership is becoming increasingly difficult. With the enemy's bold advance toward Sildvik, a further sweeping encirclement movement, and an advance toward Hundalen and Bjornfjell, are well within the realm of possibilities, as the enemy has more than sufficient strong forces at his disposal, and is fully informed of our situation. Deploying Naval Section Kothe south of Hundalen can only serve as a security measure against them.
>
> 'At the same time, the supply situation is growing increasingly difficult. For three days now, no replenishment of supplies, especially ammunition. The urgently needed reinforcements in personnel also remains on hold due to bad weather.
>
> Our situation also brings to light the fact that all reserves have been deployed to the last man, down to the available troops from the various sections, which consist of almost only naval personnel.

Due to the enemy attack of 30 May, Battalion Haussels found it necessary to shorten its widely spread-out front; the teams on Beisfjordstotta and

Resmaalaksa were pulled back, resulting in the distance to Battalion Walter widening even further.

On 31 May, the Poles continued their vigorous attacks against Battalion Haussels at near-battalion strength, and they were about to break through the middle of the German unit. After capturing the saddle north of Peak 639, they would then try to break through to Sildvik from the south-west. Their first weak attack, close to midday in Molnelven valley, was easily fended off. Then at 1630 hrs, they attacked once more in the swampy terrain of the valley with strong forces, and at the same time pushed down from Durmalsfjell accompanied by fire from their heavy weaponry. They succeeded in breaking through at individual positions of the thinly manned front, but were then brought to a standstill. At 2000 hrs, in the attempt to widen their existing breakthrough, the enemy began renewed advances. By 0130 hrs, after back-and-forth combat, with the deployment of the last reserves, these advances were finally defeated. The battlefield was strewn with fallen Polish soldiers.

On 30 May, Battalion Walther was pulled back to a new position, at which time Generalleutnant Dietl considered various reasons for pulling back the entire south front, however reluctantly. Doing so would close the large gap between the two battalions, offer a more favourable positon in terms of terrain, and at the same time create a shorter front, which could be manned more densely and eliminate the need for already scarce reserves. The left flank of Group Windisch (1st Battalion) was under threat of attack. With the help of reserves, it would be able to fall back from the Storelven valley to the high plateau of Rauberget (Peak 656), and still maintain the link with Battalion Walther north of Rombakenfjord. At the same time, this would also free up forces (3rd Company/138th) to support the seriously threatened Group von Schleebrügge.

A distinct disadvantage of this plan, however, which could not be ignored, was that the vital Stromnen Strait (which in the afternoon of 22 May had been mined by three seaplanes) would be abandoned to the enemy. This could, among other dangers, lead to deeper penetration by enemy warships into Rombakenfjord, ruling out the use of the fjord as a final landing area for German seaplanes.

Notwithstanding, the following retreat order was issued at 2300 hrs:

> Battalion Walter to the line Ornelven (3 kilometres south of Stromnen Strait)–
> Peak 638–Peak 818 (Middagsfjell).
>   Battalion Haussels to the line of Peaks 660–467–961 (Aksla) –east of Sildvik
> Lake. Each battalion will designate a company as reserves.

The retreat movements began on 1 June at 0330 hrs, and were carried out without significant enemy pressure, with new positions occupied by the end of the day. At this time, however, it was learned that Battalion Walther had given up Middagsfjell and now once again stood with its left flank 2km behind Battalion Haussels. Battalion Haussels, therefore, continued to hang in limbo. Now, in order to finally link the two battalions, the right flank of Battalion Haussels was required to retreat to Peak 788 (Sildvikfjell). With the massing of the defence of the battalion on the rocky mountains of Sildvikfjell and Aksla, two genuine natural fortresses were acquired. Like glacis, the steep cliffs of their walls would prevent a close approach by the enemy. Thus, along with the now-thawed lakes below, the bare, lonely cirques of these mountains would present the enemy with yet another natural barrier. Moreover, few forces would be needed to defend the saddle between the two dominating peaks. The advantages of this especially favourable defensive position substantially made up for the sacrifice of nearly 2km of terrain.

In the early afternoon of 1 June, the Poles managed to get themselves quite a bloody nose. They attacked in droves across the glacial snowfields of Durmalsfjell, and down toward the protruding mountain bastions. Attempting to storm up the mountain, they were badly shot up by a mountain gun that the German units disassembled and laboriously hauled to Sildviksfjell on an armoured personnel transport.[2] Under its direct fire, the assault collapsed. Surprised by the sudden use of artillery, the enemy fled in confusion. After this, there were no further attacks on Battalion Haussels, which had already suffered the loss of 15 dead since 29 May. The enemy now confined themselves to the peaks that lay in front of the battalion, occupying them with heavy weapons.

As of 1 June, Battalion Walther occupied its new position at Ornelven, from Rombakenfjord to Peak 638 (see Bibliography, 43). It held this position until the end of the conflict in the following organisation and numbers:

Parachute Company Götte 2/94 (officers/soldiers)
Naval Company Fuchs 2/72
Parachute Company Kersten 1/45
Naval Company von Freytag 4/98
Naval Company von Diest 3/68
Parachute Platoon Keuchel 2/51

Battalion reserve in front of Tunnel 8 consisted of Naval Company Meissner with 5/86, Staff 1st Company/1st Airborne Infantry Regiment, and signal platoon with 45 officers and men. The battalion's heavy weapons consisted of nine heavy machine guns and four medium mortars.

Prior to this, the enemy had subjected Battalion Walther to various degrees of pressure (by Foreign Legionnaires) along the ore railway. But the enemy neglected their first opportunity to overrun the weak and shaken naval companies at Tunnel 3, although it could have been done as a continuation of the land attack on 28 May. Even on 29 May – a day when the enemy's air force was constantly overhead – they did not escalate to larger attacks. Instead, at 1720 hrs, a British destroyer sailed into Rombakenfjord, and together with a land battery at Troeldal, heavily bombarded the defence positions at Tunnel 4. This was in preparation for a powerful foray along the ore railway that would deploy at 1800 hrs. To relieve the battalion of this enemy pressure and to forestall a possible landing to the rear, the division ordered a retreat as far as Straumsnes, which was carried out at 2300 hrs, under the protective fire of heavy weapons.[3]

During the night of 30 May and through the early morning of the next day, enemy pressure on the slopes south of the ore railway persisted amid shelling from the destroyers in Rombakenfjord. In response, at about midday, the division ordered the right flank of the battalion to retreat all the way to the Stromnen Strait. On 31 May, before midday, the French attacked along the railway again, but were turned back at the new defence line. In a makeshift effort at creating the effect of artillery, two train cars loaded with explosives were sent rolling down [towards the enemy]. At 1100 hrs, the train cars exploded at the Stromnen train station.

After 1 June passed quietly, the enemy repeatedly attempted to attack at the seam between Battalion Walther and Battalion Haussels, and to press in on the left flank of Battalion Walther from the mountains. During the morning of 2 June, the ascent of some lengthy enemy infantry columns with heavy weapons was sighted toward Middagsfjell. After this peak was occupied, the enemy carried out forays toward Peak 639: the defenders, who were airborne infantry, successfully fought them off. But by afternoon, the peak had to be abandoned to the more powerful enemy, who firmly dug in and did not carry out any further attacks.

Between 31 May and 3 June, with the intermittently clear weather, the Luftwaffe came in to offer relief to the fighters on the southern front and along the ore railway. The fighter planes attacked on 31 May, between 1700 and 1830 hrs, but their bombs also struck German positions along the ore railway, with a demoralising effect on the troops. On the afternoon of 1 June, a large number of bombers appeared once more. On 2 June, despite some partial heavy fog, there appeared 10 Stukas, eight fighter planes, and four Zerstörer Me 110s, which bombed both the enemy at the railway and Narvik itself. On 3 June, over 30 planes flew in, two of which were shot down by enemy infantry.

Then the weather took another turn for the worse. It rained almost incessantly, and in the high elevations, this meant more snow. In the snow-covered mountains, the extreme cold was made worse by a sharp north wind. A heavy fog settled in, with visibility no more than a few metres. One advantage of the ever-deteriorating weather was that it discouraged further attacks on the southern front, but up on the mountain the troops were fully exposed to its hardships. The hard rocky high terrain offered few options for shelter, leaving the men out in the open in pouring rain, whirling snow, and cold, damp fog.[4] As on the other front sectors, with no kitchens and no firewood, there were no warm rations to be brought in.

All of the scarce necessities for life and battle were hauled to the high altitude positions on the shoulders of their naval comrades, using up all of their energy once more. In rain and snow storms, the transport staff traversed swamps and snow fields and climbed the flanks of mountains, panting under their burdens. Many collapsed from exhaustion, but still, the trip had to be made twice a day, usually with only a few hours' rest to revive their fading strength.

Here, as always, Dietl was constantly on the move around the positions. The entries in his personal journal and in the war journal of Battle Group Narvik bear witness to the worries of those days and the earnest sense that things could not go on in this manner. The following journal entries bring shocking clarity to the degree of suffering and hardship during the battle for Narvik:

30 May: The troops are clearly exhausted. Constantly bivouacked out in the open in bad weather and without enough clothing, they are suffering greatly from the cold and rain. Relief is almost entirely out of the question due to scarce resources. No shelter is available.

31 May: I [Generalleutnant Dietl] know that ultimately only a very large support effort can help us.

1 June: The troops are under extreme duress. With the thin occupation, scarce weaponry, and the constant deployment without relief, which has weakened the defence crews' strength, there can be no possible defence in the usual sense of the word.

2 June: the resupply situation is growing increasingly difficult, there is a shortage of hand grenades and ammunition. Furthermore there is still a problem bringing in provisions all the way to the positions. That these can still be held is thanks to the fact that the enemy only attacks individual positions and in this way, the scarce ammunition that we have on hand can be sent to the endangered area.

For days now, no ammunition resupply has taken place. Support from the Luftwaffe against the enemy is requested constantly. But in this unfavourable weather, there is no hope.

3 June: The people live in a rocky desert with the worst equipment and insufficient clothing. The troops are being subjected to inhumane suffering.

4 June: Bitter stone desert. No shelter. 1st Battalion is badly affected by the constant bivouacking.

The troops must be relieved, but I have nothing.

Yet wherever the general found his men, he came away with the belief that even the men themselves believed that further enemy attacks could still could be defeated – but only if they had confidence that help, support, and reinforcements would arrive soon. And these had been confirmed and promised repeatedly. Battle Group Narvik would have to hold out until the promised reinforcements could engage in the battle in force. And so it was in the following words that the general addressed his mountain infantrymen, sailors, and airborne infantrymen:

I know your suffering and know what you have to get through. But you must hold out, the enemy must never be allowed to break through. It will not last much longer, help is on its way. You must only hold on for eight more days! (see Bibliography, 16)

The words 'eight more days' became a matter of faith, which was ultimately confirmed either by chance or fate when help did actually arrive almost exactly to the day. Granted, it was not sufficient help, but as it would soon turn out, the Allies were to pull out of the fight. At that moment, however, events had not yet evolved that far.

On the evening of 5 June, for the first time, a British destroyer passed unhindered through the Stromnen Strait, evading the mine blockade, and sailed to Sildvik. In consolidated fire with the French 10.5cm battery positioned at Troeldal, it struck the positions of Battalion Walther along the ore railway. Although it was a disturbing flank bombardment, it was not as threatening as a possible enemy landing in Rombakenfjord. It could just as likely take place in the rear of Battalion Walter as at the end of Rombakenfjord.

From here, by means of a quick push, in combination with simultaneous attacks by the Norwegians in the north-east, the Allies would be able to separate the German northern and southern fronts cleanly from one another at their narrowest point, between the end of the fjord and the Swedish border. The big question for the Germans was whether to constrict the front in the south as far as the Sildvik peak, in order to maintain sufficient forces for security at the end of Rombakenfjord. But this idea was temporarily set aside by division headquarters in favour of placing all hopes for recapturing the area upon the arrival of reinforcements, which was still thought possible. Even next day, when two destroyers sailed through the now clear and unprotected Stromnen Strait and bombarded the positions along the ore railway, the decision to firmly hold the current defensive line did not change. Parts of Battalion Walther and one platoon of Naval Regiment Berger (still commanded by two captains) were ordered to take over security at the end of Rombakenfjord.

More comforting news for the division headquarters was the fact that on 5 June, ski reconnaissance troops from Naval Section Kothe (and one more platoon after its release to Group von Schleebrügge at Rundfjeldet) had reported that the south-east was free of the enemy as far as 20km deep, and that the enemy in front of Battalion Haussels was behaving quietly and was observed everywhere to be bivouacking.

On the night of 5 June, Battalion Walther experienced a mishap after two low-flying air attacks on the battalion command post, which was located in a rail car. The rail car was forced into cover in Tunnel 8, and due to the incline on that stretch of tracks, the wagon began to roll, the brakes failed, and the car rolled toward the enemy. Its contents included all division orders, various documents as to strength and structure of individual units, and a situation map with precise notations and updates. A reaction force was immediately deployed, which determined that the wagon had been completely emptied. At first the greatest fear, understandably so, was that this would provide the enemy with complete information [of their deployment]. Later, it was viewed as a great advantage. With all of the many unit designations, sections, battle groups, and battalions, the enemy would have to assume there were far more forces than actually were on hand.

From 6–7 June, Battalion Walther was fired on and bombarded day and night by the destroyers that entered into Rombakenfjord, along with artillery, mortars, and enemy planes. The division understood this to be either preparation fire for an imminent major attack along the ore railway, or a landing in Rombakenfjord. In order to prevent landing attempts at their outset, the Germans planned a concentration of strong weapons in the bay east of Sildvik, with two 3.7cm anti-tank guns, two 2cm anti-aircraft guns, two anti-tank rifles, and one heavy machine gun. Any approaching destroyers would promptly be attacked by their collective fire. The comrades of the Luftwaffe attempted once more to intervene in the battle. The enemy, who had been constantly and annoyingly firing into the right flank of Battalion Walther at the ore railway, and at the battery at Troeldal, was attacked by four Ju 88s and six Zerstörer Me 110s on 7 June at 1800 hrs.[5]

In early June, according to reconnaissance troop reports, observations, and statements from deserters, the enemy had three Polish battalions (one of which was resting at Beisfjord) facing Battalion Haussels, two Foreign Legion and one French alpine infantry battalions (of which one rested in Narvik) facing Battalion Walther, two French alpine infantry battalions and the Norwegian Infantry Regiment 15 facing the left flank and centre, the 16th Norwegian Infantry Regiment facing the right flank of Group Windisch, and the 14th Norwegian Infantry Regiment facing Group von Schleebrügge.

The French hold back in front of Group Windisch

Group Windisch moved into the new position during the night of 21/22 May (see Chapter VI), and now for the first time there was a continuous, tightly closed front in the north, one that also offered advantageous terrain features.

The sector of Group Windisch now formed a defensive line with a right-angle and included the high plateau of the Haugfjeldet in the north-east at the end of the upper Jern Lake, and adjoined Group von Schleebrügge. To the south, looking out from Peak 79, Group Windisch's position covered the Stromnen Strait. The newly concentrated front allowed for an occupation in depth, and the ability to hold reserves for the section. On the right, as before, 3rd Battalion now incorporated 11th and 13th Companies (with 12th Company in reserve). To the left, with a boundary at the south end of the lower Jern Lake, it adjoined 1st Battalion. Behind its left flank was Naval Company Erdmenger.

The battalion had positioned its 3rd, 2nd, and 5th companies on the west slopes of Haugfjeldet. Adjoining them was Sector Brandl (Pioneer Platoon Leutnant Brandt, Kapitän Müller, and mountain artillerymen), deployed forward on both sides of Peak 303. At Peak 79 was 3rd Company/138th Mountain Infantry Regiment, and on Peak 211 was Section Raabe.

In terms of weapons, the battalion had four heavy machine guns, four medium mortars, and 12 light machine guns. The 2nd Company/139th Mountain Infantry Regiment as a case in point, after being filled by sailors, numbered 63 men, and had four light machine guns. Each company was assigned a heavy machine gun and a medium mortar.[6] As it was, Group Windisch had to cover a front whose width extended to three-and–a-half hours' length [sic].

Group Windisch had been provided one of the two mountain guns that had landed. Peak 668 was set up as an outpost and supply drop zone.

The next days were used for reinforcing the position to the extent actually possible in the stony terrain. The melting streams and lakes, which in the north and west protected the Haugfjeldet massif, as well as the Storelven valley, all formed a strong natural obstacle against the enemy, which they would only be able to overcome with heavy casualties. Everywhere, from the rocky pulpits and high-altitude positions of the new line on down, the German machine guns dominated the area in front of them almost without a gap.

Thus, the main concern was to first of all create shelter for the defenders, who again were positioned on the high mountains between broad snowfields. As before, there were neither trees nor brush, only monotonous mountain terrain resembling a moonscape of scree, boulders, innumerable mountain peaks, and gullies.

If during the first days of occupying the new position the sun happened to shine occasionally, the weather quickly became extremely unfavourable again. Clouds and fog settled on the mountains and surrounded the fighters in a thick, eerie veil; it rained and snowed simultaneously. Very soon the men had not a shred of dry clothing on their bodies, and crouched freezing behind their stone emplacements. It was only gradually that some wood from the valleys, located deep on the left flank of the 3rd Company/138th and Section Raabe (and who consequently had it somewhat better), was hauled up to the high plateau in a tedious climb. This wood was used in combination with stacked stones and draped tarpaulins to create meagre shelters.

Initially, the enemy conducted themselves with much restraint, and only very carefully did they push in closer with their forces to the full width of the front. They gradually occupied all of the peaks and high areas, bringing in their heavy weapons. All movements took place outside the range of German infantry weapons, so that they could not be engaged in battle.

Occupying new positions was made easier on 22 May by the vigorous deployment of German fighter planes, which by midday had heavily bombarded the enemy. In the afternoon, a major attack by the Luftwaffe with 21 Ju 88s was observed, which despite heavy anti-aircraft fire, targeted the enemy battleships in the fjords, who created a smokescreen and steered away on a zig-zag course. German fighter plane activity continued forcefully during the night of 23 and 24 May.

The only enemy contact on 22 May was with 1st Battalion on Storelven. On 24 May, the enemy felt their way closer, added reinforcements over the course of the day, and then appeared quite close to the front of 3rd Battalion. Peaks 444, 361, 418, and 377 were occupied by the enemy at night. On 25 May, a 40-strong French troop, which was passing by at Hergotten, was surprised by a reconnaissance troop from 1st Battalion under the command of the adjutant (Oberleutnant Stöber).[7] The reconnaissance troop inflicted losses of 15 enemy dead, five wounded, and two captured, and also captured a machine gun; German losses were two dead and one wounded (Oberleutnant Stöber). Next day, minor encounters took place between reconnaissance troops and the enemy occupying the high peaks. In addition, the enemy forces working their way forward between Cirkel and Jern Lakes were pushed back again.[8]

German forces repulsed a night-time foray on 27 May by the Norwegians, who were pushing more strongly against security forces between Cirkel and Jern lakes, causing heavy enemy casualties. Daily, on the left flank where 3rd Company/138th was positioned, a British destroyer sailed almost as far as the strait of Stromnen and opened fire. During its attempt to break through the strait, the ship was successfully fought off by two medium mortars on Peak 79.

Earlier, on 25 May, fearing heavier enemy attacks, the division had sent 2nd Company/138th Mountain Infantry Regiment to Group von Schleebrügge to serve as reserve behind the seam between the two battalions. On 29 May, however, 2nd Company was once more pulled out of Group von Schleebrügge.

It was still not possible to identify the intent and *Schwerpunkt* of the enemy force facing Group Windisch. Did the enemy want to attack the left flank, while pushing north in order to roll up on the mountain positions? Or, once they found a detour was impossible, would they try to break through the centre of the group between Cirkel and Jern lakes, on the seam between 1st and 3rd Battalions? Over the following days, it was concluded that something was underway in the Storeleven valley, once more against the much-tested 1st Battalion. On 28 May, artillery, mortars, and infantry guns began to fire on the positions. The next day, the enemy again showered the forwardmost positions of 1st Battalion with heavy fire, and an attack swelled to a veritable hurricane towards midnight and lasted until the morning of 30 May.

On 31 May, 1st Battalion, on the verge of recapturing the southern front, curved its left flank back toward the rock plateau of Rauberget. Those parts of the unit located north of the Stromnen Strait then had to climb up again out of the warm, green valleys to the steep and storm-swept desert of stone.

The recent shortening of the front released the 3rd Company/138th and Section Raabe, but they had to be sent to reinforce the hard-pressed Group von Schleebrügge. Section Brandl now took over the left flank.

There appeared to be a change in the situation on 31 May. Increasing battle activity began in front of 3rd Battalion. During the late afternoon of 3 June, after a bridge was built across the Holmelven valley on the eastern shore of Jern Lake, the Norwegians attempted to attack toward the south on the right flank of 3rd Battalion. At this, 3rd Battalion was given parts of 2nd Company/139th as reinforcements, and reserves (12th Company) were placed behind the threatened sector. The enemy then broke off their advance and pulled back.

Then it became quiet again. During the night of 6/7 June, enemy aircraft dropped bombs across all sectors. The next day, early in the morning, German planes bombed the annoying enemy battery north of the lower Jern Lake.

During the night of 7/8 June, a wild artillery storm broke out unexpectedly from all enemy batteries, as well as from the warships in the fjords all across the positions.[9] In addition, a great many loud detonations were heard from the direction of Narvik (as it was later learned, explosions by the retreating enemy), which could be felt even through the night's roaring snowstorm.[10]

Futile breakthrough attempts by the Norwegians in the north-east

Group von Schleebrügge had to endure the final and most difficult battles. An increasingly serious threat was building in the north-east, on the extreme right flank. The Norwegians were preparing a powerful breakthrough along the Swedish border. Yet the full extent of the enemy's preparations could not be fully determined. The enemy sounded out the new German positions, but most of their larger movements remained hidden behind impenetrable weather. Because the Norwegians stayed outside the range of the German weapons, even when seen, they remained untouchable by weapons-fire. However, in general the enemy appeared to be moving to the right, toward Peaks 620 and 698, which were soon to be the arena for fierce clashes.

The days leading up to 27 May passed quietly. The enemy carefully moved closer, bringing their heavy weapons and artillery into position. Due to lack of ammunition, any counter effort against them would be weak. It would only be possible with help from the Luftwaffe, which, back on 22 May, had bombarded the heavily occupied Kuberget. The weather was bad, and the troops suffered greatly in the wet and cold.

Group von Schleebrügge, with its right flank echeloned forward, now had the following structure:

> Sub-Sector West: 1st Company/1st Airborne Infantry Regiment with four heavy machine guns on both sides of Peak 456 (adjoining 3rd/139th).
>
> Sub-Sector Centre: 1st Company/139th with one heavy machine gun and one medium mortar on Peak 625 and north-west of this, Company Trupp, simultaneously the command post of the group at Peak 361 (Outpost II).
>
> Sub-Sector East: Naval Platoon Brauns with one heavy machine gun on Holm Peak (west of Holm Lake), Naval Company Steinecker with one heavy machine gun on Peak 620 and 698, aligned along the Swedish border.

With increasing enemy pressure primarily along the border, the division headquarters again released forces from other front sectors to strengthen the right flank, and then reorganised.

Thus, 3rd Company/138th, stationed on the left flank of Group Windisch, was pulled out and placed under the command of Group von Schleebrügge. The 3rd Company/138th took over Sector East until 30 May, occupied Holm Peak with Platoon Leutnant Hopfe, occupied Peak 620 with Company Trupp and Platoon Leutnant Körber (assigned from 2nd Company/138th), and Peak 698 with Naval Platoon Brauns. Naval Company Steinecker, which became available with the arrival of 3rd Company/138th, returned to Naval Section Kothe, which now was positioned on the Rundfjeldet, where, under the command of the division, it was tasked with securing the deep right flank.

On 28 May, the enemy employed light infantry guns, mortars, and artillery fire on the German positions, and over the next days this increased to preparatory fire. This was especially so on Sub-Sector West. During the night of 30 May, nine enemy bombers targeted Sub-Sectors Centre and East. Amid constant fire, the Norwegians worked their way closer, to within the range of infantry weapons. On the afternoon of 30 May, about two companies were seen heading south-east from the Kuberget area.

On 31 May, beginning at around 1300 hrs, the enemy approached Peak 620 from the west with several companies, with heavy fire support and under the cover of fog. Peak 620 was defended by about 90 men, with one heavy machine gun and one medium mortar. From the high Peaks 1,067 and 931, the enemy dominated the German positions with mortar and artillery fire. The enemy handled their heavy weapons well, and soon inflicted a great number of casualties. The commander of 3rd Company/138th, Oberleutnant Ploder, was also wounded. This fierce struggle lasted several hours late into the night. With three separate heavy attacks, the enemy tried to break through and onto this important peak, with the help of six aircraft.

The Germans engaged the many-times-stronger force from all sides, in small groups of three, four, and five mountain infantrymen, in hard, close-combat and hand-grenade duels. Thick patches of fog raced over the peaks, limiting visibility to 10 metres. Munitions became scarce, and hand grenades had to be conserved, used only to be put to maximum effect. For the one medium mortar, there were only six rounds available. The enemy finally succeeded in breaking through and firmly entrenched themselves on the peak, yet did not completely capture it.

In these hours of extreme need, the last division reserve, 2nd Company/138th (under Oberleutnant Renner) appeared. This company had been through all of the back-and-forth shuffling typical for the scarce German reserves:

> They landed between the 22 and 24 May, some in sea plane, some by parachute, and after regrouping, initially remained as division reserve in the area of Bjornfjell,

and were deployed on 25 May at 1200 hrs in [the] strength of 82 men to Group Windisch, where they were to occupy a reserve positon behind the seam that joined 1st and 3rd Battalions. In an arduous march over mountain and valleys, the company struggled to reach their destination. Skis could no longer be used, due to bare rock on many stretches along the way. Often sinking up to the hips in the deep, very slushy snow, the men worked their way forward. There were still frozen, mirror-like lakes to overcome, and steep, precipitous terrain. Occasionally a man would fall from the ranks and into a crevasse, crack in the ice, or snow bog, so deeply that he could be pulled out only with help of his comrades. Every 200 metres it was necessary to rest, since each man had to carry his own weapon, equipment, and all of his baggage. At 2100 hrs, the company reached its destination and set up a tent camp in a high-lying cirque.

On 29 May, the company again received the order to march toward Peak 361 (Outpost II). Once more they made a tiring march through snow and ice, across wilderness streams and dangerous snow bridges, to their assigned position, where they bivouacked. On 31 May, before midday, they received their assignment to Group von Schleebrügge. (see Bibliography, 48)

During the early morning of 1 June, the enemy continued its determined attack on Peak 620, which was now occupied by the 2nd Company/138th. Toward 0800 hrs, after 15 hours of continuous fighting, and after beating off four attacks, the peak had to be abandoned. The worn-out defenders (the two platoons of 2nd Company/138th had casualties of seven dead and 14 wounded) were pulled back to the so-called Central Peak (*Mittelhöhe*), which adjoined them in the south-west, which they occupied until about 0900 hrs. At 1030 hrs, Sub-Sector West came under heavy fire once more; the enemy also attempted to push into the main battle line at Sub-Sector East. After occupying Peak 620 and pushing eastwards of Holm Lake, however, the enemy was fought off by concentric fire from Peak 698, Holm Peak, and Middle Peak.

The hard battles over Peak 620 are described in the journal entries of 2nd Company/138th:

On Peak 620 on 31 May at about 2100 hrs, Platoon Leutnant Körber was attacked by strong enemy forces. The platoon inflicted heavy casualties on the enemy at close-combat distance with hand grenades. In the thick fog, the enemy then was able to make a surprise breakthrough, and the platoon had to continue to defend on the rear slope. Digging-in into this layered [type of] stone was not possible. The crew of the only heavy machine gun was wounded, the medium mortar had already shot up its mortar rounds, and the hand grenades were running short. Situated up on the crest of the towering mountain on the opposite side, the enemy was able to dominate the entire slope with heavy machine guns. At the same time, the platoon also came under heavy mortar fire.

Toward 2200 hrs, the enemy attacked once more, frontally, with 150 to 200 men. With hand grenades and empty weapons, our men fought them back in close combat. Grenade fire and heavy machine gun fire still struck on the rear slope.

One hour later, after heavy fire preparation, the enemy attacked once more in the same strength but was beaten back again. Now, even the light mortar had used up its last mortar rounds. The crew went back to get ammunition, but the trip there and back took about 10 hours.

Toward 1900 hrs, Oberleutnant Renner had taken command of the battle, and at midnight, 2nd Platoon, with 30 men, finally arrived bringing light mortar rounds and hand grenades. Despite the fact that it had just finished a very arduous march, the platoon immediately attempted a counter-attack, but the enemy was too strong.

On 1 June at 0245 hrs, after an air bombardment by six aircraft, the enemy attacked once more with a strength of 200 to 250 men. With the last functioning machine guns and the last hand grenades, this advance was also forced back. Shortly thereafter, two smaller forays took place. It was raining, and the troops were completely exhausted.

At 0600 hrs, the heavy shelling began again and covered the entire peak. All around were deafening booms, shrapnel and gravel whirring through the air. There were no more mortar rounds or hand grenades on hand.

At 0745 hrs, the enemy attacked with a strength of about 100 men. The 2nd Platoon occupied two small plateaus left and right in order to better provide fire support to Platoon Körber. The attack collapsed close in front of our positions.

The troops were completely drained. They had sustained 15 hours of uninterrupted battle, and almost every hour the enemy assaulted them with fresh forces. There was almost no ammunition left, reinforcements were not to be expected – it was becoming impossible to hold out any longer.

At 0800 hrs, a new attack took place, which could not be stopped. Amid the covering fire of a group from 3rd Company/138th, Peak 620 was evacuated.

Over the following days, the Norwegians continued their vigorous attacks on Sub-Sector East, which was also the right flank of Group von Schleebrügge, trying everything possible to break in near the Swedish border. The Norwegians had missed their opportunity to make a wide sweeping envelopment of the deep flank, which at one point had still been open. Now they were forced to attack frontally against the defensive front, which had been strengthened and now included the fought-over Peak 698 as its right cornerstone.

Here, 3rd Platoon of 2nd Company/138th received orders to reinforce Naval Platoon Brauns. After enduring an eight-hour march across difficult mountain terrain, and another bomb attack on the way, the platoon arrived on 1 June at around 0200 hrs. It was already obvious on 1 June that the Norwegian reinforcements from the upper Karelven valley (south of Peak 529) were pouring in, heading toward them. Early the next day, at around 0430 hrs, the Norwegians attacked Peak 698 with two or three companies. Despite repeated attempts to break in, they were beaten back in bloody close-combat with hand grenades and thrown back down the slopes. An attempted breach of the position at the so-called Centre Peak, where the entire Sub-Sector West was held back with heavy fire, was also defeated by the stubborn defence.

At 0900 hrs on 3 June, the alarm suddenly shook the defenders on Peak 698 from their sleep. Furious machine-gun fire whipped across the positions, rifle grenades burst between the rocks. Confronted with German heavy mortar fire, the approaching enemy backed off and bombarded the peak with their own heavy fire. Enemy aircraft dropped their bomb loads. The entire mountain ridge seemed to quake in the explosions. At 1400 hrs, an enemy platoon moving under cover of fog, succeeded in a breakthrough, but was thrown back again in a counter-attack. Towards 2100 hrs, the enemy attacked once more, and was beaten back again.

An attack took place directly on the Swedish border against the extreme right outpost, where four sailors were positioned high up between the rocks with one heavy machine gun. This gun inflicted 18 deaths and succeeded in repulsing the attack.

Not to be forgotten amid all of the bitter fighting are the accomplishments of the men of the resupply force (mostly sailors), who even under the heaviest of enemy fire moved in full view across the slopes and through valleys carrying provisions and desperately needed munitions. The trip took 10 hours through deep, wet snow all the way from support Peak II and back again to the positions. Yet none of the carriers gave up, and all tirelessly hauled the heavy ammunition to the keep the weapons fed.

The division headquarters saw the main threats here in the north-east, as well as in the south, and expected even stronger attacks against Group von Schleebrügge. They therefore took further reinforcement measures.

In response to the pressure of events, Naval Section Kothe was relocated toward the south, and on the afternoon of 1 June, Naval Company Steinecker was sent from Naval Section Kothe as security force on the Rundfjeldet. In addition, the division reserve Naval Company March (of Naval Regiment Berger) was temporarily relocated to Hundalen during the night of 1/2 June, and during the night of 5/6 June received the mission to relieve the battle-worn Naval Platoon Brauns on Peak 698. The medium mortar platoon from 1st Battalion/1st Airborne Infantry Regiment, which had parachuted in on 31 May with four medium mortars, was ordered to Peak 698, where it arrived on the evening of 3 June, just in time to defend against the ongoing enemy attack. Following that platoon, Airborne Infantry Platoon Leutnant Spang, with a strength of two officers and 44 men, arrived at Rundfjeldet after a march of a day and a half, went from there to Peak 615, and afterwards was also deployed at Peak 698. On 5 June, Platoon Leutnant Raabe (3rd Company/138th) finally arrived at Peak 698, having previously been assigned to Group Windisch (1st Battalion) on the left flank. Nothing demonstrates more clearly the eternally cumbersome, urgently needed patchwork by the division headquarters than the immediate deployment of all reinforcements into battle as they trickled in, or the constant, urgent regrouping to ensure any new gaps were sealed, breaches prevented, new intermediate positions occupied, and threatened sectors reinforced – a work of leadership that had to judiciously utilise each man and each weapon.[11]

Closer and closer, the enemy moved toward Group von Schleebrügge. More and more heavy weapons appeared; ever heavier artillery attacks came, throwing rounds and shrapnel on the tired defenders.[12]

When the enemy was not attacking, they were softening the German positions with constant artillery or mortar fire and dropping bombs. 'If only the weather would at least get a bit better' was an often-heard exclamation from mountain infantrymen, sailors, and airborne infantrymen, who were plagued day and night with the cold, their hands frozen stiff from continually having to reach for their weapons and hand grenades as they fought the enemy onslaught.

After some mild temperatures at the end of May, the weather had badly deteriorated again – there was now rain and more rain, interrupted by occasional heavy driving snow. A storm howled wildly across the mountains and peaks, with patches of fog, piled clouds, rain, and blinding snow that blew across the wet slippery rocks and watery snowfields. Whereas a few days earlier there had been hard snow, the water now accumulated into pools and lakes, ice and snow slush. Streams roared through ravines and crevices, and snowfields became lakes of slush. Even on skis, the going was tough, with men constantly falling and becoming stuck.

In the grey clouds of fog, besieged by alpine storms, the men crouched under thin tarpaulins. They camped in caves of layered rock, crawling deep inside to avoid the dripping rocks and boulders. Their clothing was completely soaked through, and in their wet stockings and torn boots, their feet froze. The cold wetness constantly penetrated through under-clothes. Shaking from the cold, there was no sleep. Rations were scarce and insufficient, consisting only of canned meat, hard bread (*Dauerbrot*), or captured Norwegian *Zwieback* toast. The difference between day and night was barely perceptible. Following the gray, rainy, melancholy days, there remained a bright twilight all through the night.

The strength-sapping weather conditions, however, did not prevent, the well-equipped and well-provisioned Norwegians from further attacks, focusing particularly on the capture of Peak 698, which had become a strongly occupied bastion. From 4–7 June, they took a breath, apparently in order to gather themselves for the next major assault. The constant low-intensity battles continued relentlessly, amid great hardship and sacrifice, as is described in the journal of 2nd Company/138th:

> On 4 June, Peak 698 was shelled. An enemy attack attempt was immediately choked off by mortars from the airborne infantry. Massive enemy movements were observed. The day passed with reduced levels of fire. The enemy lay opposite us in the fog, some [within] 30 metres; casualties due to head shots by enemy snipers opposite us on the slope of Peak 620. Up to now, [there are] 12 absences from wounds and frostbite. At 2000 hrs, [there's] an attempted attack in company strength, [with] continuous firing activity.
>
> One of our reconnaissance elements from [Peak] 698, while running reconnaissance in the thick fog, was able to push forward deep into the enemy rear area and was spotted in a moment when the fog suddenly lifted, then was fired on from all sides. Three men died, [and] one severely wounded man had to remain behind. Only the commander of the reconnaissance troop and two men, after they lay motionless for almost four hours, were able to work their way back once the fog set in again.

A liaison reconnaissance troop at the southern end of Holm Lake did not get far, as the snow bridge across the wild stream had broken through in the heavy rain, and the enemy was watching too sharply.

On 5 June at 0300 hrs, the enemy attacked Peak 698 again, was repulsed but continued to shell the peak with mortars.

At 0945 hrs, the enemy pushed forward with two platoons toward the southern edge of Holm Lake, but was chased back by flanking fire from [Peak] 698.

Completely soaked through from the constant snow and rain, everyone lay in their positions. Between the boulders and stone, only very scant protection is to be found from the pouring rain and falling snow. Thick fog prevents all visibility and demands all the greater attention and readiness. For many days, [there is] no warm food. The rations must be brought in daily on a march of several hours across the mountain. The men freeze so badly, that they find no sleep despite their exhaustion.

Our own Stukas are battling the enemy. Shortly after their take-off six enemy aircraft came over and attacked with bombs and on-board weapons.

At 0930 hrs on 6 June, the enemy pushed forward once more toward [Peak] 698, but the attack collapsed. Constant heavy mortar fire. Four [are] wounded by shrapnel, three men with frostbite must return to hospital, one severely wounded airborne infantryman must be carried to Bjornfjell in a 10-hour march, through deep snow and across steep mountain slopes.

In the early afternoon, an enemy platoon was repulsed. Massive enemy movements were from west to east, showing a new, larger attack is imminent.

At midnight, enemy aircraft dropped bombs. Everyone immediately sought protection between the rocks.

One last time, by now aware that their allies were pulling out, the Norwegians tried with all their might to break through on the northeast flank and to roll up the German positions, despite a violation of Swedish neutrality.

On 7 June at 0900 hrs, the Central Peak (north-west of Peak 698) came under constant pressure from two to three companies, while at the same time heavy mortar and artillery fire covered Holm Peak. Isolated fire attacks rained down on both Sub-Sectors Centre and West. At 2230 hrs, the peak fell to the superior power of the enemy, but near 1700 hrs the next day, it was retaken. Partly carried out in close-combat, often under German mortar shelling, all other enemy attacks were unsuccessful. Toward evening, German fighter planes dropped bombs on the enemy artillery positions and heavy weapons nests.

During the night of 8 June, strong mortar fire covered Holm Peak and all of Peak 698. In the enveloping fog, visibility barely reached five paces. But despite the fog, the shots from well-aimed enemy weapons still hit their targets and inflicted casualties. Suddenly, at 0230 hrs, gunfire and machine-gun bursts whistled by very close, coming from the left toward the rear. The enemy – about two companies strong – had swept around in the thick fog into the rear of the German positions, and unintentionally crossed into Swedish territory. The sailors, who were located close to the border, had to pull back. Close by and below the summit position, the Norwegians came into view. Ski Platoon Rohr (eight men of 1st Battalion/139th) had already been alerted and were close at hand. The ski platoon attacked, supported from the south by Ski Platoon Adler (21 men of 3rd Company/138th), who were in reserve at that time. Previously, half the peak had been lost, but after two-and-a-half hours of fierce close-combat, it was cleared of enemy and retaken. Anywhere the enemy still stubbornly held on, they were shot out of their rock cover by German mortars. The Norwegians suffered heavy losses, fell back, and were pursued. In the process, several machine guns were captured. Among the losses from Ski Platoon Adler were two dead and two wounded.

At 0845 hrs the same day, the enemy fired from Peak 620 onto Holm Peak in an effort to pin down the defenders there, while trying once more to capture Central Peak and to break through at Holm Lake in one last attack. At 1000 hrs, the peak was lost to the enemy, but the Germans assaulted it once more at 1430 hrs.[13]

As early as 8 June, there were rumours that the Norwegians were abandoning the northern front in several places and pulling back. Reconnaissance troops sent forward, however, still came upon tough resistance, and the entire sector of the group came under heavy artillery fire.

Narvik holds out

For division headquarters and all men of Battle Group Narvik, the final days of the battle were just as filled with tension, exciting moments, times of doubt and times of hope as they had been at the beginning of the landing on 9 April, almost exactly eight weeks earlier. On 6 June, the Finnish radio station reported a massive enemy offensive against Bjornfjell was imminent (see Bibliography, 40). The determined attacks of the enemy in the north-east appeared to underscore this, seeming to be a prelude to such an offensive. The situation in Rombakenfjord also seemed precarious, where the increased bombardment of the ore railway continued, and during the night of 7/8 June, heavy ship and cutter traffic under the protection of British destroyers gave rise to fears of a new landing at the end of the fjord and a push toward Hundalen. The situation in these sectors was no doubt tense. Sufficient reserves were no longer available to counter a simultaneous major attack in several places at once, nor could they even be made available. The resupply of reinforcements, weapons, and ammunition by air would, at this point, not suffice for any further intensive defence and conduct of battle. At the time, the 26 airborne infantrymen who landed on 7 June represented the entire remaining division reserve.

Despite the enemy offensive which the division headquarters was certain would occur on 9 or 10 June, Generalleutnant Dietl decided to hold the previous positions, without shortening the fronts any further. The decision may well have been based on news from Group XXI, finally confirming they would quickly send extensive reinforcements as agreed. A radio message recorded on the evening of 31 May held out the prospect of considerable support in five to six days. Dietl was expected to hold out until then, no matter how small the area became. Crossing over into Sweden was to be avoided if at all possible. A message received at 1500 hrs on 4 June announced the arrival of 1,800 airborne infantrymen by cargo glider. Shortly afterward, this announcement was retracted due to inclement weather. Over the course of 5 June, repeated discussions took place with Trondheim, in an attempt to promptly bring in the airborne infantrymen.[14] On two occasions, the aircraft were already underway but had to be turned around due to bad weather. At 2100 hrs, Group XXI announced by radio message that in addition to the promised airborne infantry, there would be 1,000 mountain infantry parachuting in.[15] On 7 June, Dietl decided that pulling back the front would have to depend on whether the arrival of even just one company of reinforcements could be counted on (see Bibliography, 39).

On 7 June, hopes rose for a good outcome to the battle for Narvik. Through Oberst Meindl (Regimental Commander, 112th Mountain Artillery Regiment), who had parachuted in, a secret briefing took place, according to which there was a possibility that in the near future the German fleet would go into action against the Allied naval forces in front of Narvik and Haarstad. Nothing was mentioned about a combined effort involving Battle Group Narvik and German naval forces, but Dietl hoped it would soon bring some overall relief.

However, events would soon take a very surprising turn.

'Today will see a great change in our fate,' wrote Dietl on 8 June in his personal journal. That morning, the startling news had come in that the enemy had retreated in front of Battalions Walther and Haussels and had evacuated various occupied peaks. No one knew any specifics, and above all, no one could think of a reason for it. The persistent fog had covered the enemy's retreat, so it was not determined until very late that the enemy was no longer present. In this manner, they had prevented any quick pursuit.

The division ordered Battalion Walther to immediately proceed to the line Stromnen Strait–Middagsfjell, and to push forward along the ore railway to Narvik. Battalion Haussels was ordered to immediately send heavy reconnaissance across Beisfjord in the direction of Narvik. Group Windisch was to move up its left flank (1st Battalion) to Storelven once more.

During the day, there was a growing impression that the enemy had retreated opposite Battalions Haussels and Walther (as of 8 June, consolidated into Group Meindl) all the way to Narvik. There were no more incidents of enemy contact.

At 1500 hrs, Group XXI received the information that air reconnaissance at the western exit of Ofotenfjord saw several enemy escort platoons retreating in a westerly direction.[16] No intervention by German naval forces had taken place thus far (see Bibliography, 39).

This message provided a completely new perspective of the situation. It could be assumed that in the south, the Allies had pulled out and evacuated Narvik. Dietl himself rushed forward, urging the troops to head quickly for the town.

Into the late evening, reasons for disbelief continued to surface. Toward 2200 hrs, messages arrived one after another from the north, reporting that reconnaissance troops from Group Windisch were prevented from crossing Storelven at several points by strong enemy defences from the western peak. Furthermore, strong enemy forces remained to the west and north of Cirkel Lake. In the case of Group von Schleebrügge, weapons fire was active from both sides following that day's forays.

Reports from Battalions Walther and Haussels were still delayed, as they had apparently advanced too quickly, causing communications to be interrupted for a long time. Due to a lack of cable, the restoration of telephone lines was impossible.

What was clear, however, was that the enemy intended to abandon the fight for Narvik. As for the enemy resistance that remained in the north, especially in front of Group Windisch (whose reports had been much delayed), this could be viewed as the perseverance of a combat-effective rearguard protecting the enemy's retreat and embarkation. Regretfully, the division had to forsake all notion of shifting into attack mode with strong forces, taking the opportunity to capture the retreating enemy in its moment of vulnerability. This was partly because the German troops were too weakened and affected by the previous heavy battles, but also for want of sufficient mobility, weapons, and ammunition (see Bibliography, 40).

Events now began to develop quickly. At 0115 hrs on 9 June, Group XXI announced that the Norwegian king and the government had left Tromso and had ordered the Norwegian high commander, General Ruge, to stack arms and establish communication with the German commanders. Battle Group Narvik received instructions to demand the capitulation of the commander of the opposing Norwegian troops.

At 0130 hrs, a message arrived that on 8 June at 2130 hrs, Battalion Walther, still not having come across the enemy, had marched back to Narvik. At around 1800 hrs, Battalion Haussels found Beisfjord clear of enemy forces and had likewise begun the march to Narvik.[17]

In the morning, the situation in the north was unchanged, the fronts standing opposite, still ready to fire. A troop from Group von Schleebrügge, while running reconnaissance on Peak 620 that morning, was fired on by the Norwegians, with one man killed and two taken prisoner. At 0810 hrs, a Norwegian officer appeared before the commander of Sub-Sector East (Oberleutnant Renner) as negotiator. Upon this, Major von Schleebrügge proceeded to meet with the commander of the Norwegian troops, Oberstleutnant Munte-Kaas, in order to initiate communication and negotiate an armistice. These negotiations, however, were protracted by the Norwegians, who stated that they would as of 2400 hrs, on orders and as planned, relocate to the north and open fire on the Germans as soon as they came within 2km of them.

At 1200 hrs, news arrived from Group XXI that there would be an attempt by Oslo to contact General Ruge directly and communicate to him Germany's demand for capitulation. If the response was not sent by peace envoy by 1600 hrs, all resistance would be broken by means of the utmost deployment of the Luftwaffe. Battle Group Narvik was to convey this same demand to the Norwegians.

Toward 1500 hrs, Group XXI conveyed General Ruge's reply: as of 2400 hrs, hostilities would be discontinued, and truce delegates were on their way to Trondheim and Narvik.

Over the course of the afternoon, the Norwegians slowly began to disengage everywhere, and maintaining security, they retreated unimpeded in a well-ordered manner northwards in the direction of Saetermoen. Out of respect for the flawless and honourable behaviour of the Norwegian soldiers, they were permitted a retreat march with weapons.

During the night of 9/10 June, after the Norwegians had retreated, German troops moved in all over the north.

At 0020 hrs on 10 June, the Norwegian negotiator Oberstleutnant Wrede-Holm arrived in Narvik from Ojord and was led to the division headquarters, at Spionkop, where he arrived at 0445 hrs. By 0900 hrs, the negotiations were finished and the capitulation document by the Norwegian 'Northern Army', under honourable conditions, was signed. By the evening of the same day, the troops from the northern front also reached their assigned areas – 3rd Battalion in Herjangenfjord, 1st Battalion in Bjerkvik, and Group von Schleebrügge the area east of Hartvik Lake.

The battle for Narvik was over. The battle groups under Generalleutnant Dietl had stood fast. They had faced an impossible mission, yet they mastered and fulfilled that mission all the way to the victorious end. In the evening of that unforgettable day of 8 June 1940, the fighters from the south front marched from two sides in ordered form, flawlessly aligned, and singing. But outwardly they were almost unrecognisable as German soldiers. Wearing split-open and ripped uniforms that fell hanging from their thin bodies, their faces were sunken and framed by wild beards. Here, some in jackboots or mountain boots; there, some rubber boots or lace-up shoes; blue naval trousers worn with a grey uniform blouse or Norwegian jacket; mountain infantry stirrup-trousers with a captured anorak; steel helmets, mountain caps, Norwegian caps, an airborne infantry helmet, a naval cap. Still, each carried with him his weapon – rifle, machine gun, or mortar – and carried with him his ammunition (see Bibliography, 16).

On the other side of Rombakenfjord and the ore railway, the fighters from the north front were assembling. The groups came in from all sides, the platoons moving into their muster areas, each group a colourful mix. One mountain infantry first lieutenant with a blond full beard led a barely recognisable section of mountain artillerymen, infantrymen, and sailors; a tired naval officer led a group of sailors, airborne infantrymen, and anti-aircraft soldiers. They all appeared to have aged years during the past weeks. Few of them dawdled among the others, many had been wounded, and many were sent to hospital with frostbite.

Once more, the men had to complete a final forced march lasting 15 to 20 hours, with their last ounce of strength, struggling to reach their destination. From the storm-swept rocks, and deserted mountain terrain, where even on 9 June it had snowed; from the cold, the wet, and eternal fog and then down into the valleys, where the late spring sun warmed them as they entered. Now there were houses, friendly meadows, and light green birch trees. And humans, who did not threaten one's life ...

Order of Battle of Group Dietl on 9 April

(On the day of the landing in Narvik)

(Subordinated under Group XXI)

Divisional Staff, 3rd Mountain Division

Group Narvik

(Major Haussels)
Staff of 2nd Battalion/139th

6th–8th Companies each had:	9 light machine guns (*LMG* = *leichtes Maschinengewehr*)
	2 heavy machine guns (*SMG* = *schweres Maschinengewehr*)
	3 light mortars (*le Gr. W.* = *leichte Granatwerfer*)
	2 heavy mortars
	2–3 anti-tank rifles (*Panzerbüchse*)
9th Company:	6 medium trench mortars[1]
	2 light infantry guns[2]
10th Company:	4 heavy machine guns
	Signal platoon (= *Nachrichtenzug*)
	Pioneer (combat engineer) platoon
100 men per company	

Group Elvegaardsmoen

(Oberst Windisch)
Regimental Staff, 139th Mountain Infantry Regiment
1st and 3rd Battalions (same structure as 2nd Battalion)

In Narvik

Artillery Command (Equipment with Export Echelon)
1 platoon of 83rd Mountain Pioneer Battalion
Naval Artillery Command and Anti-Aircraft Destroyer (*Zerstörer-Flak*)
(Guns with Export Echelon)
Harbour Commandant (Harbour Captain, Naval Signal Officer [M.N.O. =
Marine Nachrichten Offizier])
Narvik Sector Signal Command 463 (1 large radio station)
Anti-Aircraft Command (Advance Command 1st Anti-Aircraft Regiment
32) (Equipment with Export Echelon), later improvised
Airport Commandant Bardufoss

Order of Battle of Battle Group Dietl on 13 May[3]

(from 18 April–5 May under command of the

Wehrmacht High Command)

(*OKW = Oberkommando der Wehrmacht*)

Divisional Staff of the 3rd Mountain Division

Commanding, Generalleutnant Dietl

1a (Operations Officer), Oberleutnant Bader

Adjutant, Oberst Hermann

01, Oberleutnant Müller

Division Physician, Dr Lottner

Ordnance Sergeant (W.W.O.), Hauptmann Schreiner

Division Signal Commander

Naval Signal Officer Navy Signal Officer (M.N.O. = *Marine Nachrichten Offizier*)

Pioneer Commander, Hauptmann Oberndorfer

Signal Command

Artillery Commander, Hauptmann Emmelheinz

Naval Artillery Commander

1st Platoon/83rd Mountain Pioneer Battalion (Leutnant Brandt), 25 men

Anti-Aircraft Commander (Oberleutnant Stecken), 6 2cm anti-aircraft guns

Battle Group Narvik (Major Haussels)
Staff of 2nd Battalion/139th Mountain Infantry Regiment

Naval Battalion Freytag-Loringhofen
    (includes portions of Naval Battalion Erdmenger) (2 companies)
½ Battery of 2nd Company/112th Mountain Artillery Regiment
    (2 7.5cm guns)
2nd Battalion/139th Mountain Rifle Regiment
    (same structure as 9 April)

Naval Regiment Berger (Fregattenkapitän Berger)
(security of ore railway)

Sector Command Straumsnes
    Battalion Holtorf
    3rd Naval Company

Sector Command Sildvik
    Battalion Thiele
    3rd Naval Company

Sector Command Hundalen
    Battalion Zenker
    2nd Naval Company

Sector Command Bjornfjell
    Battalion Arnim
    2nd Naval Company

Group Windisch (Oberst Windisch)
Regimental Staff of 139th Mountain Infantry Regiment

3rd Battalion/139th Mountain Infantry Regiment (Major Hagemann)
    (structure on 9 April)

Company Erdmenger
    Naval Units

Naval Battalion Kothe
(approximately 300 men)

Company Schleebrügge
(reinforced 1st Company/139th)

Company Müller
Units of 2nd Battalion/139th

1st Battalion/139th (Major Stautner)
(without 1st Company)
2 light infantry guns given to 2nd Battalion/139th

Company Ploder
(3rd Company/138th Mountain Infantry Regiment)

½ battery of 2nd/112th Mountain
Artillery Regiment

Order of Battle of Group Dietl on 27 May

Under command of Group XXI

Divisional Staff of 3rd Mountain Division
  Division Signal Commander,
  Flivo (as of 20 May) Anti-Aircraft Commander,
  Oberleutnant Stecken (six 2cm anti-aircraft weapons)

Sector Commander, Hauptmann Brugger
  Parts of Naval Section Kothe
  1st Battalion/1st Airborne Infantry Regiment
  (with parts of units, with strength of about two companies)

Group Narvik (Major Haussels)
Staff of 2nd Battalion/139th Mountain Infantry Regiment

Naval Battalion
  Freytag-Loringhofen (as 13 May)

Company Rieger
  2nd Company/137th

Company Schweiger
  1st Company/137th Mountain Infantry Regiment

Parts of Mountain Anti-Tank Detachment 48
  4 3.7cm anti-tank guns
2nd Battalion/139th Mountain Rifle Regiment[1] (as on 13 May)
  with the attached:
  Artillery Commander, Hauptmann Emmelheinz
  Naval Artillery Commander

Demi-battery 2nd Company/112th Mountain Artillery Regiment
  2 7.5cm guns

Navy Regiment Berger (securing at the ore railway)

(as on 13 May)

Group Windisch[1]
Regimental Staff, 139th Mountain Infantry Regiment

3rd Battalion/139th[2]
  (as on 13 May)

1st Battalion/139th
  (without 1st Company, or light infantry gun platoon)

Battalion Schleebrügge
  Reinforced 1st Company/139th, Company Ploder
    (3rd Company/138th)
  1st Company, 1st Airborne Infantry Regiment

Company Erdmenger
  Navy elements

Company Müller
  Parts of 2nd Battalion/139th

Company Renner
  2nd Company/138th

Order of Battle of Group Dietl on 9 June

(Under command of Group XXI)

Divisional Staff of 3rd Mountain Division

Ordinance Sergeant [W.W.O. = *Waffenoberfeldwebel*]
Signal Officer
Signal Commander
Forward Air Controller [*Flivo*]
Anti-Aircraft Commander, Oberleutnant Stecken (6 2cm anti-aircraft guns)
Security Crew on Rundfjeldet
Elements of Naval Section Kothe

Naval Sector Kothe

One naval company given to 139th Mountain Infantry Regiment

Group Oberst Meindl

(Regimental Commander, 112th Mountain Artillery Regiment)
(not until after 8 June)

2nd Battalion/139th[1] (Major Haussels)
(Company formed from elements of Naval Company full strength with inclusion of Company Rieger)

2nd Company/137th Mountain Infantry Regiment

1st Company/137th
  Naval Company von Gaartzen

1st Battalion/1st Airborne Infantry Regiment
Captain Walther
  2 Companies

Naval Battalion Holtorf
  2 Naval Companies

1 Platoon of 83rd Mountain Pioneer Battalion

Group Windisch

Staff of 139th Mountain Infantry Regiment

3rd Battalion/139th (Major Hagemann
  (as on 27 May)

1st Battalion/139th (Major Stautner)
  (as on 27 May)

Battalion Schleebrügge
  1st Company/139th
  1st Company/1st Airborne Infantry Regiment
  2nd Company/138th Mountain Infantry Regiment
  3rd Company/138th

Naval Company (Detachment Kothe)

Naval Company March

Naval Regiment Berger

Sector Commander Sildvik
  Naval Battalion Thiele
  (two naval companies)

Sector Commander Hundalen
  Naval Captain Zenker

Sector Commander Bjornfjell
  Naval Company Arnim

British–French–Polish–Norwegian organisation of forces around Narvik on 17 April (see Bibliography, 2)

(Codename for Allied troops: 'Rupertforce')

Fleet:

Admiral Earl of Cork and Orrery
Battleship *Warspite*
Aircraft Carrier *Furious*
Cruisers *Southampton, Effingham, Aurora, Enterprise*
approximately 5 or 6 destroyers

Ground troops (in the area of Harstad):

Major-General P. J. Mackesy
24th Guards Brigade[1] (Brigadier W. Fraser)
  1st Battalion Scots Guards (Lieutenant-Colonel Trappes-Lomax)
  1st Battalion Irish Guards (Lieutenant-Colonel Faulkner)
  2nd Battalion The South Wales Borderers (Lieutenant-Colonal Gottwaltz)
  3rd Light Anti-Aircraft Battery
  229th and 230th Pioneer Company

On 10 May

Fleet:

Admiral Earl of Cork and Orrery
Battleship *Resolution*
Cruisers *Effingham, Aurora, Enterprise*
Anti-aircraft Cruisers *Cairo, Coventry, Curlew*
Aircraft Carrier *Ark Royal*
approximately 5 or 6 destroyers

Ground troops:

Britain:
24th Guards Brigade (Brigadier W. Fraser)
(as on 17.4)
    203rd Battery/51st Field Artillery Regiment
    193rd Heavy Anti-Aircraft Battery
    55th Light Anti-Aircraft Regiment
    One tank section of the 3rd King's Own Hussars

France:
27th Demi-Brigade Alpine Infantry (Brigadier-General Bethouart)
    6th Battalion Alpine Infantry
    12th Battalion Alpine Infantry
    14th Battalion Alpine Infantry

13th Demi-Brigade of Foreign Legion
    1st and 2nd Foreign Legion Battalions
    342nd Independent Tank Company
    2nd Independent Colonial Artillery Section
    14th Anti-tank Company

Poland:
Polish 1st Mountain Infantry Brigade (General Bohuecz-Szyako)
    1st Demi Brigade with 1st and 2nd Battalions
    2nd Demi-Brigade with 3rd and 4th Battalions

Norway:

Norwegian 6th Division (Generalmajor C. G. Fleischer)

IR (Infantry Regiment) 13 (as of mid-January 1940 under command of 5th Division)

IR 14

IR 15

IR 16

Varanger Battalion

Alta Battalion

Detachment Narvik

Mountain Artillery Section III (two mountain batteries, one gun battery)

Pioneer Battalion (2 companies)

Signal Company

Division troops

Fighter plane/Air Section (Tromso)

Anti-Aircraft Section

(Total of about 8,000–10,000 men, about 290 machine guns and 12 guns)

On 3 June

Fleet:

Admiral Earl of Cork and Orrery
Cruiser *Southampton*
Anti-aircraft cruisers *Cairo, Coventry*
Aircraft Carriers *Ark Royal, Glorious*
Approximately 5 or 6 destroyers

Ground troops:

Northwest Expedition Corps
Lieutenant General C. J. E. Auchinleck

Britain:[3]
24th Guards Brigade (Brigadier W. Fraser)[4]
(as on 10 May)
   6th Anti-Aircraft Brigade (Brigadier F. N. C. Rosseter)
   55th Light Anti-Aircraft Regiment with 163rd, 164th, and
   165th Batteries
   56th Light Anti-Aircraft Regiment with 3rd and 167th
   Batteries
   51st Heavy Anti-Aircraft Regiment with 151st, 152nd, and
   153rd Batteries
   82nd Heavy Anti-Aircraft Regiment with 156th, 193rd, and
   256th Batteries

France, Poland, and Norway:
(as on 10 May)

Air Force:

British Air Fighter Group (Captain M. Moore)
263rd Bomber Squadron (Gladiators)
46th Fighter Squadron (Hurricanes)
11th Observation Echelon

Total enemy forces deployed against Group Dietl
17 infantry battalions
1 company of mountain troops
1 cavalry regiment
1 machine gun battalion
1 tank company
5 pioneer (combat engineer) companies
5 field artillery batteries
2 heavy howitzer batteries
8 light anti-aircraft batteries (96 guns)
13 heavy anti-aircraft batteries (104 guns)

4 cruisers
6 destroyers
12 U-boat hunters
4 escort vessels
2 fighter squadrons
1 bomber squadron
1 battle squadron
 numerous auxiliary vessels and transporters
Total strength approximately 25,000 men

Operations Order for the Occupation of Narvik

Group XXI   Berlin, 12 March 1940
Ia 46/40 Senior Commanders
Subject: *Weserübung Nord*

Operations Order for the Occupation of Narvik

Map 1:100,000 Page Malselov, Harstad, Salangen, Ofoten, Narvik

1. Positions and organisation of the Norwegian 6th Division as well as military geographical data, see specific Appendices and the admiralty staff handbook. Coastal fortifications, see also guidance from the navy for the occupation of these structures.
2. On 'Weser Day' the *3rd Mountain Division Battle Group*, early, in a surprise operation, will take possession of Narvik, the Elvegaardsmoen exercise area (Norwegian Infantry Regiment 15), and the fortifications south of Ramsundet (narrowest fjord passageway 35km west of Narvik), and the Norwegian portion of the ore railway (Narvik–Lulea) along with the Narvik Harbour, and thereby secure for Germany the export of ore from the Swedish mines. The commander of the battle group holds military sovereign authority in the area of occupation. He does not have executive powers. He is, however, given authority to take all measures necessary for the fulfillment of his missions. For command organisation, see enclosures.
3. *Policy* for the occupation is the most *peaceful* execution possible. All measures must be taken accordingly. To avoid armed conflict it is

recommended that peace negotiators be sent in for *short* negotiations. Local resistance is vigorous and for a quick victory it is necessary to break that resistance, in order to achieve a peaceful solution. In the unlikely case of a general revolt, the deployment of all means necessary for quick victory is required. The guidance specified for conduct in Norway is to be emphasised. The occupation is to disturb the domestic life of the town, economy, and community life as little as possible.

4. For the occupation of Narvik, the initial mission of the battle group is at break of dawn, under the element of surprise, to simultaneously capture the fortifications along the fjord, the harbour of Narvik, and the exercise area at Elvegaardsmoen, and neutralise any resistance by Norwegian forces.

   a) The fortifications along the fjord are to be occupied and made defence-ready immediately with the harbour commander assigned by the navy.

   b) In Narvik, the facilities important to military and traffic systems are to be occupied to prevent the obstructing of German interest; on the other hand, the personal freedom of the population and public life must be as little disturbed as possible. The instruments of power of the occupation troops must only be apparent to the extent necessary to accomplish the purpose. Communications must be established promptly with Vizekonsul Wussow and the military commandant Oberst Sundlo, who is reportedly pro-German, in order to assert all further demands through negotiation.

   In the harbour, in cooperation with the harbour commander (harbour captain), the exit of all ships is to be prevented. As soon as peaceful progress is secured, the domestic and coastal ship traffic can be resumed. Radio traffic of the ships lying in the harbour is to be prevented …

   c) In Elvegaardsmoen, all resistance is to be neutralised …

   Sparing the sense of honour of the Norwegian armed forces must be given consideration. Release of all military members suspended from duty is to be arranged for those who are peaceful and show loyal conduct.

   d) …

5. If the breach through the fjord fortifications does not succeed due to enemy resistance, the fallback position is to be the harbour at Elvenes at Gratangsbotn (30km north of Narvik). From here, Elvegaardsmoen, Narvik, and the fjord fortifications are to be captured one after the other. While outward bound, Haarstad is to be occupied, and the Norwegian 6th Division is to be neutralised.

    a) Establishment of communication with the staff of the Norwegian 6th Division in Haarstad. A peaceful path to normalising the mutual relationship is to be sought … With respect to Tromso, initially nothing is to be undertaken, as occupation of area will be ordered later by Group XXI.

    b) The occupation of outposts in the north and north-east areas of Narvik:
    Exercise area Saetermoen at Baru, 60km north-east of Narvik. Salangen (army workshops and potential airfield) 50km north of Narvik, Bardufoss, Airport at Rusta 80km north-east of Narvik. These areas should be accessible via the large north road that begins at Narvik. The condition of the airfield installations must be determined, and as far as condition and work forces permit, the area must be readied for the landing of aircraft there. Air traffic and destruction of existing facilities must be prevented …

7. Working in cooperation with the navy:
Enclosure 5 to the Naval Warfare Command Letter No. I Operation 270/40 for Senior Commanders has gone out to the division.

8. Achieving the fastest possible connection by air to the south (Trondheim) depends on the availability of manpower to create a functioning airfield.

9. Working in cooperation with the Luftwaffe:
For anti-aircraft protection at Narvik, it is ordered that 1st Battalion/32nd Anti-Aircraft Regiment of 3rd Mountain Division is placed under direct command of X Air Corps.
Organisation: Staff, Signal Platoons 1st, 2nd, and 4th Company/32nd Anti-Aircraft Regiment.

The following are to enter Narvik:

    a) Advance party on warships echelon

    b) Equipment and munitions on the export echelon

    c) Complete personnel later

    ...

10. ...

11. *Additional forces* to Narvik will be resupplied depending on the situation, by coastal ships and air transport as follows:

    a) Initially, the elements of 3rd Mountain Division deployed around Trondheim, after being relieved by additional forces from the group.

    b) The remainder of the division by sea transport as far as Oslo, and by train to Trondheim (possibly via Sweden).

12. Signal communications:

    ...

13. Secrecy:

    ...

14. Command post of Group XXI:

    ...

Commander, Group XXI
Signed, v. Falkenhorst

The Seizing of Narvik

Enclosure 2   14 March 1940
to 3rd Mountain Division 1a Nr. 50/40 Senior Commanders

The Seizing of Narvik

1. Under the fire protection of the remaining destroyer No. 3, the staff of 2nd/139th, 8th Company, 9th Company, and 10th Company, which are on the destroyers No. 4 and No. 5 in the harbour are to land in Narvik in separate areas. After landing, the companies will proceed according to directions of the battalion commander, through the town, all the way to the north and north-west edge of Narvik and secure the landing of the remaining men on destroyer No. 3 (division staff, 7th Company, etc.).

2. The group of forces intended for Narvik (2nd Battalion/139th Mountain Infantry Regiment, without reinforced 6th Company) is to proceed through the city in a north-eastern direction and here it will secure the eastern side. Take possession of the ferry across Rombaken [sic]. In order to deal with the possible resistance of the enemy in Narvik, heavy weapons of the battalion should also be positioned on the peaks south-east of Narvik, so that they can hold the city under fire.

   In the town are important *military* and *transportation* installations that must be captured (harbour, railway and mail installations, military structures, barracks, etc.) in order to protect German aims, but on the other hand the personal freedom of the population and public life must be as little disturbed as possible.

3. The battalion appointed for the capture of Narvik is to remain as occupation force in the town, and must set up for defence, in order to prevent attempts by the enemy to land.

4. With the entry of our own ground and naval aircraft with intelligence and transport missions, in the first days there will be aircraft support in the area of Narvik (types Ju 52, Ju 90, FW 200, occasional He 111, seaplanes He 59, Do 24, Do 26, He 115). Be careful during the fire by anti-aircraft defence.

5. Signal communications: See the Special Orders for Signal Traffic. Of importance are constant radio connection and rapid messaging. These depend on:

    a) was the landing successful?

    b) the conduct of the Norwegians?

    c) which further points are occupied?

    d) first appearance of enemy naval and air forces?

    e) is there access to a landing field?

6. Secrecy: …

7. Division staff lands in Narvik and remains here until further notice

signed, Dietl

Operation in Northern Norway

Secret Subject Matter for Commanders

Enclosure E   2 April 1940

to Group XXI Ia 194/40 Senior Commanders

Operation in Northern Norway

The mission of 3rd Mountain Division is first of all the securing of Narvik and the railway to Sweden (Lulea Railway). Over and above the missions specified in the operations order for the occupation of Narvik (Group XXI 1a 46/60 for Senior Commanders of 12 Mar 40), is, after the delivery of further elements of the division, to also occupy Tromso, and prevent enemy landings. The final goal is the occupation and securing of the area of Tromso–Haarstad–Ofotenfjord–Narvik–Saetermoen–Bardufoss, both from the sea as well as in from the direction of Sweden.

The addition of more elements of the division from Trondheim to Narvik depends on the development of the situation in northern Norway and the immediate coastal area. The parts of the 3rd Mountain Division which are deployed around Trondheim and are designated to be sent here, up to their departure for Narvik, will be under the command of the 196th Division as soon as it has arrived in Trondheim.

The division must be ready at any time, with a sufficiently strong detachment, to also occupy the ore mines of Kiruna (Sweden). These preparations are to be scheduled into the calendar.

Instructions from Hitler to Dietl

The Supreme Commander of the Wehrmacht   Berlin, 18 April 1940
to

Generalleutnant Dietl

1. All information indicates that preparations by the enemy for heavy action against Narvik are underway. Long term, in consideration of your weapons and equipment you will not be able to hold out.
2. The transport and provisioning of further of our forces with artillery is not possible.
3. Your most important mission remains, despite this, to hold out as long as possible. In this way you must buy time for all the preparations, and ensure that by means of the most extreme destruction of the railway and its structures, that the ore railway and the shipping of ore will be of no use to the enemy for a long time in the future.
4. Through a battle conducted as per radio message of 15 April at 1823 hrs, and with the convening of your forces along the ore railway, you can hobble the enemy naval and ground forces for a long time, and relieve the battles being conducted at other places of the northern arena to a large extent.
5. The addition of explosives and incendiaries by long-distance air transport has been initiated. During the return flight, these aircraft will initially bring back the highly specialised personnel from the navy, who are of little value to you.

6. Convey by courier or by radio, whether after completion of your mission as stated in No. 3, you see the possibility of struggling south through the mountains with selected forces, supported by occasional drops of provisions from aircraft, and after the elimination of those unable to march, to cross the Swedish border. About the possibility of a transport by sea plane, you can reply through the courier. If either of these options be excluded, conduct yourself in a manner that preserves the stainless honour of the Wehrmacht.

signed, Adolf Hitler

Wishlist

Battle Group Narvik   29 May 1940
1a

Wishlist

1. Personnel reinforcements are still necessary.
2. The handover to the Kriegsmarine [Navy] in greater scope can only succeed if sufficient replacements arrive.
3. It is especially challenging that the troops have no artillery available. Therefore [we need] weapons and munition, in this case an opening of the route.
4. A deployment of Stukas soon.
5. Due to the impossibility of munitions resupply through Sweden, it is necessary to organise the entire munitions resupply by airdrop. The Battle Group has very scarce munitions reserves, and therefore a munitions airdrop on the air route is most urgently needed. Necessary quantities of munitions for Group XXI have already been requested, but there has been no airdrop for the last three days.
6. Due to enemy action, a great absence of weapons, replacements urgently needed. Weapons were already requested for Group XXI.
7. The unit suffers greatly due to lack of housing, as well as from clothing that is worn out and too light weight, and the impossibility of producing warm rations in large enough quantities. Urgently needed is a resupply of mountain footwear and clothing as well as tent equipment.

8. Newly arrived troops are equipped inadequately for the most part. In the case of paratroopers they have no rucksacks, coats, eating utensils, etc. The Group has no available reserves of any kind. It is therefore requested that newly arriving personnel bring all necessary equipment items with them.

...

13. Supplies will last for another 3–4 weeks, a resupply has already been promised.

signed, Dietl

Arrival of Troop Reinforcements to Battle Group Narvik by Air Transport

4 May: 1310 hrs, a Seaplane takes off with 3.7cm anti-aircraft gun and ammunition (incl. 72 grenades for mountain guns).[1]

7 May: 0830 hrs, a seaplane takes off with anti-aircraft gun.[2]

8 May: 1010 hrs, a Do 26 lands in Rombakenfjord.

2200 hrs, another sea plane lands in Beisfjord, after having been shot at in Rombakenfjord.

Arrived: 1 officer, 35 men of the 3rd Company/138th.

10 May: 1500 hrs, seaplane lands in Rombakenfjord.

1515 hrs, a second seaplane was forced to make an emergency landing in Beisfjord under strong anti-aircraft fire.

Arrived: 1 officer, 30 men of the 3rd/138th.

14 May: 1100 hrs, airborne landing at Bjornfell by 3 officers and 63 paratroopers of 1st Company/1st Airborne Infantry Regiment.

15 May: airborne landing of 22 paratroopers.

16 May: midday and afternoon, airborne landing of 1 officer and 75 paratroopers.

18 May: 1630 hrs, landing of 2 seaplanes with 1 officer and 15 men from the 2nd/138th.

20 May: 2000 hrs, two boat planes land in Rombakenfjord and bring 2 officers, 12 men of the 3rd/138th, a 3.7cm Pak[3] with crew and forward air controller [Flivo] (Hptm Kless).

22 May: 1730 hrs, 3 seaplanes arrive with 1 officer and 23 men from 2nd/138th and one 3.7cm anti-armour gun.[4]

2300 hrs, 3 more seaplanes land with 1 officer and 38 men from 2nd/138th.

23 May: For the first time, at 2245 hrs, mountain infantry jumpers land successfully after only eight days' training (only 2 slightly injured). Arrived: 1 officer, 65 men of the 1st/137th.

24 May: In the afternoon a Waal [seaplane] landed in Rombakenfjord and brought the first members of the 6th/138th.

2200 hrs, 55 men of the 2nd/137th jumped in without significant incident.

In the night 2 seaplanes landed with 154 men of the 6th/138th.

25 May: 1000 hrs, 1 officer and 53 men of the 2nd/137th landed without incident.

In the afternoon 1 officer and 44 men of the 2nd/138th jumped in, 1900 hrs, 1 officer and 53 men of the 1st/137th jumped in.

26 May: 1800 hrs, more members of the 1st Airborne Infantry Regiment (Battalion Cdr Hptm Walther, 2 officers and 78 men) were dropped in from a Ju 52.

28 May: 0010 hrs, 46 men of the 1st Airborne Infantry Regiment parachute in without incident.

0030 hrs, 1 seaplane lands carrying one mountain howitzer [Geb. Geschütz].

1930 hrs, 2 seaplanes with 3 mountain howitzers, attacked during water landing, destroyed by enemy riflemen [Jaeger]. One dead, several wounded.

29 May: 0435 hrs, 2 Officers, 63 men of the 1st/1st Airborne Infantry Regiment[5] parachuted in.

2230 hrs, 61 paratroopers dropped in by a 6 Ju 52 without destroyer protection.

31 May: 2130 hrs, 57 men jumped in with 4 grenade launchers from the 1st/1st Airborne Infantry Regiment.[6] The Jus were once again without air-fighter cover.

2 June: 2130 hrs, 2 officers, 44 men of the 1st/1st Airborne Infantry Regiment parachuted in.

7 June: 1843 hrs, Oberst Meindl jumped in with 26 paratroopers.

9 June: 0500 hrs, 20 paratroopers jumped in.

Endnotes

Chapter I

1 The commander of the destroyers (*FdZ* = *Führer der Zerstörer*) was Kommodore Bonte.

2 This was how the 2nd Battalion/139th Mountain Infantry Regiment, for instance, lost its only two light infantry cannons.

3 Contrary to the belief at that time that *Glowworm* was a scout for the British fleet, it was actually lagging behind the main destroyer unit due to engine damage, which was on its return voyage from Norway. On 8 April, it was in front of the Vestfjord, in Norwegian territorial waters, where it had laid mines to stop German ore ships from returning from Narvik.

4 Despite pressure from the Norwegian commander of the area of Narvik, Oberst Sundlo, the fortifications were never rebuilt.

5 According to W. Hubatch, just before 0600 hrs, or according to F.O. [*Felddienst Offizier* – field duty officer] Busch, between 0530 and 0600 hrs.

6 Norwegian 13th Infantry Regiment was detached from the 5th Division in mid-January and placed under the 6th Division.

7 Reported in *The Times*, 16 July 1940.

8 Later, in the war journal of Naval Battalion Erdmenger, the general noted in handwriting, 'Since I expected an attack by the Norwegians, I therefore belonged with my troops.'

9 These were the *Hardy*, *Hunter*, *Hotspur*, *Hostile*, and *Havock*.

10 *Havock* sank the German supply steamer *Rauenfels*, which was moving towards him while exiting Ofotenfjord.

11 On 12 April, during outpost patrol duty, this destroyer slashed its double bottom on an underwater rift.

12 After repeated attempts during the night of 13 April to tow the *Cossack*, it was freed on the morning of 14 April during high tide.

13 In his personal journal, Generalleutnant Dietl remarked: 'If, after the scuttling of the German destroyers, the British had gone on the attack, the situation would have become very difficult for us.'

Chapter 2

1   This ore railway had an enormous capacity, making Narvik, with its excellent quay and loading facilities, the most significant iron ore harbour of the north. Month after month, 24 trains rolled into Narvik daily, each with 41 cars, each car carrying 35 tons, which came to about 1,500 tons of iron ore per train. Over the course of one year, almost 8 million tons of premium quality ore, often with grade as high as 70 per cent, came into Narvik from the so-called 'magnet mountains.' A large portion of this went to England (see Bibliography, 3).

2   For the elevation measurements given here, it must be kept in mind that this northern area already stands at 1,000 metres above sea level, corresponding to a southern European level of about 2,500 metres.

3   Planned either for reinforcements at the entrance to Ofotenfjord, or for defence of Narvik proper.

4   Translator's note: North Base = *Basis Nord*, an anchorage area where the Russians allowed German ships to anchor.

5   In this case, just as before, Lindemann, the merchant ship captain who had been brought onboard as a consultant, had very early on described the prevailing weather conditions correctly, stating that the airfield at Bardufoss was only usable in summer (see Bibliography, 44).

6   Only one single plane was able to take off again, but not until all of the remaining fuel was collected from the other planes and a runway was hard-packed. After the sudden thaw had weakened the surface, the Ju plane could not take off again and sank in the lake.

7   The author was unable to determine whether this lack of winter equipment was due to shortage of space on the destroyers, to the need for secrecy, to an assumption that this equipment could be acquired in-country, or due to the fact that the season of the year was not taken into account.

8   Later, two 2cm flak guns each were installed at Hundalen, Norddal Bridge, and at Bjornfjell.

9   In their battle report of 13 April, the British spoke of 'the presence of coastal batteries at Narvik' (see Bibliography, 44).

10   After the division headquarters had moved to Bjornfjell, the radio tower station was delivered to them by means of a daring exploit: On the evening of 12 May, the weapons officer of the division, Hauptmann Schreiner, in the cover of rain and fog, picked up the precious equipment and carried it out of the harbour by motor boat, going around the entire Framnes peninsula and into Rombakenfjord – under the eyes of the British destroyers. At 2145 hrs, he landed below Sildvik and then the transmitter was transported to Bjornfjell, where, in the difficult weeks to come, it provided invaluable service (see Bibliography, 39).

11   As of 23 April to Straumsnes.

12 As of 26 April deployed between Naval Battalion and 8th Company/139th, on both sides of Tunnel 1.

13 Assured of British assistance, which had been promised most unequivocally on 9 April at 1800 hrs by the British ambassador in Oslo, on that day the Norwegian government broadcasted a call for military resistance against the Germans. The state of war between Norway and Germany had begun.

14 Naval ski reconnaissance troops from the Narvik Sector brought in these early reports.

15 The 1st Company/139th had, after its original mission (removal of the presumed Norwegian coastal batteries at Hamnes), entered the harbour at Narvik, but was not returned to 1st Battalion in Elvegaardsmoen, and instead, in the first days, was deployed forward as security on the ore railway.

16 This refers to a German reconnaissance troop, strength one officer/11 men, from Camp Elvegaardsmoen that had been captured by the Norwegians on 9 April. Its mission had been to establish an overland connection to Narvik.

17 According to a message from the Wehrmacht High Command (OKW) dated 19 May at 1245 hrs, Sweden refused to allow the transit of weapons and ammunition.

18 On 28 April, a reconnaissance troop that had pushed forward to 1km south-east of Ostervik (eastern shore of Bogen bay), reported: 'In Bogen Bay, four enemy destroyers, between 1130 and 1300 hrs, about 500–600 men landed. And on 29 April: Two cruisers, three destroyers, and at 1930 hrs, brisk traffic with fishing cutters heading to Haakvik.'

19 On 13 April at approximately 1500 hrs, a radio messaged arrived from Hitler: 'Narvik must be defended against attacks. If the weather is favourable, the Luftwaffe will assist. If necessary, permanently block the ore railway in the mountains. Secure Hartvik Lake as a landing strip.' (see Bibliography, 39)

On 15 April a radio message came from the Wehrmacht High Command: 'In case the situation forces giving up present positions (Narvik), create support points in the mountains, as much as possible along the ore railway, defend using support via air drop. Completely destroy the forward-most portion of the ore railway.' (see Bibliography, 41)

On 17 April a Directive from Army High Command (OKH) said: 'hold onto Narvik against the superior force.' (see Bibliography, 40).

20 The courier (Hauptmann Sternburger) had already been notified on 18 April by radio message, but did not arrive until 22 April due to bad weather. At the moment the seaplane touched down in Beisfjord, the driving snow concealed it from observation from the enemy ships lying in Ofotenfjord. The courier conveyed the Führer's directive contained in Appendix 9. At the same time, he reported that Battle Group Narvik was now to be transferred to the direct command of the OKW (a radio message of 18 April, 1900 hrs, had already confirmed this: 'Battle Group Narvik is now separated from the unit of Group XXI'). A new subordinate relationship was not mentioned (see Bibliography, 39).

21   In his memoirs, Churchill criticised his caution with the following statement: 'In a telegram General Mackesy received the order to attack and occupy Narvik with the fire support of the *Warspite* and the destroyers. As it turned out, however, General Mackesy was loath to try to take the town in direct attack and with the close support of the fleet. Lord Cork could not change his mind. It was the general's intention to hold out until about the time of the beginning snow thaw.'

22   The battalion had been brought in by ship to Salangen and there it was unloaded on 18 April (see Bibliography, 39).

23   See Chapter III.

Chapter 3

1   For structure of units, see Appendix 5.

2   The positions were taken over by the Naval Artillery Battery.

3   This was said to be a British 10cm howitzer battery.

4   On 8 May, the Hotel Royal was set on fire during the shooting. This was where the main provisions were warehoused for the entire sector. Luckily, the fire was quickly put out. The two mountain guns had only three rounds for adjusting fire and nine fire-for-effect rounds for use against enemy batteries.

5   According to a statement dated 19 May by a Polish defector, about 800 Poles were already at Ankenesfjell.

6   The enemy on the heights of Ankenesfjell, in the meantime, were reinforced by a total of four battalions.

7   The 3.7cm anti-tank gun was brought in on 22 May by seaplane and was deployed along the road at Ankenes.

8   A radio message received 26 May, at 0615 hrs, reported: 'Situation at sea on 25 May near Haarstad, several heavy and light cruisers, one carrier, two battleships, five transporters.' Headquarters Staff, Trondheim (see Bibliography, 41).

9   In the period between 23 and 25 May, both companies jumped in at Bjornfjell with parachutes after only an eight-day rapid training programme.

Chapter 4

1   This digging-in did not necessarily indicate that the enemy was planning to occupy a position here, but more to the point, it shows how quickly and thoroughly they secured the area against a possible German ambush during rest and bivouac as a result of the experience at Elvenes.

2   Strength of about 60 men, consisting of Company Trupp, Ski Platoon Bussmer and 3rd Platoon. The 2nd Platoon, still division reserve in Narvik, followed.

3   The previous positions of the 1st Company/139th north-west of Bjornfjell were taken over by a platoon from Naval Company Zenker, which also sent forward a platoon for security to the south in the Hundalen valley.

4   By levying men from all companies of the 2nd Battalion/139th, the weak Company Brucker was formed. Naval Company Erdmenger was pulled out, and its previous sector at Fagernes was taken over by Naval Company von Gaartzen, which previously had been on the right flank. Here, Naval Company von Freytag had to spread out its positions at Djupvik as far as Tunnel 5. Both companies that had been taken from the coastal front marched off on the evening of 30 April, sometimes under fire from enemy ships' cannons on the road along Beisfjord, and climbed from the southern end of the fjord though the mountains to Sildvik, where they were taken to Hundalen by train transport.

5   The degree of soldierly spirit that filled the fighters on the northern front is exemplified by the conduct of one man of the field guard. Already wounded, he remained alone at the telephone post, passed along final position reports, and then followed his comrades into the fight against the closely approaching Norwegians, but not without the valuable telephone line, which he rolled up and took with him.

6   According to statements by POWs from the Norwegian 'Alta' Battalion.

7   The intensive defence by 1st Company/139th, with its very high expenditure of ammunition, was only possible because of the smooth functioning of the resupply personnel of the company, who tirelessly hauled ammunition with self-sacrificing dedication. The resupply echelon, which was made up of those who were ill, lightly wounded, and Norwegian POWs, was always on the move, on hours-long, tiresome marches, with their improvised sleds and mountaineering backpacks. Often the men climbed twice a day under heavy loads through the deep, soft snow up to the mountain saddle and mountain slopes.

8   The division approved the relocation after the fact, in the express order of 29 April which said to hold the new positions.

9   According to captured paperwork, the enemy assumed that at Laberget there was a German presence of 400–500 men.

10 Four guns, of which presumably two were French 10cm and two Norwegian 7cm mountain howitzers.

11 According to prisoner of war statement, Norwegian 15th Infantry Regiment and French mountain infantry.

12 Two Norwegian aircraft attacked during the ground battle.

13 The earnestness with which Generalleutnant Dietl judged the situation is shown in that on 7 May he personally rushed on skis to Group Windisch, where he appeared on 8 May at 0700 hrs, in order to discuss the situation face-to-face.

14 As early as 8 May, there were once again six ship units in the fjord.

15 11th Company was reinforced by a platoon from Naval Company Erdmenger on 9 May.

Chapter 5

1 Among them was the *Grom*, the last of the Polish destroyers, sunk on 4 April at around 0900 hrs by chain bombs [*Kettenbombe*] from an He 111.

Chapter 6

1 The battleship *Resolution*, the cruisers *Effingham*, *Aurora*, and *Enterprise*, and presumably the anti-aircraft cruiser *Cairo*.

2 On 13 May, at 1010 hrs, the Trondheim aircraft commander reported that a deployment of the Luftwaffe was impossible for the time being due to the weather.

3 Toward evening of 13 May, a large number of men from Naval Battalion Kothe showed up near the division command post, shell-shocked and in complete disarray. These were primarily men of the naval company deployed at Gjeisvik. The navy men had a totally inaccurate picture of the situation, believing that the entire Group Windisch was lost. While mountain infantrymen were immediately sent forward individually, the naval personnel gathered in Bjornfjell and for the time being remained unfit for battle. By 20 May, Naval Section Kothe was reorganised.

4 The pioneer platoon was sent to Outpost III on 13 May at 1445 hrs, with orders to serve as reserve

5 Landed in Rombakenfjord between 8 and 10 May in strength of two officers/65 men.

6 Later, several men tried to cross on collapsing snow bridges but drifted off; they drowned.

7 Oberst Herrmann, General Dietl's adjutant, wrote in his personal journal: 'The infantrymen were so exhausted that some of them fell asleep next to their machine guns as they fired.'

8 As reinforcement, Leutnant Brandt's pioneer company was given three light machine guns.

9 Fifty per cent of the company, after medical examination at Outpost III, were taken to the field hospital at Bjornfjell as unfit for duty due to lung inflammations, frostbite, and foot injuries. The rest were reorganised into two platoons of 18–20 men each. On 18 May, the company received 25 men from Naval Regiment Berger as reinforcements (see Bibliography, 44).

10 Occupation of the north peak: nine men of 14th Company with two light machine guns; on the west slope of Lillebalak, two groups of four and seven men, one heavy machine gun from 15th Company.

11 One battery west of Hartvik Lake.

12 3rd Company/138th landed on 20 May by seaplane in Rombakenfjord.

13 During the night of 7 May, the division transferred one more naval platoon of Section Hauptmann Brucker, in strength of one officer to 20 men, half of whom

were integrated into the combat unit, the other half provided to the resupply echelon.

14 Formed in place of Ski Platoon Trautner from 1st Battalion.

15 The structure of company Becker: Company Trupp, two infantry groups with four light machine guns, five heavy machine guns from Company Trupp.

16 Having jumped in at midday and in the afternoon of 16 May, six men were injured in the jump. The parachute infantrymen arrived well supplied with weapons, yet they had no equipment for fighting in snow, cold temperatures, or storms. Further, they lacked any experience in mountain combat.

17 Consisting of the naval personnel of the former Naval Battalion Kothe (newly formed as Naval Section Kothe), gathered at Bjornfjell, with total strength equal to three platoons.

Chapter 7

1 Almost exclusively made up of technical naval personnel, such as boilermen, mechanics, and fitters, etc.

2 The two suburban areas of Narvik possessing piers.

3 Previously shot down five enemy aircraft.

4 Generalleutnant Dietl had to face the question of whether he ought to evacuate Narvik before, or at least just before the first signs of enemy landings, and then reposition the deployed forces in a rear area for a renewed defence. He decided to take his chances on the landing attempt. Even though one could not call Narvik a prize with high military value, the giving up of Narvik without resistance would have a strong effect on the fighting spirit of the troops, and the enemy would be handed a cheap victory that would always be represented in world-wide propaganda as German defeat (see Bibliography, 39).

5 Anti-aircraft cruisers *Cairo* and *Coventry*.

6 Cruiser *Southampton*.

7 Two French 7.5cm batteries and one Norwegian 10.5cm motorised battery

8 The boats were constructed especially for landings – flat, motorised cutters with a shallow draught, having armoured side plates protruding as high as 50cm above the waterline. Each had a crew of about 50 men with heavy weapons.

9 The radioman found himself in the midst of the advancing enemy [troops] and, after continually falling back and then fighting his way forward, finally arrived at Naval Company von Freytag at about 1130 hrs. But he could not establish a connection back to the sector commander because the counterpart station equipment there had long since been dismantled.

10 One Norwegian battalion.

11 Two bombs hit the anti-aircraft cruiser *Cairo*, killing or wounding 30 men.

12 At 0040 hrs, the division had once more demanded urgent air support, which was approved by the aircraft commander at Trondheim at 0415 hrs.

13 One battalion of French Alpine Infantry landed.

14 The sailors there held out until midday. At 1100 hrs, the station reported: 'enemy troops marching toward Narvik, in the town itself no enemy as yet. No communication of any kind with our units.' And at 1215 hrs: 'radio station blown up, as it is impossible to continue holding out.'

15 2nd and 4th Battalions of the Polish mountain infantry, some 2,000 men (3rd Battalion in reserve).

16 Jumped in on 27 May.

17 Until this point, all existing gaps in the front were ably filled by sailors. These were in fact fully combat-ready men, but did not have the training and experience for land battle to the extent needed for mountain warfare. Basically, however, while fighting in the mountain infantry unit, they were fully dedicated and performed their duty.

18 At the same time, Naval Regiment Berger received the order from the division to deploy all available forces for a counter-attack at the ore railway.

19 During the night of 24/25 May, it arrived by seaplane in a strength of 14 men.

20 Jumped in on 26/May at 1810 hrs with parts of his battalion.

21 Because only a small number of the missing men returned to the troop or were captured, the majority must be counted as dead.

22 Seaplanes with mountain guns were attacked and set on fire during the firing on 27 May at 1930 hrs, during the water landing of enemy fighters, so that only one gun could still be unloaded in time. One other gun landed by seaplane in Rombakenfjord on 28 May at 0030 hrs, at the same time that the battle for Narvik was still raging.

Chapter 8

1 The division war diary entry for the afternoon of 30 May read: 'Hauptmann Walther is apparently in Major Haussels's unit. He was clearly given instructions from the division that the troops of Naval Battalion Holtorf were to be assigned to him. Apparently however, Hauptmann Walther was not able to assert his authority immediately due to the difference in rank.'

2 Arrived on 28 May by seaplane.

3 At 2245 hrs, airborne troops from Sildvik were also provided to the battalion.

4 The troops managed on their own as well as possible. In the near vicinity, old clothing and uniform pieces of both friend and enemy were washed by those who were only mildly ill, made wearable again, and provided to the fighting troops. In this way, they could hand in their completely soaked uniforms, making partial exchanges, which could be dried near the fires in the valleys at the rear. In this manner, over the course of time the troops took on quite a multi-coloured look. Hardly any two men were uniformed alike (see Bibliography, 43).

5   By the end of the battles, with a total strength of six officers/214 men, parts of the 1st Company/1st Airborne Infantry Regiment deployed along the ore railway, with losses totaling two officers/26 men dead, two officers/39 men wounded, and nine missing in action.

6   Strength on 2 June.

7   Members of the French 14th Alpine Infantry Battalion.

8   Casualties in Group Windisch (including Group von Schleebrügge) from 19–26 May: 15 dead, 19 wounded, three missing in action.

9   Notation from author: apparently by means of this fire, the enemy wanted to conceal the beginning of their retreat movements and embarkation.

10 The casualties of 1st Battalion/139th, including the attached parts, totalled from between 9 April to 9 June: 93 dead (three officers), 167 wounded, and 124 missing in action.

11 The following examples of the two companies from 138th Mountain Infantry Regiment show how difficult it was to transport reinforcements in, owing to constant bad weather and enemy activity.

    On 8 May, 3rd Company/138th was ordered to fly from Trondheim to Narvik. Two aircraft reached their destination with its company commander (Oberleutnant Ploder), one aircraft was fired on and had to make an emergency landing, resulting in 17 men missing in action. The rest of the company – 50 men – returned to Trondheim. On 10 May, Leutnant Adler attempted to get through with the rest of 3rd Company, but succeeded only partly. Only one aircraft with Leutnant Adler was able to land in Narvik. On 12 May, a fourth attempt took place. But the aircraft were shelled over Narvik by British battleships, and, due to poor visibility, could not land and had to return to Trondheim.

    An attempt was undertaken on 14 May by 2nd Company/138th, which was also headed to Narvik (Leutnant Körber with four men from 2nd Company and eight men from the signal unit).

    After a short flight, however, the seaplane returned with a burning motor. It was not until 18 May, on the sixth attempt, that Leutnant Körber landed in Narvik with 15 men of 2nd Company/138th. Then a seventh attempt on 20 May succeeded, and Leutnant Raabe arrived with the rest of 3rd Company in Narvik. An eighth attempt, again by 2nd Company/138th, was unsuccessful. Leutnant Appel, with 28 men, did get to Narvik, but had to turn around due to bad weather conditions. The ninth attempt was undertaken on 22 May and finally, Oberleutnant Renner landed in Narvik with the bulk of 2nd Company/138th. The plan to bring in the other companies of 1st Battalion/138th to Narvik by air had to be abandoned, as it was too difficult (see Bibliography, 48).

12 Opposing Group von Schleebrügge was the Norwegian 14th Infantry Regiment with 16 guns.

13 The 2nd and 3rd Companies/138th, in all battles (mostly from Group von Schleebrügge) lost 22 dead and 25 missing in action.

14 On 19 May at 1900 hrs, a telephone connection was established for the first time with Group XXI in Oslo via Sweden (see Bibliography, 39).

15 The intent of division headquarters was to use the promised airborne and mountain infantry initially to relieve the battered Groups Windisch and von Schleebrügge, and to hold them as reserve even though at that moment a counter-attack in the direction of Hartvik Lake appeared practical. A deployment behind the enemy lines was declined, since after the previous experiences with transportation becoming bogged down, too few forces could jump in at the same time and in formation, and there were not enough suitable landing places for the transport gliders behind the enemy fronts (see Bibliography, 39).

16 On 7 June, air reconnaissance in the waters around Narvik identified one aircraft carrier, one anti-aircraft cruiser, five destroyers, two transport vessels, and two merchant ships.

17 According to statements by local citizens, most of the enemy had been shipped out from Narvik on 7 June and during the night of 7/8 June on destroyers and transport ships. Likewise, at Troeldal, during the night of 7/8 June, loading had taken place. In mid-morning of 8 June, the security forces followed. In the Stromnen Strait, on 8 June at 0100 hrs, a reconnaissance troop from Battalion Walther also observed British destroyers and several fishing steamers engaged in loading manoeuvres, but this was falsely reported as landing manoeuvres.

Appendix 1

1 Some mortars lost overboard during voyage.

2 Some lost overboard during voyage.

3 Total strength after incorporating the destroyer crews: 1,750 mountain infantry and rounded number of 2,700 navy personnel.

4 Heavy casualties in personnel, weapons, and equipment on 13 May. [translators' note: the footnotes are confused in the original. Note '1' appears AFTER note '2.' It is not possible to tell which information applies where.]

5 Each company had about 80 men.

6 Each company had about 70–80 men.

Appendix 4

1 The entire battalion had only about four medium trench mortars, and no light infantry guns.

2 Not deployed.

3 (see Bibliography, 59, 62)

4 Between 29 and 31 May, sent to Bodo.

5 Mountain Anti-Tank Section 48 (Geb. Pz.Jäg. Abt 48).

6   Same as above.
7   Same as above.
8   Same as above.
9   Same as above.
10 The 1st/1st Airborne Infantry Regiment lost four aircraft during the transporting in of troops, of which three were shot down and one had to make an emergency landing. Casualties numbered 12 dead (see Bibliography, 93).

Bibliography

Works Cited

(1) Hubatsch, Walther, *Die deutsche Besetzung von Dänemark und Norwegen 1940*, Musterschmidt-Verlag, Göttingen, 1952.

(2) Derry, T. K., *The Campaign in Norway*, Phillips and Co. Ltd, London S.W. 9.

(3) Dietl, Gerda Luise and Kurt, Hermann: *General Dietl*, Münchener Buchverlag, 1951.

(4) Churchill, W. S., *Der 2. Weltkrieg*, Band 1, Buch 2, Hamburg, 1950.

(5) Assman, Kurt, *Deutsche Schicksalsjahre*, Eberhard Brockhaus, Wiesbaden, 1950.

(6) Busch, Fritz Otto, *Narvik – Vom Heldenkampf deutscher Zerstörer*, Verlag C. Bertelsmann, Gütersloh, 1940.

(7) Heye, A. W., *Z 13 von Kiel bis Narvik*, Berlin, 1941.

(8) Hase, Georg v., *Die Kriegsmarine erobert Norwegens Fjorde*, Hase u. Koehler-Verlag, Leipzig, 1940.

(9) OKW, *Kampf um Norwegen*, Zeitgeschichte-Verlag W. Andermann, Berlin W 35, 1940; *Englands Griff nach Norwegen*, published under the auspices of the Foreign Office, Deutscher Verlag, Berlin, 1940.

(10) Mielke, Otto, *Der Heldenkampf um Narvik*, Steininger Verlag, Berlin, 1940.

(11) Fantur, Werner, *Narvik*, Junker und Dünnhaupt Verlag, Berlin, 1941.

(12) Marek, Kurt, *Wir hielten Narvik*, Berlin, 1942.

(13) Unger, Helmut, *Die Männer von Narvik*, Berlin, 1942.

(14) Böttger, Gerd, *Narvik in Wort und Bild*, Gerhard Stalling Verlag, Oldenburg, 1941.

(15) Scheuring, *Als Fallschirmjäger nach Narvik* (unpublished manuscript).

(16) Haussels, *Das war Narvik* (unpublished manuscript) (former commander of 2nd Battalion/139th Mountain Rifle Regiment).

(17) Stautner, Ludwig, *Narvik* (unpublished manuscript) (former commander of 1st Battalion/139th Mountain Infantry Regiment).

Files and document directory (Originals and/or Reproductions)
Orders and Directives

(18) Operationsbefehl für die Besetzung von Norwegen – Gruppe XXI. Nr. 20/40 g. Kdos. vom 5.3.40.

(19) Befehl für die Durchführung der Transporte zur Weserübung Nord – Gruppe XXI vom 7.3.40.

(20) Operationsbefehl für die Besetzung von Narvik – Gruppe XXI No 46/40 g. Kdos. Chefs. vom 12.3.40.

(21) Führerbefehl Nr.22094/40 g. Kdos. Chefs. vom 14.3.40.

(22) Besondere Anordnungen für den Nachrichtenverkehr Nr. 1–3. Geb.Div. Nr. 48/40 g. Kdos. vom 23.3.40.

(23) Operationsbefehl Nr. 2 – Gruppe XXI Ia 194/40 g. Kdos. vom 2.4.40.

(24) Führeranweisung an Generallt. Dietl vom 18.4.40.

(25) Anlage E zu Gruppe XXI Ia 194/40 g. Kdos. Chefs.

(26) Kampfanweisung für die Besetzung von Narvik – 3. Geb.Div. Ia Nr. 50/40 g. Kdos.

(27) Befehl für die Wegnahme der Küstenbefestigungen von Narvik Ia 3. Geb.Div. Nr. 50/40 g. Kdos.

(28) Anleitung für die Besetzung von Narvik durch das II.Geb.Jäg. Rgt. 139, Anlage 2a zu 3. Geb.Div. Ia Nr. 50/40 g. Kdos.

(29) Besetzung von Elvegaardsmoen, Anlage 3 zu 3. Geb.Div. Ia No. 50/40 g. Kdos.

(30) Divisionsbefehl für die Verteidigung des Raumes um den Ofotfjord, 3. Geb.Div Ia Nr. 115/40 11 geh. vom 11.4.40.

(31) Divisionsbefehl Nr. 1–11, 3. Geb.Div. vom 11.4.40.

(32) Schriftlicher Befehl des Abschnittkommandos Narvik vom 6.5.40 über Ausweichen.

(33) Divisionsbefehle Nr. 13–24, 3. Geb.Div. Ia vom 6.5 bis 24.5.40.

(34) Befehl Nr. 267/40 3. Geb.Div. an Abschnittskommandant Narvik vom 25.5.40.

(35) Divisionsbefehle Nr. 25–27, 3. Geb.Div. Ia vom 25.5. bis 27.5.40.

(36) Geheimbefehl 3. Geb.Div. Nr. 172/40 vom 29.5.40.

(37) Gruppe Narvik Ia Wunschzettel an OKW vom 29.5.40.

(38) Divisonsbefehle Nr. 28–38, 3. Geb.Div. Ia vom 29.5. bis 10.6.40.

War Journals, Battle Reports, and Memoirs

(39) KTB. Nr. 2 der 3. Geb.Div. (Gruppe Narvik) vom 5.4. bis 10.6.40.

(40) Persönliche Tagebuch General Dietl (Feldtagebuch) vom 5.4. bis 15.6.40.

(41) Eingelaufene Funksprüche bei Gruppe Narvik vom 12.5 bis 9.6.40.

(42) Gefechtsbericht des II./Geb.Jäg.Regt.139 vom 27. u. 28. 5.40.

(43) KTB des II./Fallschirm-Jäg.Rgt. 1 vom 21.5. bis 17.6.40.

(44) Kriegstagebuch Marine-Btl. Erdmenger vom 11.4. bis 4.6.40.

(45) Kriegstagebuch der 1./Geb. Jäg.Rgt.139 vom 6.4. bis 10.6.40.

(46) Kriegstagebuch der 2./Geb.Jäg.Rgt.139 vom 6.4. bis 10.6.40.

(47) Kriegstagebuch der 4./Geb.Jäg.Rgt.138 über den Einsatz Narvik.

(48) Kriegstagebuch des I./Geb.Jäg.Rgt. 138 über den Einsatz Narvik.

(49) Der Einsatz der 2.Geb.Art.Rgt. 112 bei Narvik.

(50) Gefechtsbericht über das Gefecht der verst. 1./139 am 16.4.40.

(51) Gefechtsbericht des I./Geb.Jäg.Rgt. 139 am 24./25. 4. bei Elvenes.

(52) Persönliche Aufzeichnungen des Btl.Kdr. I./139.

(53) Persönliches Tagebuch (Auszuege) E. Mörbt, Stab Geb. Jäg.Rgt. 139.

(54) Verlustmeldung Abschnitskommando Narvik nach Stand vom 10.7.40.

(55) Verlustmeldung I./Geb.Jäg.Rgt. 139 nach persönl. Notizen Btl.Kdr.

(56) Militarische Beschreibung der Stadt Narvik.

Enemy Intelligence

(57) Gruppe XXI Abt. Ic Nr.1/40 g. Kdos vom 4.3.40 'Derzeitiger Stand des norwegischen Heeres'.

(58) Deutsches Konsulat in Narvik vom 7.3.40: 'Narvik und die letzte politische Entwicklung'.

(59) Bericht des deutschen Militärattaches in Schweden vom 19.3.40: 'Derzeitiger Stand der Landesverteidigung Norwegens'.

(60) Gruppe XXI Ic Nr. 4/40 g. Kdos. vom 27.3.40: 'Feindnachrichtenblatt Nr. 1'.

(61) Gruppe XXI Ic nr. 8/40 g. Kdos. vom 3.4.40: 'Feindnachrichtenblatt Nr. 2'.

(62) O.K.M., 3.Abt. Skl.B. Nr. 474 g. Kdos. vom 1.4.40 Feindnachrichten über Norwegen, Nachtrag 3.

(63) Feindnachrichten über den Raum Narvik (aus Akten 3. Geb.Div., Herkunft nicht vermerkt).

(64) 6. norweg. Brig., Nr. 108 vom 19.4.40: Nachrichtenblatt Nr. 1.

Daily Orders and Capitulation Negotiations

(65) Tagesbefehl der Gruppe Narvik vom 10.6.40.

(66) Tagesbefehl der Gruppe XXI vom 9.6.40.

(67) Kapitulationsverhandlung der Gruppe Narvik mit den norweg. Truppen in Nordnorwegen vom 10.6.40 einschl. Zusätze.

(68) Abkommen des deutschen Oberkommandos in Norwegen mit dem norweg. Oberkommando vom 10.6.40.

Index

References to maps are in *italics*.